Unlock Your Financial Flow

Unlock Your Financial Flow

Manifestation Meets Money Management

Arman Lefevre

Mindful Pages

Published in 2025

ISBN: 9789371346023 (PB)
ISBN: 9789371340861 (eBook)

Published by

Mindful Pages
Imprint of Alpha Editions LLC
312 W. 2nd St #1834
Casper, WY 82601, USA

This book was developed using advanced writing tools to support the drafting and ideation process. All content has been thoughtfully curated, refined, and reviewed to ensure quality and relevance.

Content

Introduction
Where Spirit Meets Spreadsheet

Nestled quietly between the pragmatic rows of budget sheets and the shimmering allure of vision boards lies a discomforting reality—many find themselves at odds with marrying their financial decisions to their deeper values. They devour personal finance guides, attend workshops on manifestation, perhaps open investment accounts or whisper daily affirmations, yet genuine, lasting prosperity continues to slip through their fingers. This isn't a matter of lacking effort or intention. Rather, it springs from the persistent divide between two prevailing money narratives—the strategic and the spiritual—kept stubbornly apart. The premise here is daring, yet grounded: it's high time to bring these worlds together.

Take Alisha, for instance—a bright, ambitious creative who threw herself into every financial tactic imaginable. She meticulously followed conventional wisdom: automated savings, detailed expense tracking, multiple income streams. On paper, everything looked sound. Yet beneath those pristine spreadsheets lurked a persistent unease. Even a healthy bank balance couldn't dispel her anxiety. Believing the issue lay somewhere emotional, she shifted gears. She plunged into manifestation teachings, crafted vision boards, recited affirmations of abundance, and waited patiently for the universe's reply. For a while, things seemed promising—until bills mounted, freelance work dried up, and those spiritual tools started to feel less empowering, more like a form of avoidance.

The turning point came when Alisha began to approach her finances not as mere tactics or airy rituals, but as a nuanced psychological and spiritual relationship. She uncovered how her body carried scarcity imprints from childhood, recognised inherited beliefs subtly steering her choices, and found ways to weave gratitude into her budgeting practices. Crucially, she realised that the energy she brought to financial decisions mattered just as much as the numbers themselves. She didn't cast logic aside; she enriched it with intuition. She didn't abandon manifestation; she tempered it with intentional structure. The result was a transformation—not because she chose one path over the other, but because she stopped choosing between them.

Alisha's journey is far from an isolated tale. It reflects a silent struggle many endure. Traditional finance, with its emphasis on control, rationality, and external markers of success, offers sound counsel—save diligently, invest early, steer clear of debt—but often overlooks the emotional and energetic layers entwined with money. It assumes rational beings navigating predictable systems, yet human behaviour is anything but tidy.

On the flip side, spiritual and self-help circles promise abundance through belief, alignment, and the law of attraction. These teachings uplift, grant permission to dream expansively, and suggest that wealth can be summoned through thought alone. While inspiring, such approaches risk descending into wishful thinking if detached from grounded, practical action. The result? A generation caught between spreadsheets and sage sticks, between financial plans and full moon rituals—never quite settling into either peace or prosperity.

This divide isn't just theoretical—it has tangible consequences. Conventional money advice often neglects the nervous system's role, trauma's imprint, identity's sway, and the weight of cultural conditioning. Meanwhile, many manifestation practices sidestep personal accountability, undervalue strategy, or inadvertently uphold privilege. We need a fresh paradigm because the old ones, siloed as they are, address only fragments of the whole person. Fragmentation no longer serves us.

The financial landscape today demands nuance beyond binary thinking. We inhabit a world of inflation, economic swings, and digital upheaval, coupled with an intensified yearning for purpose and authenticity. People no longer merely seek to amass wealth—they want to feel well, live with integrity, and circulate resources towards a greater good. They desire their money to resonate with their values, their budgets to reflect their truths, and their investments to bolster a world they believe in. This book speaks directly to that longing.

Unlock Your Financial Flow: Manifestation Meets Money Management isn't your average financial guide, nor is it simply a metaphysical handbook. It's a synthesis—a careful weaving of spiritual energy principles and evidence-based financial strategies. It bridges inner transformation with external action, honouring both the metaphysics of abundance and the arithmetic of compound interest. Wealth, after all, is not solely what you possess—it's how you move it, steward it, and the consciousness guiding those acts.

The journey begins by peeling back the layers of your current financial habits. Chapter One dives into the roots of your money story, tracing how early family dynamics, cultural narratives, and inherited trauma sow subconscious patterns that either hinder or hasten your prosperity. You'll explore why fear of success can sometimes be more debilitating than fear of failure, and how well-meaning manifestation efforts can slip into spiritual bypass when the psychological groundwork is ignored.

Next, Chapter Two ventures into the quantum realm—not as whimsical speculation, but as a grounded model for understanding money's energetic mechanics. You'll discover how frequency alignment, emotional resonance, and the observer effect actively shape your financial reality. This chapter also introduces the concept of the Quantum Wallet—a multidimensional perspective encompassing emotion, intention, and strategic design.

Chapter Three draws us back into the body. Somatic wealth practices and nervous system regulation take centre stage, revealing that financial trauma isn't confined to the mind but resides in the physical. Drawing on polyvagal theory and somatic therapy, this section makes clear that safety is the bedrock for strategy, and that breathwork and bodily awareness can unlock capacity for increased income, risk-taking, and inner calm.

In Chapter Four, we confront narrative head-on. The internal scripts about money—what it signifies, who deserves it, and what having more says about you—exert immense influence on financial outcomes. Here, you'll find tools for cognitive reframing, introductions to wealth archetypes, and linguistic strategies to reshape your identity from within.

Then comes the practical heart of the matter. Chapter Five invites a radical rethinking of budgeting—not as drudgery, but as a sacred alignment. You'll learn to organise your spending around your highest values, detect energy leaks in your finances, and use gratitude to reshape your relationship with both income and expenditure. Chapter Six then elevates investing from a technical task to a spiritual practice. Whether your style leans towards intuition or analysis, you'll find guidance to honour your approach while engaging with real-world principles of financial growth and sustainable wealth building.

By Chapter Seven, the focus shifts to income and identity. This chapter delves into how self-worth, shadow work, and cultural conditioning set limits on earning potential. It offers exercises to strengthen your "money-receiving muscle" and create income streams aligned with both financial objectives and soulful purpose.

Chapter Eight addresses the inevitable setbacks, detours, and disappointments—not as failures, but as parts of a spiral growth process where progress deepens and evolves. You'll gain tools for navigating financial disruptions without losing flow, including mindset resets and emotional recalibration techniques.

Finally, Chapter Nine takes a wider view—your legacy. Conscious wealth is about circulation, not hoarding. This closing chapter explores generational healing, intentional generosity, and visionary impact planning, posing the question: what kind of ancestor do you hope to become?

The conclusion weaves all threads together, reminding you that financial flow is as much a state of being as a matter of having. To unlock your financial flow is to move from fragmentation to wholeness, from fear to fluidity, from scarcity scripts to sovereign stewardship. Managing money, then, becomes an act of shaping meaning, identity, energy, and impact.

This book is for the rational mind disillusioned by cold, impersonal advice. It's for the spiritual seeker frustrated by visions that falter without structure. It's for entrepreneurs, creatives, caregivers, and changemakers who believe wealth should not only feel good but do good and be good. Above all, it's for those ready to stop pitting soul against strategy—and finally let them work in concert.

Welcome to a new paradigm of money.

Chapter 1
Money Myths and Mind Games

Before we even begin to attract or manage wealth in a way that truly reflects who we are, there's a more elusive, often overlooked truth to confront: much of what we think we believe about money wasn't really chosen—it was inherited. These beliefs aren't the product of deliberate thought or conscious decision-making; rather, they seep into us quietly, absorbed through experience, observation, and repetition. In this way, many of us move through life following financial scripts written long before we had a say. This chapter lifts the veil on those ingrained narratives, tracing their origins, exploring their influence, and offering a route towards deliberate financial rewiring.

At the core of this investigation lies financial schema theory, a psychological lens that reveals how deeply rooted money beliefs form, typically in childhood, and continue to steer our adult behaviour—mostly beneath the surface of awareness. These schemas function like internal blueprints, cognitive templates that shape what money means, who deserves it, how it should be handled, and what it reveals about our identity. Much like the emotional patterns we inherit through attachment, financial schemas develop within the context of family interactions, societal cues, and cultural conditioning.

Picture, if you will, a child raised in a home where money was synonymous with tension. Arguments over bills were commonplace, and phrases like "we can't afford that" or "money doesn't grow on trees" were etched into daily conversation. Even if this child later earns a comfortable wage, they may still harbour financial anxieties, compulsively guard their funds, or shy away from checking their bank balance. Their nervous system, wired early on, learned to associate money with conflict and insecurity—a pattern that no amount of adult rationale can simply override without conscious work.

On the flip side, some inherit a contrasting schema: money as a marker of self-worth. Perhaps they were only lauded for material success or taught that love and acceptance hinged on performance and productivity. Such individuals might become relentless high achievers, driven by an undercurrent of fear that they are never quite enough, perpetually chasing more yet rarely feeling fulfilled. Whatever the shape these beliefs take, financial schemas do more than dictate spending or saving habits; they influence our very sense of safety, identity, and belonging.

And here's where the mind games begin in earnest. Among the most subtle yet pervasive is what Gay Hendricks terms the 'upper limit problem'—a subconscious brake that kicks in when life starts to look too good. Success surges upward, opportunities line up, only for self-sabotage to rear its head. Suddenly, a careless mistake is made, a pointless argument erupts, or procrastination sneaks in. Not out of fear of failing, but fear of what success demands—visibility, responsibility, or stepping into unfamiliar roles.

Neuropsychology sheds light on this phenomenon. The brain's amygdala, designed to protect survival rather than nurture success, often prefers the known discomfort of scarcity over the perceived threat of abundance that feels unearned or unsafe. Our emotional set points—those familiar feelings we habitually return to—act much like thermostats for our well-being. If your baseline is worry or guilt, your nervous system will steer you back to those states, even when external circumstances suggest you could relax. Hence, those caught in cycles of under-earning are often not lazy or undisciplined; rather, they have mastered self-limitation in subtle, intricate ways.

This also clarifies why some who diligently practice the Law of Attraction find themselves stuck or disheartened. They visualise wealth, recite affirmations, and raise their vibration, yet the desired results remain frustratingly out of reach—or vanish soon after appearing. This is often a case of manifestation bypassing: a nuanced denial where spiritual language obscures uncomfortable truths, unhealed wounds, or necessary, practical action. Instead of confronting their fears around money or their avoidance of financial systems, they may cling to magical thinking, mistakenly believing that positivity alone suffices.

But manifestation isn't about pretending that all is well. It's about genuine alignment—which demands courage, clarity, and consistent choices. When positivity is wielded as a defence rather than a source of empowerment, it morphs into a gilded cage masquerading as freedom. Those who successfully weave manifestation into their financial lives do so by honouring both emotional realities and pragmatic demands. They recognise that energetic frequency and financial spreadsheets are not enemies but collaborators in the dance of creation.

To break free from these invisible loops, awareness must come first. One of the chapter's most valuable tools is the Emotional Currency Scale, a diagnostic instrument designed to help you assess your feelings around money. By rating your emotional responses in key domains—receiving income, paying bills, discussing finances, investing, and giving—you begin to chart your internal financial terrain. For example, feeling excitement when money arrives but guilt when spending might suggest a belief that money is 'good' only when hoarded, not circulated. Or if investing triggers fear, it could point to unresolved trauma linked to risk and uncertainty.

This exercise is far from a judgement; it's an invitation to awareness. Just as a physician cannot treat what goes unseen, you cannot shift your financial patterns without first illuminating them. The Emotional Currency Scale acts as both mirror and map—reflecting your current state and signalling potential pathways forward. Used regularly, it cultivates a practice of self-honesty and energetic clarity.

To deepen this inquiry, consider this thought experiment: what if you suddenly inherited £10 million? At first glance, many imagine this would bring instant joy, security, or freedom. Yet when pressed to explore beneath the surface, surprising emotions emerge—panic, guilt, disbelief, even fear. Would your relationships change? Could you trust yourself to steward such wealth? Would passion remain your compass, or would the absence of financial pressure leave you adrift? This reflection exposes not only your dreams but also your resistance to abundance—a rare glimpse into those shadowy corners where money still signifies danger, alienation, or loss of self.

Real lives illustrate the potency of these ideas. Take Ravi, a tech consultant who habitually undercharged despite high demand and a stellar portfolio. When he finally dared to raise his rates, he was gripped by physical unease. Through coaching and self-exploration, he uncovered a childhood memory: his father's harsh judgement of wealthy clients as greedy and exploitative. Unknowingly, Ravi had internalised a belief that charging more compromised his integrity. Once he rewrote this story, his income doubled—and more crucially, his peace of mind returned.

Then there's Amara, a yoga teacher who embraced manifestation zealously. She meditated, visualised consistently, and kept a gratitude journal religiously. Yet financial instability persisted; she struggled to pay rent, ignored tax obligations, and evaded systematisation. Her breakthrough came only when she paired spiritual discipline with grounded financial planning, stabilising and growing her income in tandem.

These narratives underscore a vital truth: financial growth isn't solely about doing more—it's about becoming different. It calls for stepping beyond inherited scripts and unconscious emotional set points into conscious authorship. To do this requires embracing discomfort, unpacking assumptions, and rewiring responses at neurological, emotional, and behavioural levels.

Throughout this chapter, you'll be prompted to reflect, journal, and map your emotional connections to money in detail. This foundation is indispensable. No budget, investment plan, or manifestation ritual alone can forge lasting wealth if your subconscious resists it. But once you identify and rewrite those inner scripts, you open the door to abundance—not just in figures, but in confidence, ease, and empowerment.

Money myths and mental blocks don't vanish through knowledge alone; transformation is essential. This chapter marks your starting point: a careful excavation of the layers silently shaping your financial world until now. It invites you to look where you've hesitated, feel what you've ignored, and take up the pen to author a new money story—one that honours both your heritage and your freedom.

The Inherited Blueprint: How Your Money Beliefs Were Formed

Before we make our first purchase, receive our first allowance, or open our first bank account, we have already absorbed a complex web of beliefs about money. These beliefs often operate beneath the surface of conscious awareness, guiding our behaviours, shaping our emotional responses, and constraining our financial potential. They don't originate from logic or financial literacy—they are absorbed through observation, repetition, and emotional imprinting during childhood. Much like the foundations of a house, these early patterns form our *financial blueprint*, a deeply ingrained map that silently influences every money decision we make. To understand how to transform our financial reality, we must first trace the origins of this hidden architecture.

At the centre of this exploration lies *financial schema theory*, a concept rooted in cognitive and developmental psychology. A schema is a mental framework—an internal structure we use to interpret and predict experiences. Financial schemas are specific variations of these frameworks, encompassing beliefs about scarcity, worthiness, control, risk, and the social meaning of money. These schemas are not innate; they are learned. And once internalised, they tend to become self-reinforcing, shaping our interpretations of events and confirming our biases.

These internal scripts begin forming in early childhood, often through indirect messaging rather than explicit teaching. A child does not need to be told "money is dangerous" to internalise that belief. They may witness parents arguing over expenses, feel the tension in a household where bills go unpaid, or experience embarrassment over wearing second-hand clothes. Conversely, a child in a wealthy household may receive the unspoken message that love, attention, or status are tied to material displays. The emotional charge around these early experiences imprints them deeply into the nervous system, encoding beliefs not only in the mind but in the body.

Research in attachment theory and early emotional development supports this. The work of psychologists such as John Bowlby and Mary Ainsworth has shown that our earliest relationships—especially with caregivers—form templates for how we relate to safety, trust, and self-worth. These templates extend into our relationship with money, which becomes a proxy for these deeper needs. If love was conditional on performance or success, money may later symbolise approval. If unpredictability marked the home environment, financial security may feel elusive, even in adulthood.

One of the most revealing aspects of financial schema theory is how these inherited beliefs can operate independently of actual financial status. For instance, someone raised in scarcity may carry the belief that there is never enough, even if they have accumulated wealth. They might hoard money, avoid investments, or experience guilt when spending—patterns not born of circumstance, but of conditioning. Alternatively, someone who internalised the idea that money is corrupting may unconsciously repel wealth through under-earning, poor planning, or self-sabotage. In both cases, the individual is not responding to the present, but to an emotionally charged narrative from the past.

A compelling real-world example is that of Martin, a senior executive earning a six-figure salary. Despite his professional success, Martin frequently found himself anxious about money. He refused to upgrade his living conditions, rarely spent on leisure, and obsessively monitored his accounts. In therapy, he uncovered childhood memories of his parents going bankrupt, including nights when electricity was cut off. Even though Martin's current financial reality was stable, his body still anticipated collapse. His nervous system had never recalibrated to safety. It wasn't until he began to consciously separate past from present—through somatic work, journaling, and re-parenting exercises—that his anxiety subsided and his relationship with money softened.

Cultural context also plays a powerful role in shaping financial blueprints. Societal narratives around money are embedded in everything from religious teachings to national economies. In some cultures, wealth is seen as a divine reward; in others, it is associated with greed and moral decay. Gender norms compound this further. Women, in particular, have historically been socialised to defer financial decision-making or associate wealth with loss of femininity. Even today, despite increasing financial independence, many women report guilt or fear around earning more than a partner, investing assertively, or prioritising their own material needs.

The legacy of colonisation, systemic inequality, and generational trauma adds further complexity. For communities historically excluded from wealth-building systems, money becomes charged not only with personal meaning but with collective wounds. The trauma of poverty, exploitation, or displacement does not simply dissipate with a generation's financial progress. Epigenetic research, such as that conducted by Rachel Yehuda on intergenerational trauma, suggests that stress responses can be biologically inherited. This means that even when individuals achieve material success, they may carry subconscious fears, inherited shame, or a baseline of hyper-vigilance that distorts their financial behaviour.

Take the case of Leila, a first-generation university graduate from a low-income immigrant family. Despite landing a well-paying job in tech, she consistently undercut her own value in negotiations and felt uncomfortable with her growing savings. She later realised that she was carrying a deep-seated loyalty to her family's struggle, equating wealth with betrayal. Her financial schema was not just about personal security—it was entangled with identity, belonging, and survivor's guilt. Only by recognising these layers could she begin to create a relationship with money that honoured both her heritage and her aspirations.

So how do these schemas evolve—or dissolve? The first step is recognition. Most people operate on financial autopilot, unaware that their decisions are less about strategy and more about story. By identifying the dominant narrative running the show, individuals can begin to re-author their experience. Tools like financial journaling, inner child dialogue, and schema-focused therapy can illuminate the scripts at play. Even simple reflective questions—

What did I learn about money growing up? Whose beliefs am I carrying? When do I feel safe or unsafe with money?—can catalyse significant shifts in awareness.

But awareness alone is not enough. Emotional processing is essential. Because these schemas are not purely cognitive, intellectual insights must be integrated somatically. This might involve working with the body through breathwork, tapping (EFT), or somatic experiencing to release the physiological tension associated with old financial wounds. It might also mean engaging in relational healing—having honest conversations with family members or support networks to disrupt secrecy, shame, and silence around money.

Once the emotional charge is softened, behaviour change becomes possible. New financial habits—whether it's tracking spending, negotiating pay, or investing with confidence—can now be encoded without triggering the old alarms. These actions serve not just as strategic improvements, but as neural rewiring mechanisms. Each new behaviour that contradicts an outdated schema sends a signal to the brain: it is safe to receive, manage, and grow wealth.

To support this process, visualisation techniques can be powerful. For example, guided imagery that invites the individual to imagine a childhood scene involving money—but this time, with their adult self present, offering comfort or new perspective—can shift the emotional association tied to that memory. Neuroplasticity research confirms that the brain does not distinguish sharply between real and vividly imagined experiences. Thus, re-imagining the past becomes a form of healing, not fantasy.

Financial education also plays a vital role, but only when paired with emotional awareness. Teaching someone how compound interest works is useful—but it won't change their behaviour if they believe investing is reckless or undeserved. Effective financial learning must speak to both the mind and the heart. It must honour the fact that money is not just numbers—it's narrative, identity, memory, and energy.

Ultimately, transforming your inherited blueprint is an act of liberation. It is the decision to question what was passed down, to interrupt unconscious patterns, and to design a financial life that reflects conscious values rather than unconscious programming. It is not about blame; it is about authorship. Whether your past was marked by scarcity, excess, or instability, you are not bound to its terms. You have the capacity to rewrite the rules, to upgrade the emotional software running your financial life, and to create a new legacy—one rooted not in reaction, but in resonance.

To begin this work, ask yourself: what were the unspoken money rules in your home? How did the adults in your life behave around wealth or lack? What messages did media, religion, or community reinforce? And perhaps most importantly—what beliefs are you ready to release?

Understanding the inherited blueprint is not a one-time revelation; it is an ongoing excavation. Each layer you uncover offers more freedom, more clarity, and more power. As you continue through this book, remember: your financial future doesn't have to echo your financial past. Awareness is the first form of wealth. From that awareness, everything begins to flow.

The Sabotage Loop: Why You Fear Success (More Than Failure)

It is tempting to think that fear of failure is what holds people back from achieving their financial goals. After all, failure is often equated with shame, risk, and the loss of control. Yet beneath the surface, a more paradoxical fear operates—*the fear of success*. While this may seem counterintuitive, psychological research and personal development insights suggest that success can be just as threatening as failure, especially when it challenges our emotional baseline. The phenomenon known as the *Upper Limit Problem*, introduced by Gay Hendricks in *The Big Leap*, illuminates this hidden dynamic. It describes the internal thermostat of wellbeing we all carry—an unconscious comfort zone for how much happiness, wealth, love, or ease we believe we are allowed to experience. When life begins to exceed that internal threshold, many people unconsciously sabotage their success in order to return to a familiar state of struggle.

The concept hinges on what psychologists call *emotional set points*, a term popularised in both neuropsychology and behavioural economics. Just as a thermostat regulates the temperature of a room, emotional set points regulate our internal state. These set points are shaped by early life experiences, relational dynamics, and core beliefs about what is safe, deserved, or possible. If your set point is anchored in scarcity, then abundance may feel threatening, even if it's exactly what you've been striving for. The moment you begin to experience more money, recognition, or ease than your nervous system is accustomed to, discomfort arises—not because something is wrong, but because it's unfamiliar.

This discomfort often shows up in subtle, insidious ways: procrastination after a promotion, overspending after receiving a windfall, forgetting to send an important email that would seal a major deal. These behaviours are not conscious rejections of success; they are protective strategies designed to restore emotional equilibrium. To the untrained mind, this looks like laziness or inconsistency. To the attuned observer, it's a sign that someone has hit their *upper limit*—and their subconscious is doing everything it can to bring them back down to where they feel emotionally congruent.

Neuroscience offers compelling insight into why this happens. The brain is wired for predictability and safety, not growth and expansion. The amygdala, which governs our threat detection systems, scans constantly for deviation from the familiar. When we step into unfamiliar success, the brain may interpret this as danger—not because success is harmful, but because it is novel and uncharted. As neuropsychologist Dr. Rick Hanson notes, the brain has a negativity bias; it is far more attuned to potential threats than rewards. This bias can lead us to subconsciously downplay or even dismantle our own wins, not out of masochism, but out of a misguided attempt to feel "normal."

Real-world stories highlight how pervasive and varied this phenomenon can be. Take James, a small business owner who spent years struggling to reach profitability. After finally landing a major client and doubling his revenue, he suddenly began missing deadlines and avoiding client calls. Within six months, the client terminated the contract. James was devastated, but later admitted that he had begun to feel overwhelmed by the pressure to maintain success. The money had arrived, but emotionally, he still identified as someone fighting for survival. Prosperity became a threat to that identity—and his behaviour adjusted accordingly.

Or consider Tanvi, a first-generation professional from a working-class background. When she was offered a senior role with a six-figure salary, her initial excitement was quickly replaced by anxiety. She found herself unable to make decisions, second-guessing her expertise, and withdrawing from colleagues. Beneath the surface, she felt guilty for surpassing the financial status of her family, as if her success would alienate her from her roots. Her sabotage wasn't about fear of the job—it was about fear of the identity shift that success required.

These cases are not anomalies; they reflect a broader truth about how human beings adapt to their perceived limits. When success threatens to disrupt our self-concept or relational bonds, we often choose familiarity over expansion. This choice is not made rationally; it is encoded into the nervous system. But with awareness and support, it can be rewritten.

The first step in dismantling the sabotage loop is recognising its presence. This often requires pausing to examine the moments when progress seems to backfire. If every time you receive a financial breakthrough you feel an inexplicable sense of dread or guilt, your emotional set point may be reacting. If success is followed by chaos, illness, or self-inflicted crises, it may be a sign that your internal thermostat is set too low. The goal is not to judge these reactions, but to understand them as protective mechanisms developed at a time when safety meant staying small.

Once identified, the upper limit pattern can be softened through *emotional reconditioning*. This involves gradually expanding your capacity to hold more positive emotional states—success, ease, wealth—without triggering shutdown. Somatic practices are particularly useful here. Techniques such as breathwork, vagal toning, and body scanning can help regulate the nervous system as it encounters new levels of abundance. When the body feels safe, the mind is more likely to interpret success as sustainable rather than threatening.

Additionally, *identity work* becomes essential. If you have always seen yourself as the underdog, the fighter, or the struggler, success may feel like a betrayal of that identity. Reframing identity in a way that includes success—not as an exception but as an expression of your evolving self—is critical. This may involve visualisation, inner child work, or rewriting internal narratives. For example, instead of telling yourself, "I'm not the kind of person who makes a lot of money," you begin to affirm, "I'm someone who is learning to receive and sustain abundance with ease and integrity."

Another powerful reframe is to see success not as a final state, but as a fluid process. When we view success as a destination, we attach to it enormous pressure—what if we can't maintain it? What if we're exposed as a fraud? But when success is reframed as an ongoing relationship, complete with learning curves, fluctuations, and redefinitions, the pressure dissipates. It becomes something we can dance with, rather than something we must protect or defend.

Financial planning can also be a grounding tool to support the integration of success. Having clear, values-based goals, automated systems, and a long-term vision can reduce the overwhelm that often accompanies sudden financial growth. The key is to ensure that your external strategies are in alignment with your internal capacity. If your body is in panic but your spreadsheet says you're thriving, you have a mismatch that must be resolved—not just by crunching numbers, but by expanding safety.

Therapeutic modalities such as Internal Family Systems (IFS), schema therapy, and psychodynamic counselling can also be instrumental in addressing deeper blocks. These approaches allow individuals to connect with the younger parts of themselves that learned to equate visibility with danger or success with abandonment. By re-parenting those inner parts, it becomes possible to rewrite the rules they've been living by.

One of the most effective realisations someone can have is that *self-sabotage is not a flaw—it's a form of protection.* When we understand sabotage as a loyal but outdated strategy, we can meet it with compassion rather than shame. This shifts us from adversaries of our own behaviour to allies of our own transformation.

To reflect on this for yourself, consider moments in your life when things were going remarkably well—financially, professionally, relationally. Did anything unravel shortly after? Did you downplay your success, create unnecessary conflict, or withdraw from joy? What part of you felt unworthy, unprepared, or unsafe in the presence of abundance? These questions are not easy, but they are liberating. They bring the subconscious into the light.

Ultimately, the fear of success is not about success itself—it's about what success threatens to change. It challenges our beliefs, disrupts our roles, and invites us to grow into versions of ourselves we may not yet fully recognise. But on the other side of that fear lies immense freedom: the freedom to receive without guilt, to expand without sabotage, and to succeed without collapse.

The sabotage loop can be broken—not by force, but by awareness, compassion, and incremental expansion. When you raise your emotional set point and begin to feel safe with more, you not only achieve success—you learn to *inhabit* it. You stop falling back. You stop turning down your brightness to fit the dimming patterns of your past. And you begin to live from a place of sustained flow, where prosperity is not a spike, but a state.

Manifestation Gone Wrong: When Positivity Becomes Denial

The modern self-help landscape is saturated with promises of limitless abundance, magnetic attraction, and the power of positive thinking. At the centre of this movement lies the Law of Attraction—an idea that our thoughts, emotions, and intentions shape the reality we experience. This concept, popularised by works such as *The Secret*, has captivated millions with its compelling suggestion: think abundantly, and abundance will follow. While rooted in genuine psychological and metaphysical insights, the application of manifestation principles has, in many cases, drifted far from their original intent. The danger lies not in the belief that our inner world shapes our outer reality—but in the seductive oversimplification of this process, where positivity becomes a form of denial, and spiritual insight is reduced to a performative mantra.

The Law of Attraction, when wielded responsibly, offers valuable guidance. Cognitive behavioural psychology supports the idea that our beliefs influence our behaviours, which in turn shape outcomes. Visualisation, goal-setting, and emotional alignment all have their place in cultivating motivation and persistence. Neuroplasticity, the brain's capacity to rewire itself based on thought and experience, lends scientific weight to the idea that focused intention can change internal and external realities. However, issues arise when these tools are used to bypass discomfort, evade personal accountability, or ignore the complexity of lived experiences.

One of the most pervasive misapplications of manifestation arises from what psychologists call *toxic positivity*—the insistence on maintaining a cheerful, high-vibration attitude at all costs, even in the face of grief, fear, injustice, or failure. When individuals are told to "just focus on the good" or "raise their vibration" in response to deep pain or systemic barriers, they are not being empowered; they are being silenced. This creates a double-bind where expressing fear, anger, or frustration is seen as spiritually immature, while repressing those emotions is rewarded as enlightened thinking.

The consequences of this are profound. People internalise the idea that any misfortune is their fault—that illness, financial hardship, or loss must be the result of low-frequency thinking or flawed visualisation. This worldview not only lacks compassion, but it also distorts reality. It neglects structural inequalities, inherited trauma, and the unpredictable nature of life itself. It replaces nuanced understanding with magical thinking, encouraging individuals to spiritualise avoidance rather than build resilience.

A striking example of this dynamic is seen in the case of Clara, a freelance wellness coach who followed every manifestation protocol with religious zeal. She crafted vision boards, scripted her ideal life, and spoke daily affirmations into her mirror. But when her business plateaued, she doubled down—not on strategy or skill-building, but on positive thinking. She refused to acknowledge her mounting debt, ignored emails from clients asking for more structure, and convinced herself that the universe would 'provide' if she just stayed in alignment. By the time Clara sought support, she was not only financially depleted but emotionally numb—confused as to why her unwavering optimism hadn't translated into real-world stability. Her story is far from unique.

What Clara, and many like her, fell into was a form of *spiritual bypassing*—a term coined by psychologist John Welwood to describe the use of spiritual ideas and practices to sidestep unresolved emotional issues, psychological wounds, or behavioural challenges. In the context of money, spiritual bypassing often looks like reframing every setback as a "test from the universe," dismissing practical financial planning as too "low vibration," or believing that any discussion of scarcity is itself a magnet for more lack. These patterns prevent growth rather than support it. They encourage stagnation under the guise of enlightenment.

To understand why this happens, we must look at the emotional appeal of simplified manifestation teachings. In a world marked by uncertainty and insecurity, the promise of control—of being able to think your way into wealth or love or health—offers immense comfort. It provides a sense of agency, particularly for those who have felt powerless. But that comfort can become addictive. If you believe that your mindset is the only variable that matters, then you can avoid the discomfort of complexity: the slow grind of building a business, the vulnerability of asking for help, the discomfort of facing your own contradictions.

However, true empowerment lies not in denial, but in integration. Manifestation principles work best when paired with self-awareness, strategic action, and emotional literacy. Positivity, when grounded in authenticity, becomes a fuel for perseverance—not a mask to hide behind. And visualisation, when informed by reality, becomes a tool for creative expansion—not a means of escaping responsibility.

Neuroscientific research supports this integrated model. Studies on motivation, such as those conducted by psychologist Gabrielle Oettingen, show that visualising success is only effective when paired with what she calls *mental contrasting*—the practice of envisioning both the desired future and the obstacles that must be overcome to reach it. Participants who engaged in mental contrasting were significantly more likely to follow through on their goals than those who only focused on the positive outcome. This suggests that realism, not unrelenting optimism, is the key to effective manifestation.

Similarly, trauma research reveals that for individuals with dysregulated nervous systems—often shaped by childhood adversity or chronic stress—forcing positivity can be counterproductive. The body cannot be tricked into feeling safe by affirmations alone. Instead, it requires regulation, processing, and repair. Practices such as somatic experiencing, emotional freedom technique (EFT), and mindfulness-based stress reduction offer more sustainable paths to alignment. When used alongside visualisation or intention setting, they allow for a more embodied, integrative manifestation practice—one that honours both light and shadow.

A more constructive approach to manifestation acknowledges that emotions are data, not enemies. Fear signals that something matters. Anger indicates a boundary has been crossed. Sadness shows where healing is needed. Rather than being obstacles to abundance, these emotions are guides—pointers to where deeper integration is required. When we suppress them in the name of staying positive, we ignore vital feedback and risk building on unstable foundations.

Consider Amir, a product designer who spent years repressing his financial anxiety by repeating affirmations like "I am financially free" and "Money flows to me effortlessly." While these statements were aspirational, they weren't believable. His body didn't feel safe, and his spending patterns didn't reflect alignment. When he finally paused to listen—to admit his fear, examine his habits, and forgive himself for past mistakes—he was able to take new actions. He built a budget, sought a mentor, and gradually stabilised his finances. The turning point wasn't more positivity; it was more presence.

This distinction between *true positivity* and *performative positivity* is critical. True positivity arises from trust, which is built through consistent alignment between thought, feeling, and action. It is not a mask, but a mood born of integration. It acknowledges setbacks without being defined by them. Performative positivity, on the other hand, is brittle. It cracks under pressure because it lacks depth. It is sustained by image, not embodiment.

The broader cultural implications of this are significant. When positivity is weaponised—as in cases where people are told to "vibe higher" rather than confront injustice or inequality—it becomes a form of gaslighting. It individualises systemic problems and implies that anyone struggling must simply be thinking the wrong thoughts. This undermines not only empathy but social change. True abundance is collective. It acknowledges context. It invites both personal responsibility and communal awareness.

To move beyond denial, we must cultivate what the Buddhist teacher Pema Chödrön calls *courageous presence*—the willingness to stay with discomfort long enough to extract wisdom. This doesn't negate the value of visioning, scripting, or affirmations; it simply puts them in their rightful place as tools, not doctrines. When these tools are used in concert with self-inquiry, strategic thinking, and emotional processing, they become genuinely transformative.

For those engaging with manifestation practices, the invitation is not to abandon positivity but to deepen it. Ask not only what you want to manifest, but *why*. What part of you is seeking validation, security, or escape? Are your affirmations building belief—or masking fear? Are you aligning with abundance—or avoiding accountability?

Ultimately, manifestation is not about getting everything you want; it's about becoming the kind of person who can sustain what you receive. That process is rarely linear, and it is never purely mental. It is emotional, behavioural, spiritual, and embodied. When we honour that complexity, we stop bypassing and start building. We shift from magical thinking to meaningful action, from denial to discernment, and from superficial alignment to sustainable flow.

Only then does manifestation truly work—not as a fantasy, but as a deeply integrated process of growth, expansion, and embodiment.

The Emotional Currency Scale: Measuring the Hidden Forces Behind Financial Flow

Money is rarely just about money. Behind every transaction, budget, or investment lies a complex network of emotions, memories, and subconscious beliefs that silently shape how we earn, spend, save, and give. While financial literacy offers practical tools, and mindset work attempts to shift internal narratives, there remains a missing link in many people's relationship with money: emotional awareness. Without understanding how we *feel* about money—how our nervous system reacts to receiving it, spending it, or even thinking about it—we cannot sustainably change our financial outcomes. This is where the concept of the *Emotional Currency Scale* becomes transformative.

The Emotional Currency Scale is not a budget planner, nor is it a psychological quiz designed to label you. It is a diagnostic tool—a mirror that reflects your emotional relationship with money across key areas of financial life. Unlike traditional financial assessments, which focus solely on numerical data or knowledge gaps, this scale maps your emotional responses to different money-related scenarios. It reveals where you are energetically open to flow and where, often without realising it, you are blocking it. By measuring the emotional "charge" in areas such as earning, spending, investing, saving, and giving, the tool helps you identify the specific emotional imprints that either support or sabotage your financial wellbeing.

The idea behind this scale draws from multiple interdisciplinary frameworks. It is informed by affective neuroscience, which explores how emotions shape perception and decision-making; somatic psychology, which understands the body as a site of stored emotional memory; and behavioural finance, which studies the cognitive biases and emotional heuristics behind financial choices.

Together, these fields demonstrate what we intuitively know but often fail to articulate: money decisions are not made in a vacuum. They are made in bodies shaped by past experiences, within cultural narratives, and under the influence of deep emotional patterning.

To illustrate this, consider the case of Darren, a high-earning consultant who found himself perpetually stressed despite financial abundance. On paper, his finances were impeccable: diversified investments, emergency savings, zero debt. Yet whenever he checked his bank accounts, he experienced a spike in anxiety. He avoided opening emails related to billing and felt a persistent sense of scarcity. When Darren completed the Emotional Currency Scale, it became clear that while he felt ease in *earning* and *saving*, he had strong negative associations with *managing* and *spending* money—linked, as it turned out, to his childhood experiences of instability and parental conflict around bills. These emotional triggers were invisible in a spreadsheet but powerful enough to undermine his experience of security.

The scale itself encourages individuals to rate their emotional responses to various financial activities on a spectrum—from ease and empowerment on one end, to anxiety, shame, or avoidance on the other. For example, how do you feel when you receive unexpected income? Elated or suspicious? When you pay a large bill, do you feel empowered, neutral, or resentful? When you consider investing, does it evoke curiosity or fear? These seemingly simple questions open a profound inquiry into the *emotional climate* of your financial life.

Why does this matter? Because emotion precedes behaviour. According to the somatic marker hypothesis, pioneered by neuroscientist Antonio Damasio, decision-making is not purely rational—it relies heavily on emotional signals that guide us toward or away from certain choices. If those signals are miscalibrated—if, for example, you associate investing with danger due to past losses or parental caution—you may unconsciously avoid wealth-building strategies despite intellectually knowing their importance. Similarly, if giving money feels like losing power because of an unresolved boundary issue, generosity may become a source of resentment rather than fulfilment.

Mapping these patterns through the Emotional Currency Scale does more than raise awareness; it creates a roadmap for transformation. Once you identify the areas where emotional resistance exists, you can begin to gently recondition your responses. This is not about forcing positivity but about fostering *emotional congruence*—a state in which your thoughts, feelings, and actions are aligned. For instance, if spending brings up guilt, instead of overriding it with affirmations, the work is to explore the root of that guilt. Did it come from a family belief that enjoying money is selfish? Was it reinforced by a past relationship where spending led to conflict? Only by addressing the emotional origin can sustainable change occur.

Real-world examples underscore the value of this approach. Leena, a yoga teacher in her late thirties, struggled with undercharging for her services. She rationalised it as staying "accessible," but deep down she felt unworthy of charging more. After engaging with the Emotional Currency Scale, she recognised a pattern: ease in giving and serving, but a block in receiving. Her discomfort with charging appropriately traced back to childhood messages that money was only earned through hard, unpleasant work. Teaching yoga, which she loved, didn't feel "deserving" of good money. This emotional incongruence was driving her pricing decisions. Once she processed this belief, she restructured her fees, and—perhaps more importantly—she stopped apologising for them.

Beyond individual healing, the scale also helps highlight relational patterns around money. Partners, families, and teams often experience conflict not because of differing financial goals, but because of misaligned emotional currencies. One partner may view saving as safety, the other as restriction. One may enjoy spontaneous spending as a form of self-expression, while the other sees it as irresponsible. By naming these emotional differences, the scale can be used as a tool for dialogue, compassion, and collaborative planning.

To make the Emotional Currency Scale practical, it should be revisited regularly—much like checking a financial dashboard or reviewing a wellness tracker. Emotions shift with context. What felt empowering during a season of abundance may feel different during a downturn. Regular engagement with the tool allows you to track emotional progress, not just financial results. Over time, this builds emotional agility: the ability to respond to financial life with flexibility, insight, and self-compassion.

Importantly, this approach does not negate the value of traditional financial tools. It enhances them. A budget without emotional awareness can become a source of shame. A savings plan without attention to emotional triggers can feel restrictive. A wealth strategy without alignment with values can leave even the most successful individuals feeling hollow. The Emotional Currency Scale acts as a bridge between the numbers and the narrative—making money personal, dynamic, and human.

Critics of emotionally-oriented finance sometimes argue that focusing on feelings detracts from objective planning. Yet, the data tell a different story. Behavioural economist Richard Thaler, in his Nobel Prize-winning work, showed that people do not behave like rational calculators when it comes to money. They follow mental shortcuts, emotional cues, and contextual nudges. To ignore this is to design financial advice for robots, not real people. Integrating emotional awareness into financial planning is not indulgence—it's intelligence.

Furthermore, acknowledging emotional responses does not mean being ruled by them. It means understanding them, so they no longer operate unconsciously. Just as a good CEO considers market sentiment alongside financial statements, a financially empowered individual considers emotional patterns alongside numerical targets. This is not about fragility; it is about full-spectrum awareness.

Ultimately, the Emotional Currency Scale invites us to see money not as a detached tool, but as a relationship—a mirror of our inner world, our past conditioning, and our capacity to evolve. By tuning into this relationship with honesty and curiosity, we create the conditions for flow. Not just financial flow in the outer world, but emotional and energetic flow within ourselves.

In this way, the scale is not merely an assessment—it is an act of self-inquiry. It challenges us to ask: Where do I feel open with money? Where do I contract? What stories are encoded in those reactions? And most importantly, what would it feel like to experience financial life with more freedom, more truth, and more peace?

Money moves where emotion allows. The clearer the emotional channel, the stronger the flow. By using the Emotional Currency Scale as both a mirror and a compass, you begin to locate the blocks, release the tension, and rewire your relationship with money—not as a source of stress or confusion, but as a dynamic expression of your inner alignment. This is where true abundance begins—not in the numbers, but in the nervous system. And from there, the outer shifts follow.

Thought Experiment: If You Inherited $10 Million Today...

It is a compelling fantasy, almost universally shared: the sudden arrival of life-changing wealth. The imagined phone call from a solicitor, the forgotten great-aunt, the surprise windfall—ten million dollars, all yours, tax-free. No more grinding at the job you resent, no more anxiety about bills, no more limits on your choices. Just complete, unassailable financial freedom. Or so it seems.

But what happens when this fantasy is treated not as escapism, but as a diagnostic tool? The thought experiment—"If you inherited $10 million today, what would you do?"—offers far more than entertainment. It provides a revealing mirror into our inner relationship with money: the dreams we cling to, the values we hold dear, and the fears we try to suppress. It excavates subconscious narratives and emotional blocks that govern our financial behaviour, often more powerfully than any spreadsheet or strategy ever could.

This exercise, deceptively simple in form, is psychologically potent. It disarms the usual rationalisations people have about why they're not pursuing what they want—because it removes the obstacle of money. When money is no longer a limiting factor, what is left? What do we actually desire? And, more uncomfortably, what are we afraid of?

At the heart of this experiment is an invitation to bypass the surface-level assumptions that shape our everyday thinking. Most people assume that their financial goals are pragmatic: pay off the mortgage, save for retirement, maybe travel more. But when given permission to dream without restraint, more layered truths often emerge. Beneath the initial fantasies of luxury cars or tropical villas lies something more profound—desires for autonomy, significance, rest, expression, or healing. Just as importantly, latent fears and guilt often surface too.

Consider the case of Priya, a marketing executive who did this exercise as part of a leadership retreat. When asked what she would do with $10 million, her immediate response was, "I'd quit my job, travel the world, and write a novel." But moments later, her expression shifted. She admitted that the idea of having that much money actually made her uneasy. "What if people started expecting things from me? What if I became a target? What if I messed it up and lost everything?" Her fantasy revealed not just a longing for creative freedom, but also a fear of visibility, trust, and self-worth. The thought experiment didn't just illuminate her dreams; it also exposed the internal narratives standing in their way.

This internal ambivalence is common. Financial psychologists have long noted that many people harbour a paradoxical relationship with wealth: they consciously desire abundance but subconsciously fear it. This fear often stems from early conditioning—messages that wealth is corrupting, that it isolates, or that it brings pressure rather than peace. For those from modest or working-class backgrounds, sudden wealth can trigger identity dissonance: a conflict between their current self-concept and the one they believe is required to handle significant money. These tensions, if unaddressed, become upper limits that quietly constrain ambition and sabotage financial growth.

The $10 million thought experiment also provides a canvas upon which to map values. When people articulate what they would do with sudden wealth, they often unconsciously reveal what matters most to them. Some speak about donating to causes, starting community projects, or supporting family members. Others speak of building something lasting—a school, a business, a creative legacy. These desires are not frivolous; they are value statements. They point to core motivators—purpose, contribution, connection—and expose the gap between current financial habits and authentic aspirations.

Take Jeremy, a software engineer who described how, with $10 million, he would fund mental health programmes in underprivileged schools. Yet when asked how he currently allocates his resources, he admitted that his spending was largely reactive—driven by stress, convenience, or social comparison. The exercise helped him recognise the dissonance between his deeper values and his day-to-day financial choices. It was a wake-up call—not to wait for a windfall to live in alignment, but to begin making value-based decisions now.

Beyond values and fears, this exercise also brings to light fantasies that may be compensatory in nature. For instance, someone who imagines buying multiple homes, luxury items, or extravagant experiences may not be shallow or materialistic. Instead, they may be attempting to soothe unmet needs—belonging, safety, or self-worth—through symbolic consumption. Rather than judging these impulses, the key is to understand what emotional voids the fantasy is trying to fill. In doing so, individuals can begin to meet those needs more directly and sustainably, without relying on a financial miracle to deliver emotional healing.

It is important to note that this exercise is not merely hypothetical. The emotions it evokes—whether excitement, shame, resistance, or clarity—are real indicators of one's current financial psychology. They reveal how much capacity one has to receive, manage, and hold wealth. This emotional capacity is just as crucial as practical acumen. Without it, even the most sophisticated strategy will falter.

Behavioural economics offers further support for the insights drawn from this thought experiment. Research by Nobel laureates Daniel Kahneman and Amos Tversky on *loss aversion* shows that people are more motivated by the fear of losing money than by the prospect of gaining it. This explains why some individuals panic at the thought of managing large sums—even hypothetically. The fear of losing something valuable or making a public mistake can be paralysing. Similarly, *status quo bias*—the tendency to prefer things as they are—helps explain why some fantasise vividly but struggle to take even small steps towards those dreams. The comfort of the familiar, even if suboptimal, often outweighs the perceived risk of change.

To make the most of this exercise, it must be approached with honest curiosity rather than performance. There are no correct answers. Whether you dream of solitude on a farm or a penthouse in Manhattan, what matters is the *why*. What are you hoping to feel? Who are you hoping to become? And which parts of that vision are available to you right now, in smaller but still meaningful ways?

Consider Ruth, a schoolteacher who imagined using her hypothetical inheritance to spend more time with her children and take up painting again. She was startled to realise that neither of those desires required $10 million. What they required was permission—permission to prioritise joy, creativity, and presence. The exercise became a portal through which she re-evaluated her time, budget, and boundaries. Wealth, she realised, was less about accumulation and more about alignment.

The deeper lesson of this experiment is that money is not the goal—it is the amplifier. It magnifies who you are, what you value, and how you relate to power, security, and freedom. If your current beliefs around money are rooted in fear, guilt, or shame, a financial windfall is unlikely to resolve those feelings. In fact, it may intensify them. Conversely, if your relationship with money is grounded in clarity, purpose, and emotional regulation, wealth becomes a tool—not just for personal ease, but for meaningful impact.

This is why the $10 million question is so powerful. It invites you to live from the *inside out*, to define wealth not by external metrics but by internal congruence. It encourages you to align your financial behaviour with your authentic self—not in some distant future, but now.

As you sit with this question, resist the urge to rush into planning. Instead, observe your reactions. Do you feel excited, overwhelmed, sceptical, energised? What parts of the fantasy feel real? What parts feel out of reach—and why? What limiting beliefs arise when you imagine holding significant wealth? These reflections are not just mental exercises; they are keys to unlocking your next level of financial and personal expansion.

The $10 million thought experiment is not about the money. It's about emotional truth. It's about recognising the gaps between what you say you want and what you're currently allowing. It's about surfacing the subconscious contracts you've made with yourself around what you're worthy of, what's possible, and what success will demand of you. Most importantly, it's about reclaiming authorship over your financial narrative—so that when real abundance arrives, it finds a home that is ready to receive it.

You may never inherit $10 million. But the clarity you gain from imagining it can be worth even more. It allows you to start living—and spending—with intention. It brings unconscious scripts to the surface and reminds you that the essence of what you seek through money—freedom, peace, creativity, generosity—can begin right here, with awareness, courage, and choice.

Chapter 2
The Quantum Wallet

We tend to view money as a straightforward, material entity—a mere instrument exchanged for goods and services. Yet, beneath this practical veneer lies a far richer reality: money is, in fact, energetic. It carries with it intention, emotion, and meaning. It reflects who we are, signals our values, and influences how we interact socially. If we pause to examine this through the intersecting prisms of neuroscience, quantum physics, and behavioural psychology, it becomes clear that the way we draw money towards us—or push it away—is not solely a matter of logic but also of vibration. This chapter invites you to consider wealth in its full complexity by introducing a concept that might at first seem abstract but is grounded in cutting-edge science: your Quantum Wallet.

"Quantum Wallet" may sound like jargon from a sci-fi novel, yet it describes something very tangible—how your thoughts, emotions, and energetic state shape the movement of money in your life. And no, this isn't mere metaphor. Contemporary advances in physics and neurobiology back what ancient wisdom has long taught: consciousness influences reality. Where you direct your attention matters. Your emotional tone signals opportunity or resistance. The coherence of your inner energy influences whether your goals materialise or remain distant hopes.

At the root of this lies what is sometimes called frequency finance—a burgeoning field that fuses vibrational science with financial behaviour. To grasp it, we need to recall a fundamental truth of quantum mechanics: matter itself is energy. What appears solid to the eye is actually composed of vibrating particles and waveforms, sensitive not just to external forces but to observation itself. The famed double-slit experiment demonstrated this strikingly—particles behave differently when observed. This so-called "observer effect" isn't merely a quirky oddity; it hints at the profound power of attention in shaping what becomes real.

Applied to money, the observer effect acts as a metaphor, though a powerful one, for intention. Where your conscious focus lands—your visualisation, your strategy, your emotional investment—literally shapes outcomes. Vague or passive financial goals? They remain unrealised potential. But clear, emotionally charged objectives supported by aligned action? They grow ever more likely to manifest. This isn't wishful thinking; it's energetic precision in practice.

Take Rayna, a social entrepreneur caught in a cycle of feast and famine, her brand's growth wavering between hope and hesitation. For years, she attracted moments of success—grants, viral exposure—only to retreat in anxiety. When she teamed up with a coach versed in somatic techniques and energy psychology, a subtle shift occurred. They used emotion-mapping to anchor her financial aims in sensory detail—how success would truly feel, how she would carry herself, the person she would become. Months later, Rayna's revenue doubled and, crucially, she felt aligned in a way she never had before. This is frequency finance in action.

Our nervous system plays a crucial role in this dynamic. Acting as the bridge between inner experience and the outside world, it constantly scans for safety and opportunity. An often-overlooked factor is the influence of mirror neurons—those remarkable brain cells firing not only when we act but also when we witness others acting. These neurons underlie empathy and social learning but also something that might be called financial contagion: the unconscious soaking up of attitudes, fears, and expectations about money from those around us.

If your circle is steeped in scarcity—people worried about bills, resisting growth, or harbouring resentment towards wealth—it becomes incredibly difficult, neurologically and emotionally, to maintain an abundant mindset. Your nervous system mirrors their tension and contraction, usually without you even realising it. Conversely, spending time among those who relate to money with confidence, gratitude, and integrity can rewire your emotional baseline. You internalise new standards of what is normal, safe, and achievable. Environment, then, is far more than physical; it is profoundly energetic.

Social neuroscience supports this view. Studies reveal that emotions are contagious and that financial behaviours—whether saving, spending, or investing—are shaped by our social networks. For example, research published in the *New England Journal of Medicine* found that obesity spreads through social circles not due to shared diets but through shifting norms. The same applies to money. Your financial thermostat is, to some extent, a product of your relational field.

This insight points towards the need for intentional practice. Building your Quantum Wallet requires attention not just to digits but to narrative and feeling. Traditional vision boards can inspire but often remain too static, too symbolic, to catalyse true change. What we need is Visualisation 2.0: a richer, embodied approach to manifestation that integrates movement, emotion, and storytelling.

Instead of pinning up images of luxury cars or holiday villas, this new method asks you to *live* your visualisations in the present. Rehearse your future through your body—walk, speak, act as though you already inhabit your desired financial reality. Script narratives that capture not just what you want, but how you think and feel when it is yours. Neuroscience tells us the brain struggles to distinguish sharply between real and vividly imagined experiences. Pairing visualisation with physical embodiment and emotional engagement activates neuroplasticity—the brain's remarkable ability to forge new pathways towards different habits and responses.

Consider Leo, a freelancer stuck on the same income level for five years. His ambitions were clear, yet his body betrayed disbelief—tight shoulders, shallow breath—whenever he imagined earning more. With coaching, Leo learned to combine his goals with deep breathing, movement, and affirmations. Instead of passively meditating, he paced while repeating: "I deliver immense value. I hold more income with ease. I invest from trust." Over time, his nervous system adjusted to wealth as a safe and attainable state. His confidence soared, he negotiated better fees, and his income rose steadily.

Central to this practice is a journaling tool we call *Build Your Quantum Wallet.* This isn't a mere transaction log; it is a living map of your financial identity—how you relate to money on emotional, energetic, and strategic levels. Questions prompt reflection: What frequency do I associate with receiving money? What am I truly open to financially—and what do I unconsciously reject? Which beliefs cap my financial ceiling? How does my body respond to the idea of holding greater wealth? These inquiries create coherence between what you intend and how you embody it, making your financial goals feel both possible and familiar.

They also expose gaps—those awkward spaces where your declared ambitions don't yet align with your internal state. Maybe you want to grow your income but freeze whenever it's time to invest in yourself. Perhaps financial freedom is your stated aim, yet you procrastinate on basic tasks like budgeting or invoicing. Such discrepancies are not failures but invitations—to realign. To build a Quantum Wallet means bringing every aspect of yourself into harmony: thoughts, feelings, habits, and nervous system regulation.

The message here is a profound one: wealth is not merely earned; it is attuned. Money flows when your values, emotions, behaviours, and actions sing in unison. But when your mind craves more while your body shrinks back, or when your ambitions expand while your self-image contracts, money hesitates.

You needn't become a physicist or neuroscientist to grasp or apply this. What matters is becoming a conscious observer of your own inner field—the thoughts you nurture, the feelings you replay, the environments you inhabit, and the stories you tell yourself. The Quantum Wallet is no mystical fantasy but a grounded, evidence-informed framework for aligning your inner landscape with external prosperity.

This chapter will lead you step-by-step through that journey: beginning with the science of frequency and brain function, advancing through sophisticated visualisation methods, and concluding with a practical journaling system to chart your financial energy. By the end, you won't just understand what a Quantum Wallet is—you will have begun crafting one. Not by apps or ledgers, but through alignment, awareness, and a renewed relationship with wealth itself.

Frequency Finance: What Science Says About Vibes and Value

We are increasingly recognising that money is more than a transactional medium—it is a reflection of energy. While traditional financial education focuses almost exclusively on numbers, strategies, and behaviours, a deeper layer of reality is often left unexamined: the energetic frequency from which those behaviours arise. This is not metaphorical fluff or new-age rhetoric. The emerging field of "frequency finance" bridges quantum physics, neurobiology, and behavioural science to illuminate how our inner state—our "vibration"—affects our capacity to attract, sustain, and expand wealth.

To understand frequency finance, we must begin with a foundational principle from quantum mechanics: everything is energy. What appears solid is, on a subatomic level, made up of particles vibrating at various frequencies. These particles do not exist in isolation, but in constant interaction with their environment. The implications are profound: the observer affects the observed, intention can influence matter, and coherence of frequency can determine the stability or breakdown of complex systems. These are not fringe hypotheses; they are well-established principles in modern physics. When extrapolated into the domain of personal finance, they suggest that the way we *feel*, think, and direct attention is not merely psychological—it is energetic.

But what does "frequency" mean in practical, observable terms? In physics, frequency refers to the number of oscillations a wave completes in a given period. In human terms, frequency can be understood as our predominant emotional and physiological state. Emotions have measurable electromagnetic signatures. Studies using EEG and heart rate variability (HRV) technology show that emotions like gratitude and love produce coherent, high-frequency patterns, while stress and fear generate disordered, low-frequency fields. The HeartMath Institute has pioneered research in this area, demonstrating that heart-brain coherence—achieved through regulated breathing and positive emotional focus—can enhance cognitive function, emotional resilience, and even influence the external environment through electromagnetic resonance.

This isn't spiritual romanticism; it's empirical. If our emotional state has a vibrational pattern, and if that pattern influences both perception and action, then it logically follows that financial decisions are being made from either a state of coherence or dissonance. Coherent states promote clarity, focus, and calm decision-making. Dissonant states generate impulsivity, confusion, and avoidance. This insight alone has massive implications for how we approach money.

Consider Nadia, an interior designer who constantly felt on edge around her finances. Despite earning well, she was chronically under-saving and over-spending. No budget or app seemed to fix the issue. Through coaching, she realised that her nervous system was perpetually activated—stuck in a subtle but persistent fight-or-flight state due to childhood instability around money. This dysregulated frequency was clouding her judgement, leading her to avoid financial planning because it unconsciously reminded her of threat. Once she began practising daily coherence techniques—heart-focused breathing, gratitude journaling, and intentional presence—her relationship with money shifted. She began budgeting not from fear, but from empowerment. Her savings grew, and so did her peace.

Frequency, then, is not about wishing or willing wealth into existence. It is about *entrainment*—a term from physics and biology that describes the synchronisation of rhythmic systems. Fireflies entrain their flashing patterns; human menstrual cycles entrain when cohabiting; and your internal energetic field entrains with the dominant energies around you. If you frequently dwell in stress, shame, or lack, you entrain your nervous system—and eventually your behaviour—to scarcity. If you cultivate coherence, alignment, and positive anticipation, you begin to entrain to abundance. These are not moral states; they are physiological conditions. And they are trainable.

Crucially, this reframes the conversation about wealth from being purely tactical to being vibrationally strategic. It explains why two people with similar skills and opportunities can produce radically different outcomes. One might operate from a low-frequency state of doubt and contraction, subtly repelling opportunity. The other, from trust and receptivity, naturally becomes magnetic to aligned outcomes. Entrepreneurs often describe this anecdotally: "Things just started flowing," "Clients came out of nowhere," "I didn't push—it just clicked." These are expressions of energetic alignment manifesting in material results.

There is also a compelling parallel here with behavioural economics. Daniel Kahneman and Amos Tversky's research into prospect theory shows that humans are not rational financial agents. We are highly susceptible to emotional framing, loss aversion, and cognitive biases. When we are in a dysregulated or incoherent state, these biases are amplified. We become more risk-averse, less creative, and more likely to default to short-term thinking. Frequency work—whether through meditation, somatic regulation, or intentional gratitude—interrupts this reactivity. It increases access to the prefrontal cortex, the brain's executive centre responsible for planning, self-control, and goal-setting.

This is why frequency finance is not about replacing spreadsheets with spirituality. It is about integrating both. Money is inherently multidimensional. It is numbers and neurology, vibration and value, strategy and story. When we ignore its energetic component, we remain in a partial paradigm—one that often leaves people overwhelmed, ashamed, or disempowered despite their best intentions.

One of the most compelling realisations in frequency finance is that wealth is not something we chase; it is something we *resonate with.* Just as tuning forks of the same frequency vibrate together, your internal frequency can either harmonise with or repel financial opportunity. This does not mean that wealth comes without effort, but that aligned effort produces exponentially greater returns than effort born of stress and self-doubt.

Practically, this means examining your own financial frequency across various dimensions. How do you feel when you receive money? When you give it? When you talk about it? What physiological and emotional state do you occupy when you budget, invest, or make spending decisions? These questions are not indulgent—they are diagnostic. They help uncover the invisible drivers behind visible results.

Take the example of Theo, a software developer who had read dozens of books on investing but still hadn't started. He cited "not enough time" or "waiting for the right moment." In truth, he felt physically anxious every time he opened his brokerage account. Through coaching and breath-based regulation practices, he traced this anxiety back to his father's volatile relationship with money and his own perfectionism. Once he began doing just five minutes a day of heart coherence breathing before financial tasks, the anxiety subsided. He opened his first investment account, automated small contributions, and gradually built a diversified portfolio—all because he aligned his frequency first.

This is the essence of frequency finance: regulate before you calculate. Align before you act. Visualise before you strategise. These are not soft skills; they are core competencies for a new paradigm of wealth-building that honours the full spectrum of human experience—body, mind, and field.

One powerful metaphor for this is tuning a radio. If you want to hear classical music but your dial is set to heavy metal, it doesn't matter how badly you want Beethoven—you will get distortion. Your internal frequency is the dial. When you adjust it to match the signal you want to receive—calm, confidence, alignment—you increase your receptivity. You become clearer, more grounded, and more discerning. Money, like music, flows best through clear channels.

This chapter, and those that follow, will provide both the theoretical foundations and practical techniques for adjusting your financial frequency. You will explore how to identify energetic blocks, how to use your physiology as an ally, and how to craft rituals and routines that support coherence. You will also learn how to measure your emotional responses to money—not to judge them, but to understand the story they are telling.

Because at its core, frequency finance is not about chasing a number. It's about creating a field—a field of energy, awareness, and intention that invites wealth not only to arrive, but to stay. It recognises that money is not just what you earn; it is what you embody. And that the most powerful wealth strategies are not those that bypass the nervous system, but those that *integrate* it.

The future of finance is vibrational. It is grounded in science, elevated by self-awareness, and activated by coherence. As you deepen your relationship with these principles, you will begin to notice something subtle yet unmistakable: money no longer feels like a source of stress or an external pursuit. It begins to feel like an extension of your inner state—a natural, responsive element of a life lived in alignment. That is the promise of frequency finance. And it begins not with force, but with frequency.

Mirror Neurons and Financial Empathy: How Our Environment Shapes Our Wealth Psychology

In the discourse on money and mindset, much attention has been given to individual beliefs, behaviours, and strategic habits. We are urged to change our thoughts, upgrade our narratives, and take decisive action toward financial goals. While these personal development tools are valuable, they often overlook a powerful, under-acknowledged force in wealth psychology: the influence of our environment. More specifically, the way our nervous system unconsciously attunes to the emotional states of those around us—especially when it comes to scarcity or abundance. At the centre of this phenomenon lies a fascinating neurological mechanism: *mirror neurons*.

Discovered in the 1990s by Italian neuroscientists studying macaque monkeys, mirror neurons are a class of brain cells that fire not only when we perform an action, but when we observe someone else performing it. These neurons are believed to be essential for empathy, imitation, and learning through observation. They are the biological basis of our ability to 'feel with' others.

When someone nearby winces in pain, your mirror neurons activate as if you too were hurt. When you see someone smile or relax, your brain mirrors that state, creating a subtle but real shift in your own emotional and physiological response.

While most commonly discussed in the context of empathy or social bonding, mirror neurons also have profound implications for our relationship with money. Financial states—like joy, anxiety, generosity, or fear—are not just psychological; they are *energetic and emotional frequencies* that can be absorbed through interpersonal proximity. We don't just learn financial behaviours by watching others; we *feel* our way into financial patterns, often unconsciously adopting the emotional tone of those we spend the most time with.

This helps explain why two people with the same income, education, and access to opportunity can have vastly different outcomes in how they earn, spend, or grow wealth. It is not just what they know—it is what they have absorbed through their relational ecosystem. If you are surrounded by individuals who view money as a source of anxiety, guilt, or competition, your nervous system may mirror that state, creating internal dissonance even if your intellectual beliefs point toward abundance. Conversely, if your environment normalises conversations about investment, generosity, or empowered earning, you are more likely to feel regulated and confident in your own financial decisions.

Consider the case of Emily, a rising entrepreneur who had recently transitioned from a salaried role into self-employment. She had read every financial book recommended to her, joined online courses, and hired a coach. Yet despite having the knowledge and strategy, she found herself hesitating to pitch her services, undercharging clients, and feeling intense guilt around money. Through deeper reflection and somatic therapy, Emily traced her discomfort back to her early social environment. She grew up in a community where wealth was regarded with suspicion, and financial ambition was quietly shamed. More recently, her close friends continued to speak about money as elusive, unfair, or morally compromising. Even as she consciously tried to rewire her beliefs, her nervous system was mirroring a constant background frequency of financial contraction. Her breakthrough came not from learning new strategies, but from expanding her community to include people who viewed money as a creative, empowering force.

The role of environment in shaping financial outcomes is supported by research in behavioural economics and social psychology. Nicholas Christakis and James Fowler, in their landmark study on social networks, found that behaviours like smoking, obesity, and even happiness are *socially contagious*. If a friend of your friend gains weight, your likelihood of gaining weight increases—even if you have never met that person. The mechanism? Shared norms and the mirror effect of emotional modelling. If this is true for health and lifestyle, it is equally true for financial behaviours. What your peers normalise becomes your unconscious baseline.

This is not to say that you are a passive product of your environment. Rather, it is a call to become *consciously selective* about the energetic and emotional ecosystems you inhabit. Your nervous system is always listening. It picks up cues of safety or threat, permission or restriction, possibility or limitation—not just from your internal dialogue, but from the subtle dynamics around you. If every conversation about money in your social sphere is laced with stress, scarcity, or moral conflict, your capacity to embody abundance is inevitably constrained.

One of the most potent applications of this insight lies in designing what behavioural scientist BJ Fogg calls a "contextual architecture." Rather than relying solely on willpower or mindset shifts, we can shape our environment to support the internal states we want to cultivate. This means not only curating physical spaces—such as a clutter-free budgeting zone or a dedicated area for money journaling—but also cultivating social spaces that reinforce financial empowerment. Whether it's joining masterminds, following financially literate thought leaders, or intentionally spending more time with those who model wealth with grace and generosity, these decisions rewire not only your thoughts but your physiology.

Moreover, financial empathy—the ability to *feel* the financial state of others—is not always an asset. While empathy builds connection and compassion, unregulated empathy can lead to enmeshment, guilt, or self-abandonment. This is especially true for caregivers, empaths, or individuals in helping professions, who often unconsciously take on others' money stress. They may delay raising prices, hesitate to receive, or overgive out of a mirrored fear that they will be seen as selfish or uncaring. Learning to differentiate *sympathy* from *mirrored scarcity* becomes an act of financial sovereignty.

Boundaries, in this context, are not just psychological—they are neurological. Practices that re-anchor you into your own frequency, such as grounding breathwork, somatic tracking, or reflective journaling, are essential tools for interrupting the mirror reflex when it leads to disempowerment. They allow you to feel with others without losing yourself. To support others without sabotaging your own financial wellbeing. To observe scarcity without absorbing it.

This capacity to remain energetically distinct is especially critical in environments where financial trauma is widespread—within families, partnerships, or communities healing from systemic injustice. While empathy for others' struggles is a vital part of collective healing, over-identification can erode personal agency. True empowerment does not mean disconnecting from those who struggle, but holding a grounded and coherent state that offers stability to the system. In this way, *your nervous system becomes a permission slip*—not just for your own abundance, but for others to expand into theirs.

Real-world examples underscore this principle. When start-up incubators place emerging entrepreneurs alongside seasoned founders, the newer cohort not only learns skills but begins to *embody* the cadence of confidence, strategic thinking, and bold vision. The mirror effect accelerates integration. Similarly, in mentorship-based wealth circles, participants often report that the biggest shift isn't tactical—it's emotional. Seeing someone who looks like them, with a similar background or identity, model financial fluency creates a neurological opening that says, "This is safe. This is possible. This is who I can become."

The most meaningful shifts in your financial life may not come from more effort, but from better resonance. From spending less time in scarcity-saturated environments and more time in spaces that regulate and inspire. From tracking not only what you earn or save, but *how you feel* around money, and who you feel that way with. These subtleties become your financial nervous system's blueprint—one that either contracts in defence or expands in trust.

Ultimately, mirror neurons are a reminder that money is not just personal—it is relational. Your beliefs do not live in isolation. They are shaped in conversation, reinforced through proximity, and embedded in emotional fields. Recognising this allows you to make empowered choices—not just about your financial goals, but about your financial environment.

Ask yourself: Who am I mirroring? What financial energy do I absorb unconsciously? Where am I most expansive—and who am I with when that happens? These questions are not intellectual exercises; they are diagnostic gateways to a new level of financial clarity and coherence.

To build wealth is not only to shift your mindset. It is to tune your nervous system to new frequencies. To align your body and environment with the emotional tone of prosperity. And to remember that sometimes the most profound upgrade isn't internal—it's relational. Because your nervous system already knows how to mirror. The key is choosing what, and who, it mirrors next.

The Observer Effect and Wealth: How Attention Shapes Financial Reality

In the world of quantum physics, one principle has sparked enduring fascination and philosophical reflection: the observer effect. It suggests that the act of observation is not passive; it influences the very outcome being observed. Though rooted in the subatomic behaviour of particles, the implications of this idea extend far beyond the lab. When we apply this principle to human intention and financial life, a powerful insight emerges—*what we observe with focus and emotional engagement tends to materialise.* Attention, it turns out, is not only a cognitive process. It is a creative force.

The observer effect was famously demonstrated through the double-slit experiment, where particles of light or matter exhibited different behaviour depending on whether they were being observed. When left unmeasured, they behaved like waves—fluid, full of possibility. When observed, they collapsed into particles—fixed, measurable outcomes. The experiment shook the foundations of classical physics, challenging the assumption that reality exists independently of the observer. Instead, it posited that the conscious act of observation participates in shaping reality itself.

For many, the connection between quantum mechanics and personal finance may seem far-fetched. Yet when examined through the lens of psychology, neuroscience, and behavioural economics, the parallels become surprisingly tangible. Observation, in this context, can be understood as focused awareness—directed attention, imbued with intention, expectation, and emotion. It is the quality of presence we bring to a goal, the way we visualise our future, the depth of our engagement with a desire or vision. And just like in the quantum field, this observation changes things.

In financial terms, this means that what you consistently focus on begins to shape your experience—not through magic, but through a cascade of neurological and behavioural shifts. The brain's reticular activating system (RAS), a network of neurons in the brainstem, filters the massive amount of sensory information we receive and allows us to notice what we deem important. When you set a financial intention—whether to increase your income, build savings, or launch a business—your RAS starts scanning for relevant opportunities, patterns, and signals in your environment. You literally begin to *see* what you previously ignored. What once appeared random becomes meaningful. The act of intentional observation primes your mind to participate actively in constructing the reality you desire.

Take for example the case of Michael, a corporate analyst who spent years plateaued at the same salary. Although he aspired to financial growth, he rarely examined his goals beyond vague desires. After working with a financial coach, he began tracking a specific intention: to increase his income by 30% within 12 months. Every morning, he reviewed his goal, visualised himself already living with that outcome, and recorded the actions he could take to align with it. Within three months, he received an unexpected job offer at a competitor firm with a significant pay rise. Michael described the experience as uncanny—but it wasn't luck. It was the result of sustained, intentional observation triggering both subtle internal recalibration and the proactive behaviours that followed.

This dynamic is well-documented in psychological literature. Studies on *implementation intentions*—specific plans that link a future goal with concrete action steps—show that people who write down and regularly revisit their goals are significantly more likely to achieve them. The combination of focused attention and structured planning activates neural circuits related to motivation and habit formation. What is striking is how these outcomes mimic the quantum principle: goals left in abstraction remain as uncollapsed waves of possibility. Goals observed—clearly defined, emotionally engaged, and consistently revisited—collapse into outcomes.

Yet the observer effect is not merely about goals. It also applies to *how* we observe ourselves. The narratives we repeat, the identities we reinforce, and the expectations we carry become self-fulfilling prophecies. If you habitually observe yourself through the lens of lack—"I'm not good with money," "I never follow through," "Abundance is for others"—you reinforce those energetic states. The act of internal observation solidifies these self-concepts, influencing both behaviour and physiology.

Neuroscientific studies show that the brain is experience-dependent and plastic throughout life. Self-directed neuroplasticity—the process of using conscious thought to rewire neural pathways—is a powerful tool for reshaping financial identity. When you observe yourself with intention, choosing to hold an image of the empowered, capable, financially fluent self, you activate new patterns of perception and response. This is not about pretending or affirming without conviction. It is about training your attention to dwell in possibility rather than perpetuate limitation.

Consider Aisha, a graphic designer who grew up with strong family narratives around frugality and financial fear. She internalised the belief that wealth was unstable, and that pursuing money would compromise her integrity. Despite her talent, she undervalued her work and avoided high-paying clients. Through reflective observation practices—including daily scripting, visualisation, and somatic grounding—she began to change her internal lens. She no longer just wanted to earn more; she started *seeing herself* as someone who could. This subtle but critical shift in observation preceded a major shift in her business: she doubled her prices, attracted aligned clients, and finally felt congruent with financial expansion.

Attention, then, is not neutral. It is a vector. Where it points, energy follows. And what is observed consistently, with emotion and clarity, begins to materialise—first in perception, then in action, and eventually in results.

However, it is important to distinguish between *active observation* and *passive wishing.* The observer effect is not a loophole in the laws of effort or accountability. It does not suggest that merely thinking about money will cause it to appear. Instead, it points to a more nuanced truth: that when we bring conscious, regulated, emotionally engaged attention to our financial life, we prime our entire system—neurological, behavioural, and energetic—to align with our desired outcomes. The effect is not instantaneous, but it is cumulative and profound.

One of the most effective tools to harness the observer effect is *structured visualisation.* This goes beyond imagining wealth or success in abstract terms. It involves deliberately rehearsing the internal state, behaviours, and outcomes associated with your goal. Visualise not only the result—such as the number in your bank account—but also the process: how you show up, the decisions you make, the energy you exude. Studies in sports psychology show that mental rehearsal can create neural changes almost identical to physical practice. Applied to financial life, this means you can begin *living* the frequency of wealth before external evidence arrives.

This practice becomes even more potent when paired with somatic regulation. If you visualise abundance but your body responds with tension or fear, you're unlikely to sustain that frequency. The observer effect is not purely cerebral; it is embodied. By combining breathwork, emotional attunement, and presence, you create coherence—where thought, feeling, and physiology align. In this state, observation becomes not just mental activity but energetic calibration.

In collective settings, the observer effect explains why shared intention amplifies outcomes. Group meditations, visioning sessions, or mastermind circles create what physicist David Bohm called *shared fields of coherence.* When multiple people focus their awareness on a unified goal—especially when anchored in emotion and clarity—shifts occur not only within individuals, but across the field. This is not just metaphysical speculation; research in social neuroscience and psychoneuroimmunology suggests that collective attention can affect emotional regulation, stress levels, and even biological markers.

At its core, the observer effect invites a radical responsibility: to become the conscious steward of your attention. In a world saturated with distraction, anxiety, and noise, this is no small task. But it is essential. Because what you habitually observe, you energise. And what you energise, you eventually realise.

Ask yourself: What do I observe daily? Do I observe limitation or expansion? Scarcity or possibility? Do I fixate on what's missing, or do I attend to what's emerging? These questions are not rhetorical—they are mirrors. They reflect the quality of consciousness you bring to your financial life. And they offer a doorway into a new kind of prosperity—one that is not merely measured by external numbers, but by internal alignment.

To live intentionally is to observe with purpose. To build wealth, in this quantum-informed sense, is to become a precise, disciplined observer of your inner and outer world—curating your focus, training your perception, and inhabiting your vision long before it manifests. Because the moment you observe something with sustained attention and embodied belief, it begins to move out of the abstract and into the actual.

In this sense, wealth is not just something you pursue. It is something you learn to *see*. And in the act of seeing—clearly, consistently, and coherently—you begin to bring it into being.

Visualisation 2.0: Beyond the Vision Board

For decades, vision boards have occupied a central space in the world of personal development and manifestation. Collages of dream homes, luxury cars, tropical holidays, and inspiring quotes adorn the walls of countless aspiring entrepreneurs, creatives, and spiritual seekers. The underlying idea is simple and seductive: if you can see it, you can believe it, and if you believe it, you can achieve it. Yet, while this approach to visualisation can ignite short-term inspiration, many find themselves disillusioned when the promised outcomes fail to materialise—or worse, when those outcomes arrive but fail to deliver the anticipated emotional satisfaction.

This disconnect arises from a critical oversight: traditional visualisation practices often remain superficial. They focus on symbols and outcomes but neglect the internal mechanisms that actually create and sustain transformation. The images may be curated, but the emotions are rarely engaged with depth or precision. The goals are defined, yet the nervous system is left behind. What's needed is an evolution—a next-generation framework for visualisation that honours the complexity of human behaviour, emotion, and embodiment. This is where *Visualisation 2.0* enters.

Visualisation 2.0 is not about discarding vision boards altogether. Rather, it's about transcending their limitations by incorporating scientifically grounded techniques that activate the body, clarify intention, and integrate emotional resonance. It is a multidimensional approach to manifestation that engages the full self—cognitive, emotional, physiological, and narrative.

At the core of this upgraded practice lies a concept known as *emotion-mapping*. While traditional visualisation asks, "What do you want?", emotion-mapping asks, "How do you want to *feel*?" Neuroscience consistently shows that emotions are the fuel behind behaviour. The limbic system, the brain's emotional centre, plays a pivotal role in encoding memory, shaping decisions, and signalling safety or threat. If your visualisation does not evoke a compelling emotional state, it lacks the neurological imprint necessary to influence sustained action. Conversely, when a goal is paired with a strong emotional signature—such as joy, pride, peace, or confidence—it becomes anchored in the nervous system as a felt reality, not a distant hope.

Consider Sasha, a coach who had spent years visualising a six-figure business. Her vision board was elaborate and meticulously updated each year. And yet, her income plateaued, her confidence wavered, and her motivation fluctuated. It wasn't until she worked with a somatic practitioner that she realised her visualisation practice was missing emotional coherence. The images excited her intellectually, but emotionally, they triggered anxiety, unworthiness, and pressure. Through emotion-mapping, she began identifying the feelings she genuinely desired—ease, spaciousness, creative flow—and aligned her visualisations accordingly. Instead of simply picturing the result, she rehearsed the *emotional experience* of living from that frequency. Within months, not only did her income increase, but her relationship to her work became more joyful and sustainable.

The second pillar of Visualisation 2.0 is *embodiment*. This refers to the practice of activating the body as a participant in visualisation, rather than relegating the experience to the mind. Studies in sports psychology and neuroplasticity confirm that mental rehearsal paired with physical activation can rewire neural pathways more effectively than mental imagery alone. Athletes who mentally practise their routines while engaging in micro-movements or breath synchronisation perform better under pressure than those who visualise in a static state.

Embodied visualisation means feeling the goal in your muscles, breath, posture, and presence. It is walking as the person who already holds that success. It is breathing as if the anxiety has lifted.

It is standing, sitting, and speaking with the gravity of self-trust. This does not require theatrical performance. Often, subtle shifts are the most powerful: a deeper breath, a relaxed jaw, a shift in gaze. These somatic cues send feedback to the brain that the desired state is already being lived. The body, as a storehouse of emotional memory, begins to encode the experience as real—and acts accordingly.

James, a financial advisor transitioning into coaching, exemplifies the power of embodiment. For months, he struggled to communicate his new identity, often defaulting to vague language or downplaying his skills. Through embodied visualisation, he began each day with a five-minute practice: standing tall, imagining himself delivering high-impact sessions, and repeating a simple phrase—"My voice carries clarity and value." Within weeks, he noticed a shift in his tone, posture, and the way clients responded to him. His revenue followed suit. The change was not in his strategy but in his *state*—and that state was cultivated through embodied rehearsal.

The final element that distinguishes Visualisation 2.0 from its predecessor is *narrative scripting*. This involves writing or speaking from the perspective of the "future self" who has already achieved the desired outcome. Unlike affirmations, which can sometimes feel forced or disconnected from one's current reality, narrative scripting engages the imagination in a more immersive and believable way. It taps into the storytelling architecture of the brain, which is primed to understand the world through narrative structure.

When you write a letter from your future self, journal a "day in the life" of your financial future, or record an audio message celebrating a milestone, you are not only engaging the prefrontal cortex (responsible for goal-setting and planning), but also the hippocampus (which encodes memory) and the amygdala (which tags experiences with emotional significance). The effect is a richly textured simulation that the brain and body begin to accept as familiar. And what is familiar feels safe. And what feels safe becomes easier to act upon.

Narrative scripting also addresses a key blind spot in traditional visualisation: identity. Many people visualise outcomes that conflict with their current self-concept. They want to earn more, but still see themselves as underdogs. They want freedom, but subconsciously believe they must always hustle to deserve it. Scripting allows the new identity to speak—not in generic mantras, but in personal, emotionally resonant terms. Over time, these scripts begin to reshape self-perception, dissolving internal resistance and building congruence between vision and identity.

For example, Jordan, a non-profit director pivoting into consultancy, found it difficult to internalise the idea of earning significantly more. He respected money, but felt uneasy charging high fees. Through scripting, he began to write weekly letters from his future self—a respected consultant working with mission-driven organisations, living in financial ease, and mentoring others. These letters evolved from awkward fiction to authentic dialogue. He began to feel not like he was *pretending*, but like he was *remembering* a version of himself he had suppressed. That shift paved the way for bold action: launching his brand, raising his rates, and embracing visibility.

Together, emotion-mapping, embodiment, and narrative scripting create a triad of depth that elevates visualisation from mood-boosting ritual to strategic rewiring. They transform desire into lived experience, making goals feel not just possible, but *personalised, embodied, and emotionally anchored.* This is not about tricking the mind. It is about aligning the full self with the frequency of fulfilment—before the evidence arrives.

What's critical to understand is that these practices are not linear. They are iterative. Some days, the emotions will come easily; others will require recalibration. Some scripts will feel electric; others will fall flat. The key is consistency, not perfection. Visualisation 2.0 is not about controlling the future—it's about *preparing the nervous system to receive it* with grace and coherence.

This next-level approach is not only more effective; it is more honest. It acknowledges that change is not merely intellectual. It is emotional. It is cellular. It is energetic. And when we engage with our desires through the full spectrum of experience—not just with curated images or lofty goals—we begin to move from aspiration into embodiment.

To visualise effectively is not to escape reality. It is to shape it—from the inside out. With clarity. With emotional integrity. And with the willingness to become the kind of person who can hold what they once only hoped for. That is the promise of Visualisation 2.0. And it is a practice, not a performance. A process, not a shortcut. One that, when embraced fully, transforms the dream not into a destination, but into a lived frequency.

Interactive Practice: Build Your Quantum Wallet

What if your financial reality wasn't just a reflection of your income, expenses, and investments, but also a manifestation of your inner alignment—your beliefs, your emotional frequency, and the story you tell yourself about money? In a world increasingly recognising the interplay between energy, consciousness, and material outcomes, the idea of a *Quantum Wallet* moves us beyond traditional finance into a more nuanced, integrated model. This is not about metaphysical escapism or bypassing practical skill. Rather, it is an invitation to define your financial identity at a quantum, emotional, and strategic level—deliberately and consciously.

At its core, the Quantum Wallet is a concept that merges financial intention with energetic congruence. It represents the vibrational signature you carry around money, shaped by your nervous system, your self-concept, your generational inheritance, and your capacity to receive. The construction of this wallet begins not with external tools, but with deep self-inquiry. To "build" it is to become the architect of your inner financial ecosystem—a space where mindset, embodiment, and strategy coexist in harmony.

This interactive journaling practice is not a one-time exercise. It is an ongoing dialogue between who you've been, who you are becoming, and who you are ready to be. It blends insight from quantum theory, somatic psychology, behavioural finance, and narrative identity theory to offer a multidimensional map of wealth creation. It assumes that money is not merely a goal, but a mirror—and that what it reflects depends on how clearly you are aligned internally.

To initiate the process, you begin by mapping your *current financial frequency*. This includes assessing your dominant emotions around earning, spending, saving, and investing. Do you feel anxiety when money enters your account? Guilt when you spend on yourself? Tension when you discuss money with others? These are not just fleeting feelings; they are embedded signals that influence your financial behaviour. Neuroscientific studies show that decision-making is heavily influenced by emotional tagging—associations your brain has built through past experiences. If earning is tagged with stress, you may unconsciously repel it. If saving is tagged with deprivation, you may sabotage it. Identifying these patterns is the first act of energetic decluttering.

Once you have acknowledged your current frequency, the next step is to articulate your *desired financial identity*. This is where the quantum aspect of the exercise becomes tangible. In quantum mechanics, particles exist in a field of probabilities until they are observed—until the observer's focus collapses them into a definite state. Similarly, your financial identity contains multiple possibilities. But only one becomes dominant: the one you observe most consistently through thought, feeling, and behaviour.

In this exercise, you are invited to observe yourself into the identity you choose. Not hypothetically, but narratively and emotionally. Who is the version of you that earns, holds, and circulates money with grace? How do they think, feel, speak, and act? What habits do they embody? What boundaries do they uphold? And, critically, how do they *feel* when engaging with money—not only when it's flowing in abundance, but also when navigating uncertainty?

Consider Arjun, a data consultant who spent years undercharging because of a deep-rooted belief that asking for more would alienate clients. His financial strategy was sound, but his identity was fragmented. When he engaged with the Quantum Wallet exercise, he realised his self-image was still anchored in a younger, deferential version of himself. Through narrative scripting, he wrote daily journal entries from the perspective of his future self: a confident, well-compensated consultant whose value was recognised and respected. He paired this with breathwork to ground the emotions, allowing his nervous system to register safety in expansion. Within three months, Arjun increased his rates by 40%, retained his top clients, and reported feeling more relaxed during sales conversations. He didn't just change his behaviour—he shifted his frequency.

The Quantum Wallet also demands a look at the *environmental and relational field* you operate within. Since mirror neurons attune us to the emotions of those around us, your wealth identity is shaped not only by your beliefs, but by the financial tone of your ecosystem. Are you surrounded by scarcity narratives, subtle competition, or martyrdom around money? Or by people who view wealth as a tool for purpose, generosity, and growth? Your wallet cannot be built in isolation. It is energetically connected to the relationships, media, and social contexts you engage with daily.

Another component of this practice is establishing a *strategic pathway* that aligns with your energetic and emotional profile. This is where your Quantum Wallet becomes more than a journaling tool—it becomes a bridge between embodiment and execution. You begin to identify the aligned vehicles for wealth generation. Do you thrive in structured environments, or prefer fluidity? Are you most creative when collaborating, or when in solitude? What kind of financial planning methods soothe your system rather than stress it? These strategic choices, when informed by emotional intelligence, are far more sustainable than generic advice. Wealth is not built by adopting the "best" system, but by creating a system that reflects your authentic frequency.

This strategic layer also invites you to measure progress through *resonance*, not just metrics. Traditional finance focuses on numbers alone—income levels, profit margins, ROI. While these are important, the Quantum Wallet asks you to also track your emotional shifts: Do you feel safer receiving? Do you procrastinate less when reviewing your finances? Are you more present when spending? Do you experience more peace when investing? These are not soft metrics—they are the precursors to long-term, meaningful financial expansion.

Real-world examples further illuminate this approach. Take Yvonne, an artist who oscillated between creative flow and financial chaos. When she began building her Quantum Wallet, she realised that she had internalised the archetype of the "starving artist." Through guided journaling, she re-authored her money story, crafted rituals to energetically separate creative work from financial survival, and began treating her business practices as an extension of her artistry. The result was not only increased revenue but a profound internal shift: she no longer resented financial tasks—they became acts of devotion to her future self.

The practice also works across income levels. Rajiv, a tech executive earning a substantial salary, still felt scarcity due to generational trauma and an internalised fear of loss. His journaling revealed that his self-concept was frozen at a time when his family had lost everything in a financial crisis. Through daily observation of his current abundance—paired with somatic practices that helped his body feel safe in having—he recalibrated. He didn't need more income. He needed more *permission* to enjoy what he already had. His Quantum Wallet helped him identify the emotional leaks that no amount of money could plug.

As you engage with this practice, expect resistance. Your current identity will not surrender easily. The nervous system, primed for familiarity over fulfilment, may signal discomfort when you begin to embody a new financial frequency. This is not regression—it is recalibration. Each time you revisit your journal, you are not simply writing; you are *observing*, collapsing the wave of potential into the form of your choosing.

Building your Quantum Wallet is not about scripting an idealised fantasy. It is about crafting a living, breathing architecture of financial identity that feels emotionally coherent, energetically aligned, and strategically grounded. It invites you to bring precision to your desires, clarity to your habits, and compassion to the parts of you that still hesitate.

The journaling prompt is simple, but its depth is profound: *Who am I as a financially empowered being? What does that version of me think, feel, do, and believe? And what would it look like to start living from that state today—even in small, symbolic ways?*

In answering this, you are not forecasting a distant future. You are encoding it—neurologically, emotionally, and energetically—into the present. Because wealth, in this paradigm, is not something you build from the outside in. It is something you *align with*, from the inside out.

Your Quantum Wallet is not a container for your money. It is a container for your *alignment.* And when you build it with intention, what flows into it reflects not just your work, but your worth. Not just your ambition, but your integrity. And not just your goals, but your evolution.

Chapter 3
Anchoring Abundance in the Body

For all our intellectual grasp of money—our carefully crafted goals, endless spreadsheets, and morning affirmations—real financial transformation doesn't start solely in the mind. It actually begins in the body. Beneath the surface of figures and stories lies a physiological terrain, shaped by memory, experience, and the primal instinct to survive. This chapter delves into how our somatic state—our nervous system's sense of safety or threat—profoundly colours whether money feels like a doorway to opportunity or a trigger for distress. To cultivate lasting wealth, the first step is to anchor abundance firmly within the body.

This might sound a touch abstract until you consider the countless examples: the freelancer who consistently undercharges despite a stellar portfolio, the business owner who endlessly postpones sending invoices, or the investor who panics and exits the market at the faintest sign of turbulence. These behaviours rarely arise from ignorance or poor decision-making alone. More often, they reveal somatic stress left unprocessed—nervous systems conditioned by experience to link money with danger.

Enter the emerging discipline of somatic wealth, which offers a compelling explanation. Rooted in somatic experiencing—a trauma-sensitive therapeutic approach developed by Dr Peter Levine—this perspective acknowledges that trauma isn't simply a memory stored somewhere in the brain; it is etched into the body. When faced with overwhelming experiences—be they acute financial shocks, chronic scarcity, or inherited generational wounds—the body learns to associate particular cues with threat. These might be internal sensations, like the surge of excitement at a payment notification, or external triggers, such as glancing at a daunting bank statement. Either way, they spark subconscious survival responses: freeze, flight, or fight.

These reactions are orchestrated by the autonomic nervous system, with a special role played by the vagus nerve—a central player in

Dr Stephen Porges' polyvagal theory. The vagus nerve, a key part of the parasympathetic nervous system, governs our capacity for rest, digestion, and social connection. When it's functioning well, we feel safe, curious, and creative. When dysregulated, anxiety, withdrawal, or reactivity take hold, even if no immediate threat exists.

Applied to finances, this means that our ability to take measured risks, invest in ourselves, negotiate firmly, and act decisively isn't merely a matter of will or intellect. It's intimately tied to whether our physiology senses safety. You simply cannot outthink a nervous system trapped in survival mode. No matter how many financial courses you complete or mindset mantras you recite, they won't stick if your body is in fight-or-flight.

This realisation flips the conventional wealth-building script. Safety must come before success—not as procrastination or indulgence, but as the very bedrock. When the body feels secure, the prefrontal cortex—the brain's centre for rational planning and executive function—remains engaged. When the body perceives danger, rational thought shuts down and reactive instincts take over. This explains why so many make impulsive or avoidant financial choices under pressure: biology hijacks reason.

To root abundance in the body, we need to cultivate practices that calm and regulate the nervous system. Breathwork stands out as one of the simplest yet most potent tools. Deliberately slowing the breath and engaging the diaphragm sends reassuring signals to the vagus nerve, nudging us away from the sympathetic (fight-or-flight) state towards the parasympathetic (rest-and-respond) mode. With time, this rewires the nervous system to tolerate growth—to remain composed when income rises, opportunities knock, or visibility expands.

Consider Clara, a creative entrepreneur who, for years, unknowingly capped her earnings. Every time she secured a high-paying client, she'd procrastinate, question her worth, or even fall ill. On paper, Clara's business acumen was solid: marketing, networking, ongoing education. Yet her body had learned to link success with stress. Through somatic coaching and breathwork,

Clara developed a ritual of "resourcing" herself—connecting to feelings of safety, grounding, and pleasure before sending invoices, raising prices, or investing further. Within a year, her income doubled, and more importantly, burnout diminished significantly. Her financial breakthrough wasn't due to a new strategy; it came from recalibrating her nervous system.

The stories like Clara's are not anomalies but glimpses of what becomes possible when financial growth aligns with somatic intelligence. In this chapter, you will learn to recognise your body's default reactions to money-related stress—whether it's freezing at budgeting, avoiding debt discussions, or pushing too hard for stability. You'll be introduced to foundational somatic tools: grounding techniques, orienting exercises, and micro-movements designed to signal safety to the brain.

Crucially, you'll also explore the distinction between perceived financial threat and real danger. Often, the nervous system reacts to perfectly benign triggers—a declined payment, a late invoice, a tense money conversation—as though life-or-death. Recognising the gap between past trauma-driven reactions and present reality creates the space to respond with clarity, not reflex. This is not about dismissing financial challenges or slipping into wishful thinking; it's about cultivating enough somatic spaciousness to face issues lucidly.

We will also examine the emotional body—how feelings like shame, guilt, grief, or anger embed themselves deep within our relationship to money. Often, financial trauma transcends numbers, tapping into what those numbers symbolise. Debt may represent failure; savings might evoke abandonment rooted in family history. These emotional imprints live not just in the mind but in fascia, muscles, and nervous system. Somatic awareness helps bring these patterns to light, enabling transformation and healing.

The implications stretch beyond personal wellbeing. Anchoring abundance in the body disrupts cycles of scarcity handed down through generations. It allows us to embody regulated wealth—expanding without collapse, giving without depletion, receiving without fear. This work holds special importance for marginalised or historically excluded communities, where financial trauma intertwines with systemic injustice. Somatic wealth offers a path to reclaim not only money but dignity, agency, and energetic sovereignty.

Throughout the chapter, you'll be guided through practices, reflections, and integrative exercises aimed at helping you regulate, realign, and reconnect. Building a somatic relationship with money that isn't driven by fear or fantasy but grounded in presence. This doesn't mean banishing all stress—it means developing resilience to navigate financial expansion without losing yourself.

To attempt wealth-building without anchoring it in the body is like constructing on shifting sand. Rooting abundance in the body, by contrast, establishes a foundation unshakable: a nervous system increasingly capable of holding more life, more choice, more freedom. This is no quick fix. It's a lifelong return to safety as the starting point of every financial step.

In this way, we cease chasing abundance as something external, and begin cultivating it from within. We stop oscillating between burnout and collapse. Instead, at the deepest cellular level, we start to feel: it is safe to expand, safe to rest, safe to receive, and safe to prosper. Not just as a concept, but as lived reality. This—always—starts in the body.

Somatic Wealth: Where the Body Stores Scarcity

We tend to think of financial behaviour as the product of rational thought—decisions made through deliberate planning, logical risk assessment, and careful cost-benefit analysis. But research across neuroscience, trauma psychology, and behavioural economics reveals something far more complex: much of what we do with money is not cognitive, but *somatic*. Our bodies remember what our minds forget. They encode, store, and respond to financial trauma in ways that shape our everyday choices—sometimes years or even decades after the original experience. Understanding this physiological imprint is the foundation of *somatic wealth*, a transformative lens through which to view money not as a detached tool, but as an emotionally and biologically charged relationship.

Somatic experiencing, a therapeutic modality pioneered by Dr Peter Levine, provides a key framework here. It posits that trauma is not just a story or a psychological event, but a biological one—an unresolved survival energy stuck in the nervous system. When a person encounters a threat—real or perceived—and is unable to fully fight, flee, or freeze and complete the stress response, the body stores that incomplete energy in the musculature, fascia, and autonomic pathways. These unprocessed stress cycles show up later as chronic tension, hypersensitivity, avoidance, or emotional dysregulation.

When applied to the realm of finance, this understanding is revelatory. Financial trauma may not involve physical danger, but it frequently activates the same biological mechanisms. The child who witnessed their parents argue about unpaid bills; the young adult who was humiliated by a landlord for late rent; the immigrant who survived economic instability or war; the entrepreneur who lost everything during a market crash—each of these experiences embeds somatic cues that can influence future responses to money. These imprints often go unrecognised, yet they resurface in adulthood as anxiety when checking a bank balance, dissociation when discussing investments, or guilt when receiving financial abundance.

One striking example comes from DeShawn, a corporate executive who had achieved significant financial success but remained haunted by a fear of losing everything. Despite a secure income, growing assets, and a stable home life, he regularly experienced panic when making large purchases—even those aligned with his goals. Working with a somatic coach, he identified that his body held unresolved memories from a childhood eviction. As a seven-year-old, he had watched silently while bailiffs removed furniture from their flat, his body frozen in helplessness. Although he never spoke of it again, that unresolved trauma lingered in his physiology. Until that survival energy was acknowledged and processed, no amount of financial stability could quiet the fear. His nervous system had coded prosperity as a *temporary illusion*—always one misstep from collapse.

Somatic wealth recognises this disconnect and invites us to bring the body back into the conversation. Instead of trying to override fear with logic or mask discomfort with affirmations, it calls for presence, regulation, and integration. This begins by cultivating *body literacy*—the ability to sense what is happening internally, to track shifts in sensation, and to identify the subtle cues of activation or contraction around financial topics. For instance, when you imagine receiving a large sum of money, do you feel expansion or constriction? Warmth or tension? Groundedness or vertigo? These sensations are not arbitrary. They are your body's barometer, signalling whether money feels like safety or danger.

Crucially, these signals are not always accurate—they are protective, not prophetic. The nervous system does not distinguish between past and present; it only tracks perceived safety. If money once equated to chaos, then even positive financial change can register as threat. This is why people often resist abundance not because they don't want it, but because their body *fears it*. The fear may not be conscious, but it manifests behaviourally: procrastination, undercharging, impulsive spending, hoarding, or avoidance of financial visibility.

Understanding somatic wealth also reframes how we approach financial education. Most traditional programmes assume that people struggle with money because they lack knowledge or discipline. But this approach fails to consider the *somatic capacity* to implement change. You cannot teach budgeting to someone whose nervous system goes into fight-or-flight at the sight of numbers. You cannot teach investment strategy to someone whose body freezes in the face of risk. Before there is action, there must be regulation.

Somatic tools offer pathways toward this regulation. Grounding exercises, breathwork, orienting (noticing the environment through the senses), and resourcing (connecting with sensations of safety) can help recalibrate the nervous system. These practices don't just create momentary calm—they build *capacity*. Over time, they expand the window of tolerance, allowing individuals to stay present with financial discomfort rather than dissociate or react.

Case studies abound with transformative outcomes from this approach. Leila, a small business owner, discovered that her inability to scale her offerings wasn't due to poor time management, as she had assumed, but to a deep freeze response. Whenever she neared financial growth, her body shut down—mirroring the immobilisation she had felt during her parents' bankruptcy years earlier. Through somatic therapy, she learned to track the early signs of shutdown (tight throat, shallow breathing, blank mind), and instead of pushing through or collapsing, she began using gentle movement and paced breathing to stay regulated. This embodied awareness translated into action: she hired help, raised her rates, and began saving consistently for the first time in her life.

One of the most overlooked aspects of somatic wealth is its role in *receiving*. Many people, particularly those with caregiving tendencies or complex trauma, are conditioned to associate receiving with danger, shame, or obligation. Their bodies brace against generosity. Compliments are deflected. Payments are dismissed. Opportunities are minimised. This isn't modesty—it's physiological resistance. If receiving once led to punishment, resentment, or abandonment, the body will learn to avoid it. Rewiring this response requires more than positive thinking; it demands repeated experiences of safe receiving, coupled with somatic anchoring to recondition the body's expectation of support.

The broader implications of somatic wealth extend into collective and intergenerational healing. Financial trauma is rarely individual. It is embedded in histories of displacement, colonisation, racial injustice, and patriarchal control. For many communities, scarcity is not just an economic condition—it is a somatic inheritance. Reclaiming safety around money, then, becomes an act of resistance and reclamation. When a first-generation graduate invests without panic, or when a mother from a marginalised community charges her worth without apology, it is not just financial—it is ancestral work. It sends a message to the nervous system, and to the next generation: "It is safe to thrive."

Practical application begins with awareness. Pay attention to your body's signals when interacting with money. Where do you hold tension when thinking about debt? What happens to your breath when checking your bank account? What posture do you assume when discussing pricing or asking for a raise? These micro-cues are diagnostic—they point to stored narratives waiting to be acknowledged and integrated.

From there, you can begin to re-pattern. Use breath to anchor into the present when reviewing finances. Pair financial tasks with sensory grounding (such as holding a weighted object or lighting a candle) to counteract activation. Speak aloud affirming truths *while noticing how they feel in your body*. If discomfort arises, pause and explore it—don't override it. Over time, this practice builds *somatic congruence*—where your cognitive goals and your nervous system's sense of safety are aligned.

Ultimately, somatic wealth is not about eliminating fear. It is about increasing the *capacity to stay present* with fear without being ruled by it. It is about reclaiming the body's role as an ally in financial wellbeing, not a saboteur. And it is about realising that abundance isn't something you force into existence—it is something you *learn to feel safe holding*.

By bringing the body into the financial conversation, we begin to build wealth from the inside out. Not as a bypass, but as a deep integration. Not as a temporary mindset shift, but as a rewiring of the very foundation from which all financial decisions arise. When the body no longer carries the weight of unspoken scarcity, a new kind of prosperity becomes possible: one rooted in regulation, resilience, and embodied trust. That is the essence of somatic wealth—and it starts with listening to the signals you've long been taught to ignore.

The Polyvagal Theory of Prosperity: How Emotional Regulation Shapes Financial Risk and Resilience

Prosperity is often framed as a matter of mindset, discipline, or strategy. Rarely is it seen as a function of *physiology*. Yet the more we learn from neuroscience and trauma-informed psychology, the clearer it becomes that our ability to make, manage, and multiply money is deeply influenced by the state of our nervous system. At the heart of this understanding lies the *polyvagal theory*—a groundbreaking model developed by Dr Stephen Porges that explains how our body's sense of safety shapes our behaviour. Applied to the context of finance, it suggests that your capacity to take risks, weather uncertainty, and remain calm under financial pressure is not just a trait—it's a *state.* And that state is governed in large part by a single, powerful structure: the vagus nerve.

The vagus nerve, the longest cranial nerve in the body, travels from the brainstem down through the throat, heart, lungs, and digestive tract. It is a cornerstone of the parasympathetic nervous system and plays a critical role in regulating stress responses, emotional regulation, social engagement, and gut instincts—all of which are intimately tied to how we experience money. Whether you panic when making investment decisions, freeze when confronted with budgeting tasks, or find yourself oscillating between overwork and avoidance, chances are your vagus nerve is involved.

Polyvagal theory helps us understand why some people remain grounded and strategic in the face of financial challenge, while others spiral into anxiety or immobilisation. It posits that the nervous system operates through three primary states. The first is *ventral vagal activation*, a state of safety, connection, and engagement. When we are in this state, we feel calm, focused, and capable. It is the ideal physiological condition for making thoughtful decisions, taking measured risks, and engaging in complex planning—precisely the capacities required for financial growth.

The second state is *sympathetic activation*, often referred to as the fight-or-flight response. Here, the body prepares for immediate action: heart rate increases, digestion slows, focus narrows. While this state can be useful in short bursts—such as negotiating a high-stakes deal or making a rapid investment decision—chronic sympathetic activation leads to hypervigilance, impulsivity, and burnout. Financially, it shows up as compulsive spending, hoarding, micromanagement, or excessive risk-taking born of desperation.

The third and most misunderstood state is *dorsal vagal shutdown*, a form of physiological collapse associated with helplessness, fatigue, and dissociation. In this state, the system goes offline to conserve energy in the face of overwhelming threat. It manifests as procrastination, avoidance of money tasks, paralysis in decision-making, or a sense of numbness around financial goals. People in this state often describe themselves as "bad with money" or feel chronically stuck, despite having the knowledge and skills to move forward.

Understanding these states is key to what we might call *financial self-regulation*. Most people assume that better financial outcomes require more willpower or better strategy. But as polyvagal theory reveals, if your nervous system is in survival mode, no strategy will stick. The real challenge is not just behavioural—it is biological. To act differently, we must *feel safe enough* to do so.

Consider Olivia, a freelance consultant who consistently underpriced her services despite a decade of experience. When asked why, she said, "It's just easier—I hate confrontation." Yet when she began somatic coaching informed by polyvagal theory, it became clear that raising her rates triggered a sympathetic spike: shallow breathing, clenched jaw, tunnel vision. Her body interpreted assertiveness as danger—a remnant of childhood experiences where speaking up led to punishment. By learning vagal regulation techniques—such as vocal toning, rhythmic breathing, and gentle movement—she slowly trained her system to remain in ventral vagal state during fee conversations. The result wasn't just more income, but a deeper sense of personal agency and calm.

This is the essence of *prosperity through polyvagal awareness*: recognising that financial choices are made not in a vacuum, but within the constraints of our nervous system. Risk tolerance is not fixed—it is flexible, dependent on how safe or threatened we feel. Emotional regulation is not just a soft skill—it is a core financial competency.

The practical applications of this are profound. Before making a significant financial move—be it launching a business, investing in a course, or restructuring debt—the question should not be "Is this the right decision?" but "*Am I in the right state to make this decision?*" If the body is in sympathetic overdrive or dorsal collapse, you are less likely to access long-term thinking, empathy, or clarity. If the body is in ventral vagal tone, you are more likely to evaluate options with discernment, communicate effectively, and follow through with confidence.

One of the most powerful tools for supporting vagal tone is *breathwork*. Slow, deep, diaphragmatic breathing stimulates the vagus nerve, reducing heart rate and shifting the body into parasympathetic dominance. This isn't just about feeling calm—it's about accessing a physiological state where your prefrontal cortex (the part of the brain responsible for decision-making, foresight, and impulse control) can function optimally. Regular breathwork practice has been shown to reduce cortisol, increase heart rate variability, and improve emotional regulation—all of which directly impact your financial behaviour.

Another tool is *interoception*, the ability to sense internal bodily states. Research shows that people with higher interoceptive awareness are better at managing uncertainty and tend to make more congruent decisions. When applied to finance, this means learning to *feel* the difference between a regulated yes and an anxious impulse, between aligned expansion and fear-driven overreach. Interoception helps you tune into your "gut" not as a metaphor, but as a neurological reality.

The vagus nerve also governs the *social engagement system*, which influences how we relate to others during financial interactions—whether negotiating contracts, collaborating with partners, or asking for support. When vagal tone is high, we are more likely to maintain eye contact, modulate our voice, and stay attuned to cues of connection or rupture. These microbehaviours build trust and ease, both essential for long-term financial relationships. When tone is low, however, we become abrupt, avoidant, or overly appeasing—patterns that can erode partnerships and undermine negotiations.

This has particular relevance in high-stakes or high-visibility financial contexts. Entrepreneurs pitching investors, employees requesting raises, or leaders navigating economic downturns all require not just intelligence and preparation, but *nervous system resilience*. Polyvagal-informed training can mean the difference between stumbling under pressure and showing up with coherence, confidence, and adaptability.

Real-world transformations continue to illustrate this connection. Take Jeremy, a startup founder who froze during investor pitches despite rehearsing extensively. His body would go cold, his voice thin, his thoughts disorganised—classic signs of dorsal vagal response. Through polyvagal-informed somatic work, he learned to bring himself into ventral state before presenting—using vocal resonance, positive memory recall, and co-regulation with a trusted colleague. As his state changed, so did the outcome: his pitches became more fluid, his presence more grounded, and his funding efforts more successful.

The implications for policy and education are equally important. If we want to foster true financial literacy, we must teach people not just *what* to do with money, but *how* to inhabit a physiological state in which financial decisions become safe to make. Schools, community programmes, and coaching frameworks should integrate nervous system education as part of financial wellness. This is particularly vital for communities that have experienced systemic marginalisation or economic trauma, where vigilance and shutdown are not dysfunctions, but adaptations.

Ultimately, the polyvagal theory of prosperity reminds us that success is not a disembodied concept. It is lived in the tissues, felt in the breath, expressed through the voice. It is less about conquering fear and more about cultivating regulation. Not through force, but through *attunement*—to the self, to others, and to the present moment.

Financial growth, then, is not just a product of what we know or do. It is a function of *how safe we feel while doing it.* When the body feels safe, the mind becomes strategic. When the nervous system is regulated, the vision becomes reachable. And when the vagus nerve is engaged, prosperity ceases to be a distant goal—it becomes a lived, embodied state. Not a peak to reach, but a rhythm to sustain.

Safety Before Strategy: The Somatic Prerequisite for Smart Financial Decisions

In the world of personal finance, it is widely assumed that smart decisions stem from sound strategies. We are taught that if we simply gather the right information—budget efficiently, invest wisely, save diligently—success will follow. Yet countless individuals find themselves paralysed in the face of these very strategies. Despite knowing what to do, they avoid spreadsheets, procrastinate on investment decisions, or make erratic financial moves under pressure. The disconnect is not a lack of intelligence or information. It is a lack of *safety.* True financial readiness begins not with strategy, but with *nervous system regulation.* In other words, it is not just what we know about money that matters—it's how safe we feel when engaging with it.

The idea that safety must precede strategy may appear counterintuitive in the high-performance world of wealth-building. But when we understand how the brain-body connection governs behaviour, the logic becomes undeniable. When a person feels unsafe—emotionally, psychologically, or physically—their brain shifts from the prefrontal cortex (the centre of rational planning and foresight) into more primal regions like the amygdala and brainstem. These structures are responsible for survival-based responses: fight, flight, freeze, or fawn. In this state, long-term thinking shuts down. Risk tolerance collapses. Creativity dims. And the very strategies that might support growth become inaccessible, irrelevant, or even threatening.

This is why someone might, for example, know that investing in a long-term index fund is a rational move, yet feel a visceral panic at the idea of parting with their savings. It is why entrepreneurs who are skilled and visionary may still hesitate to launch their offers, raise prices, or hire support. Their sense of safety—not their intellect—is what determines whether strategy is usable or sabotaged. The nervous system, not the spreadsheet, is calling the shots.

The growing field of neurofinance—where neuroscience meets money management—corroborates this understanding. Research shows that stress impairs financial decision-making by increasing impulsivity and reducing the ability to process complex information. In states of heightened arousal, people become more loss-averse, more reactive, and more prone to black-and-white thinking. Conversely, when individuals feel safe and regulated, they are more likely to assess risk accurately, delay gratification, and think strategically. In short, *regulation creates access to rationality.*

A powerful case study is that of Amir, a talented creative director who had recently inherited a modest but significant sum from a family member. On paper, he was financially literate. He'd read investment books, understood market principles, and had access to trusted advisors. Yet the money sat untouched in his account for over a year. Every time he tried to make a move—whether investing in a portfolio, launching a project, or even transferring it to a high-yield savings account—he felt his chest tighten, his mind go blank, and an overwhelming urge to delay. It wasn't until he began working with a somatically-informed financial coach that the pattern became clear: the inheritance, while a gift, was also linked to grief, survivor's guilt, and deep uncertainty. His body did not feel safe holding or using the money.

Through practices that combined breathwork, mindfulness, and slow, titrated exposure to financial tasks, Amir gradually built a new sense of internal stability. He learned to notice the moment his nervous system started to activate, and to pause—not to retreat, but to *regulate.* Over time, he reclaimed his agency, made a thoughtful investment in a socially responsible fund, and used a portion of the money to start a design mentorship programme in honour of his late relative. None of this required new financial education. It required *safety.*

This brings us to the central tenet of this subchapter: *mindfulness is the gateway to investment readiness.* While many associate mindfulness with meditation cushions or quiet contemplation, its truest form is presence—being aware of your internal state in real time, without judgement. When applied to financial decisions, mindfulness allows you to track the moment your body shifts from engagement to contraction. It helps you discern the difference between a rational hesitation and a trauma response. And it offers a pause long enough to choose a new path.

Mindfulness also disrupts the narrative that financial decisions must be made in a state of pressure. High-pressure environments—like last-minute deals, market panics, or urgent deadlines—often force individuals into dysregulation. The most aligned decisions tend to emerge when one is grounded, centred, and connected to their values. Slowing down is not the same as avoidance; it is a *strategy of integration.* It ensures that action is informed not just by external advice, but by internal congruence.

Practical tools for cultivating this safety-first approach begin with *interoceptive awareness*—tuning in to your body's signals before, during, and after financial tasks. Notice your breath, muscle tone, posture, and heart rate as you open a budgeting app, discuss money with a partner, or meet with an advisor. If you feel activation—tightening, heat, or numbness—pause. This is a cue that your system may be bracing. Take a few deep, diaphragmatic breaths. Place your hand on your heart or belly. Shift your gaze to a neutral object in the room. These subtle practices are not a detour from financial empowerment—they *are* the doorway.

Safety also means acknowledging and working with personal and ancestral money trauma. For many individuals—particularly those from historically marginalised or economically precarious backgrounds—money has never been safe. It has been tied to instability, shame, or even survival. Strategies that ignore this context often backfire. True readiness involves integrating these histories with compassion and clarity, creating new associations of safety around financial action.

This integration is not only psychological but behavioural. Taking micro-steps in a regulated state builds capacity. For example, transferring a small amount into an investment account—not with a sense of urgency, but with ritual and intention—can help build trust between the body and the financial process. Each act of congruent action reinforces the message: it is safe to grow. It is safe to engage. It is safe to expand.

This principle is especially important in high-stakes financial decisions such as entrepreneurship, investment, or up-levelled earning. These moves require risk. But not all risk is created equal. *Calibrated risk*—the kind that leads to sustainable prosperity—requires a baseline of internal safety. When this is present, the risk feels alive, expansive, and meaningful. When it is absent, the same move can feel overwhelming, chaotic, or self-abandoning.

Carmen, a business coach, offers a compelling illustration. She had scaled quickly and was encouraged to hire a large team. Strategically, the numbers added up. But something felt off. Her sleep was erratic, her digestion flared, and she noticed irritability and disconnection from her work. When she paused to listen to her body, she realised she was operating from sympathetic overdrive—chasing growth without anchoring safety. Instead of expanding, she stabilised. She restructured her calendar, built in somatic support, and took time to re-engage with her vision from a grounded place. When she eventually hired, it was slower—but far more sustainable.

The broader implications of "safety before strategy" are immense. Financial education must evolve beyond knowledge transmission to include *nervous system literacy*. Coaches, planners, and educators should be equipped not just to explain investment vehicles, but to recognise signs of dysregulation in clients. They must understand that when a person stalls on implementing a plan, it may not be resistance—it may be unresolved fear. Safety is not optional. It is foundational.

In a culture that glorifies speed, hustle, and ambition, the wisdom of regulation is often overlooked. Yet those who build wealth with resilience, joy, and integrity are almost always those who have learned to listen to their bodies. They know when to act, when to pause, and how to return to centre. Their strategy is not divorced from self-awareness—it is born of it.

To make sound financial decisions, your body must feel secure enough to hold both the uncertainty of the present and the possibility of the future. Without that security, no amount of data or planning will create coherence. But with it, strategy becomes more than a cognitive exercise—it becomes a lived, embodied practice of trust.

Safety is not the opposite of growth. It is its *precondition*. And when we honour that truth, our financial decisions become more than transactions. They become expressions of clarity, courage, and regulation. They become the foundation for a prosperity that is not just material, but deeply, and sustainably, felt.

Breathwork for Financial Clarity: Shifting from Fight-or-Flight to a Receiving Mindset

In modern personal finance discourse, clarity is often spoken of as a mental function—about spreadsheets, goals, and strategic decision-making. Yet those who work at the intersection of somatics and financial behaviour have come to understand a more nuanced truth: *clarity begins in the body*. It is not merely the product of cognitive processing, but of nervous system regulation. When the body is bracing—tight, shallow-breathing, reactive—clarity recedes. And when the body softens—grounded, rhythmic, and safe—clarity returns. Nowhere is this connection more evident than in the transformative practice of breathwork.

Breathwork, long known within yogic and meditative traditions, is gaining recognition across neuroscience, psychology, and trauma-informed coaching as a direct and powerful way to regulate the autonomic nervous system. It serves as a bridge between unconscious physiological responses and conscious choice. For those navigating financial uncertainty, high-stakes decisions, or long-held money anxieties, breathwork offers a rare and vital opportunity: to shift from survival reactivity into receptivity. From contraction into clarity. From grasping into groundedness.

This shift is not merely symbolic. It is measurable. Studies in psychophysiology have shown that slow, diaphragmatic breathing enhances vagal tone—the capacity of the vagus nerve to regulate stress responses. High vagal tone is associated with increased heart rate variability, reduced cortisol levels, and improved emotional resilience. These physiological states, in turn, are directly correlated with better decision-making, improved impulse control, and a greater ability to assess risk accurately—all essential for sound financial behaviour.

Consider the case of Rahul, a small business owner who found himself cycling between scarcity-driven overworking and financial freeze. Despite multiple certifications and a loyal client base, he struggled to manage his revenue and routinely sabotaged profitable opportunities. When invited to try breathwork, he was sceptical. "I need numbers, not new-age techniques," he said. But within weeks of practising a simple rhythmic breath pattern—inhale for four counts, exhale for six—before engaging with financial tasks, he noticed subtle shifts. The urge to avoid his accounts lessened. His thinking felt more spacious. He began separating the emotional charge from the numbers. Over time, he transitioned from reactive flurries of financial activity into calm, consistent stewardship. Breath didn't just calm his nerves—it *returned him to himself.*

The science behind this effect lies in how breath influences the *sympathetic and parasympathetic branches* of the nervous system. When we are in a state of fight-or-flight, our breath becomes shallow, rapid, and often restricted to the upper chest. This fuels a loop of physiological arousal, making it harder to focus, trust, or plan. Conversely, when we intentionally slow and deepen the breath, especially through extended exhales, we activate the parasympathetic response—specifically the ventral vagal state associated with safety, connection, and executive functioning. This state is the foundation not only for calm, but for creativity and clarity.

In the context of financial decision-making, this is critical. Whether reviewing a budget, preparing for a negotiation, or choosing between competing investments, the state of the nervous system colours perception. Under stress, a neutral fluctuation in the market can feel catastrophic. A minor cash flow delay can feel like failure. Opportunities appear as threats, and abundance feels unsafe. Breathwork interrupts this distortion. It allows the mind to recalibrate and see the situation for what it is—not through the filter of trauma, but through the lens of presence.

Another vital function of breathwork in financial transformation is its capacity to open the *receiving channels.* While much attention is given to earning, saving, and spending, few explore the embodied skill of *receiving.* For many, especially those with histories of financial instability or relational trauma, receiving—whether money, support, recognition, or opportunity—triggers discomfort. The breath constricts. The posture tightens. The nervous system reverts to protective vigilance.

This physiological resistance to receiving is not a character flaw. It is often the residue of past experiences where receiving was linked to danger—strings attached, obligations imposed, or punishments delivered. Over time, the body learns: to receive is to risk. Breathwork, when practised with awareness and safety, begins to unravel this association. It creates a container where receiving becomes a felt experience of safety, not threat.

Sophia, a senior executive with decades of career success, encountered this dynamic unexpectedly. When offered a promotion with significant financial increase, she found herself spiralling into self-doubt and overwhelm. "I know I've earned this," she told her coach, "but something about it feels wrong." As they explored further, it became clear that receiving the new role activated memories of an earlier career experience where success had led to burnout and betrayal. Her body had collapsed into dorsal vagal shutdown—low energy, detachment, and indecision. Through guided breathwork that emphasised lengthening the exhale and visualising safe expansion, Sophia slowly reconditioned her system to receive recognition and compensation *without collapse.* She accepted the role, but more importantly, she received it into her system with alignment and capacity.

The practice of breathwork does not need to be complex to be effective. One of the most accessible techniques involves simply extending the exhale longer than the inhale. For example, inhaling for a count of four and exhaling for a count of six helps activate the parasympathetic system. When practised regularly—even for three to five minutes—this pattern trains the body to associate stillness with safety. Over time, it becomes a physiological anchor, available even in moments of high financial stress.

Another approach is *box breathing*—inhaling, holding, exhaling, and holding again for equal counts (often four or five). This creates a rhythmic structure that stabilises attention and soothes erratic nervous system responses. Particularly useful before high-stakes financial conversations or moments of decision-making, this breath pattern builds coherence between the heart, brain, and body.

It is important to note that breathwork is not a bypass. It does not replace financial strategy, literacy, or action. Rather, it is the *condition* that makes those things more effective. It prepares the soil so that planning can take root. It shifts the state so that the strategy can land. It softens the body so that abundance, when it arrives, can be held without sabotage.

Critically, breathwork also invites us into a deeper trust in timing—what many call "divine timing" or "universal flow." When the breath is erratic, our timelines are desperate. When the breath is steady, our timelines become trusting. This does not mean inaction or complacency. It means releasing the illusion that urgency creates effectiveness. It means making decisions from a state of grounded presence, not scarcity-induced panic.

This principle is particularly relevant in a culture that often idolises urgency. "Act now," "Buy before midnight," "You're missing out"—these are not just marketing tactics; they are nervous system triggers. They prey on fight-or-flight responses. Breathwork is a radical act of refusal. It is a reclamation of agency. It says: *I will not be hurried into disconnection. I will act from alignment, not adrenaline.*

Integrating breathwork into financial life does not require adding more to an already full plate. It requires *pausing* before action. It means checking in before checking out your accounts. It means arriving in your body before arriving at the meeting. It means giving yourself three minutes of breath before that client call, that budget session, that investment review. These micro-practices create macro-shifts. They return sovereignty to the individual.

Ultimately, breathwork is not about becoming a calm person. It is about becoming a *present* one. It is about creating an inner environment where clarity is possible, risk is manageable, and receiving is safe. It is not a technique—it is a practice. A remembering. A return.

As you engage with your financial life—whether through planning, earning, saving, or sharing—ask yourself: *What is the state of my breath?* And if it is shallow, fast, or held, do not judge it. Just notice. And then gently, kindly, begin again. Inhale. Exhale. Regulate. Receive.

Because in the space between one breath and the next lies your access to wisdom, alignment, and the kind of clarity that no spreadsheet alone can provide. This is breathwork for financial clarity. And it changes everything.

Case Study: From Panic to Prosperity — How Somatic Work Helped an Entrepreneur Transform Financial Anxiety into Sustainable Growth

Financial anxiety is rarely just about money. It is a physiological experience—visceral, reactive, often paralysing—that originates not in spreadsheets but in the nervous system. For many entrepreneurs, especially those operating without a safety net or navigating complex personal histories with money, anxiety is the silent undercurrent that shapes business decisions. It interferes with pricing, constricts strategic thinking, and sabotages scalability. This case study explores how one entrepreneur's transformation from chronic financial panic to prosperous ease was made possible not through more aggressive tactics or productivity hacks, but through *somatic work*—a regulated return to the body that changed everything, including her bottom line.

Meet Eliana, a 39-year-old brand strategist who had been self-employed for nearly eight years. By all external measures, she was successful: a full client roster, glowing testimonials, and a steady income that supported her modest lifestyle. Yet beneath the surface was a constant hum of anxiety. Despite her achievements, Eliana lived in dread of checking her accounts. She avoided tax conversations with her accountant. She undercharged despite years of industry experience. She'd land high-profile clients, then lose sleep over whether she was "delivering enough." Most tellingly, every time she approached a higher income bracket, she found a way to slide back to a familiar but stressful financial baseline. The ceiling was invisible, but the pattern was undeniable.

When she began somatic coaching, Eliana didn't expect it to affect her finances. "I thought we'd talk about boundaries or burnout," she recalled. "I didn't realise my nervous system was running the whole show." Her first session revealed what cognitive mindset work had failed to reach: a body that equated financial growth with threat. Subtle physiological cues emerged as she discussed her income goals—tightness in her chest, shallow breathing, clenched hands. Her voice would speed up when she spoke about raising her rates, then drop when she mentioned potential backlash or losing clients. Her coach didn't rush to fix the anxiety; instead, they focused on noticing it.

This process of *somatic tracking*—paying close attention to internal sensations in real time—became the cornerstone of Eliana's transformation. Rather than force herself to override discomfort, she learned to name it: "There's heat in my throat." "My stomach just dropped." "My shoulders are up again." This non-judgemental awareness began to interrupt the automatic stress loops that previously drove her behaviour. Over time, she developed the capacity to pause and *stay with* the sensations, instead of avoiding or reacting to them.

Eliana also began to explore the *origin stories* of her financial anxiety. Through somatic inquiry—guided reflections that connected bodily responses to past experiences—she uncovered memories that had lived dormant but active in her system. A particularly formative one involved watching her single mother cry over unpaid bills, the shame thick in the air, as Eliana stood silently in the hallway, not knowing how to help. Her child's body had absorbed the lesson: money equals distress. Responsibility equals danger. Success equals burden. These were not thoughts—these were *somatic truths*, encoded in the tissues.

As these associations surfaced, Eliana didn't need to relive them traumatically. Instead, her coach guided her through *resourcing exercises*—simple but profound practices that anchored her body in safety while revisiting emotional material. Visualising a warm blanket, placing a hand over her heart, orienting to safe objects in the room—all of these allowed her nervous system to rewire its response to financial cues. Instead of bracing for collapse, she began to cultivate a felt sense of grounded expansion.

This internal shift began to ripple outward in practical, measurable ways. Within a month, Eliana raised her baseline rate by 15%, and for the first time, no client pushed back. She began separating her personal and business accounts—something she had postponed for years due to unconscious discomfort. Most significantly, she began implementing a practice called *financial embodiment mapping*: each week, before reviewing her finances, she would spend five minutes in diaphragmatic breathing, then track her bodily sensations while looking at her income and expenses. When tension arose, she would pause and apply a grounding technique—movement, breath, or gentle self-touch—before proceeding. Over time, the task that once spiked her anxiety became emotionally neutral, even empowering.

The results were not instant, but they were cumulative. Within six months, Eliana's monthly income had grown by 35%. By the end of the year, she had more than doubled her annual revenue. But what surprised her most wasn't the numbers—it was her *experience* of the numbers. "I'm not afraid of success anymore," she said. "Or rather, when I am, I know how to meet it." That distinction marked a new kind of prosperity—one built not on avoidance or force, but on regulation and presence.

Her relationships also shifted. With greater financial confidence came healthier boundaries with clients. She stopped over-delivering out of guilt or fear. She restructured her offerings to reflect her actual energy capacity, rather than a scarcity-fuelled sense of obligation. These choices, though strategic, were rooted in somatic safety. Her body no longer defaulted to appeasement. Instead, she acted from a state of coherence—a felt alignment between value, expression, and reception.

Eliana's story is not an outlier. It reflects a growing body of evidence suggesting that financial dysregulation is not merely behavioural—it is embodied. Many entrepreneurs, especially women and those from marginalised or under-resourced backgrounds, carry somatic imprints of financial trauma that no amount of financial literacy can override. Until the body feels safe, the brain will sabotage. Until the nervous system trusts, the strategy will stall.

This is why somatic work must become a central pillar of financial coaching and entrepreneurial development. It is not a supplement to real business acumen—it *enables* it. Without it, we risk treating symptoms (underpricing, overworking, avoidance) without addressing the source. With it, we unlock a deeper layer of transformation that is both sustainable and scalable.

From a theoretical standpoint, Eliana's case also supports key insights from polyvagal theory. Developed by Dr Stephen Porges, this model explains how the vagus nerve governs states of safety and threat, determining whether we are able to engage socially, think creatively, or collapse into survival modes. Eliana's early shutdown response to money tasks reflected a dorsal vagal state—characterised by disconnection and numbness. Through somatic tools, she began to access ventral vagal tone—a state of social engagement, emotional resilience, and strategic foresight. This shift was not intellectual; it was *embodied.*

Her story also challenges common assumptions about motivation and mindset. For years, Eliana had been told to "push through" her discomfort. To hustle. To fake confidence until it stuck. But these strategies had only reinforced her dysregulation. The moment she stopped trying to override her body—and began to listen to it—her behaviour changed. Not from willpower, but from *integration.*

This case study offers several practical insights for entrepreneurs and financial professionals:

First, somatic safety is not a luxury—it is a prerequisite. Financial clarity, courage, and creativity all depend on a regulated nervous system.

Second, behaviour follows physiology. If you're stuck in avoidance, procrastination, or financial sabotage, the question is not "What's wrong with me?" but "What does my body need to feel safe right now?"

Third, somatic tools—though often subtle—are powerful. A breath pattern, a grounding gesture, or a shift in posture can change your capacity to engage with complex financial decisions.

Finally, true prosperity is not measured solely by income growth. It is felt in the capacity to *receive*, to *rest*, and to *respond* to money from a place of dignity and trust.

Eliana's transformation—from panic to prosperity—did not follow a straight line. It was non-linear, relational, and profoundly embodied. And it stands as a testament to what becomes possible when we stop treating the body as a barrier to financial success and start recognising it as the foundation. Because when the body feels safe, prosperity stops being a future destination. It becomes a present-moment experience—lived, known, and sustained.

Chapter 4
Reframing the Financial Narrative

Our relationship with money is far more than a simple tally of earnings and expenses; it is deeply entwined with the stories we tell ourselves—often without realising that many of these narratives have been passed down to us, quietly, over years and generations. These inherited scripts, forged in early childhood and reinforced by family, culture, media, and personal experience, shape the invisible frameworks guiding our financial behaviour. Whether it's the quiet, nagging thought of "I'm hopeless with money" or the suspicion that "wealth inevitably corrupts," such beliefs don't merely mirror our reality—they actively construct it. And yet, how many navigate their financial lives without ever pausing to question where these deep-seated stories originated, or whether they still serve us?

This chapter invites a moment of pause—a chance to examine the architecture of your financial self-image. This isn't about blame or reductionism; it's an act of conscious authorship. If your money story has been shaped by fear, shame, scarcity, or a sense of unworthiness, simply changing your habits won't suffice. You need to rewrite the narrative underneath. In doing so, you reclaim more than just control over your finances—you reclaim sovereignty over the identity that money has long coloured or distorted.

Let's start with a fundamental truth: you didn't choose your original money story. Like an old script handed down without your consent, it was written for you before you even knew you were a character. Some messages were explicit—a parent cautioning, "Money doesn't grow on trees," or a teacher warning, "You'll never earn from that." Others were subtler, more insidious: watching a caregiver silently sacrifice their wellbeing to support others, teaching you that earning comes with guilt, or that success must be hidden to belong. These messages don't just lodge in your thoughts; they settle deep within your nervous system, shaping how comfortable you feel with visibility, ambition, or receiving.

Over time, these stories become self-fulfilling prophecies. Believing "I'm irresponsible with money" makes it less likely you'll engage with your finances, perpetuating disorganisation. Thinking "rich people are greedy" can, often unconsciously, push you away from wealth—even if part of you desires it. These aren't trivial opinions; they are core beliefs that hold your behaviour in place.

Psychology calls this cognitive schema formation—the development of internal frameworks through which we interpret new information. Schemas shape what we notice, how we remember, and what we expect. When a financial schema is built on scarcity or inadequacy, even promising opportunities get filtered through suspicion or unworthiness. The first step to shifting this is awareness: noticing these scripts when they arise and asking, "Whose voice is this? Is this belief true? Useful? Or simply inherited?"

Reframing is no naïve optimism or forced cheerfulness. Rather, it is a deliberate, psychologically grounded practice of crafting alternative narratives that feel both believable and empowering. Drawing on cognitive behavioural therapy and narrative coaching, this chapter shares evidence-based approaches to loosening limiting beliefs. For instance, instead of "I'm terrible with numbers," a shift to "I've struggled with financial systems before, but I'm discovering methods that work for me" is subtle, yet profound—it opens a door to action while respecting your reality.

To deepen this work, we turn to wealth archetypes, rooted in Jungian psychology. These patterns of belief and behaviour reveal the roles we unconsciously adopt around money. Perhaps you identify with The Martyr, whose worth hinges on sacrifice and who feels guilt at earning more than others. Or The Magician, who trusts in abundance and creativity but struggles with structure. Maybe The Miser, who clings tightly to control, fearing generosity will drain resources. These archetypes aren't boxes to confine you, but mirrors—tools of compassion that reveal habitual patterns. Later in the chapter, you'll have the chance to pinpoint your dominant archetype through a reflective quiz, setting the stage for integration and growth.

Language, too, plays a crucial role in reshaping identity. Our inner dialogue acts as a feedback loop, reinforcing the beliefs we habitually voice. Here, psycholinguistics—the study of how language shapes thought—comes into play. Research indicates that regular exposure to positive, personalised affirmations can literally rewire neural pathways. Yet, the secret lies in resonance. A phrase like "I am a money magnet" may feel empty if it clashes with your experience. Instead, this chapter guides you to craft affirmations that fit your nervous system's current window of tolerance—phrases that gently stretch your self-concept without snapping it.

For example, if "I am financially free" feels too far-fetched, you might begin with "I'm learning to feel more confident around money each day." These affirmations, spoken aloud or written consistently, act as small nudges, gradually shifting your identity from scarcity to sufficiency, and then towards expansion. The aim isn't fantasy but emotional alignment—the harmony between belief, feeling, and behaviour.

To deepen this reflection, you'll be invited into a thought experiment: Who would you be if money were unlimited? It's a provocative question that often sparks fantasies or discomfort. But this isn't an exercise in material excess—it's a way to explore how much your identity is tethered to financial limitation. If survival were no longer a concern, how might you work, create, love, or lead? What qualities would emerge? And what does that reveal about the invisible constraints you currently accept as fixed?

Such reflection often brings hidden scripts to the surface—around worthiness, responsibility, or morality. Some discover a fear that wealth might estrange them from their community. Others uncover long-suppressed desires for rest, creativity, or activism that only feel safe once survival is assured. These insights aren't merely psychological—they are strategic. When you see how tightly income and identity are entwined, you gain the power to consciously disentangle them.

Throughout this chapter, you won't merely analyse your beliefs—you'll rewrite them. With tools drawn from coaching, psychotherapy, and integrative finance, you'll begin replacing inherited scripts with conscious narratives. Not because your old stories were false, but because they were incomplete—written from survival, not agency. Now, you are ready to author from a place of choice.

This is the heart of reframing your financial narrative: moving from unconscious inheritance to deliberate authorship. It is reclaiming your voice, your values, and your capacity to shape the story money tells about you—not as a tale of lack or excess, but as a reflection of truth.

Money is never just about transactions. It is a story we inhabit. And every story can be rewritten. This chapter hands you the pen—the rest is yours to write.

The Narratives We Tell (and Sell): How Internalised Money Scripts Shape Behaviour

Money is not neutral. It arrives entangled in stories—some inherited, others absorbed, many internalised so deeply that they operate beneath conscious awareness. These money scripts are the quiet narratives we live by: "I'm terrible with money," "You have to work hard for every penny," "Rich people are selfish," "More money, more problems." Though they may appear as harmless clichés or passing thoughts, they are in fact powerful cognitive frameworks that shape our perception, our behaviour, and ultimately, our financial outcomes.

The psychologist Brad Klontz, a leading voice in financial therapy, introduced the concept of *money scripts* to describe the unconscious beliefs we develop about money, typically in childhood. These beliefs are context-dependent, often formed in response to our familial environment, cultural messages, and early emotional experiences. Once formed, they become default settings—heuristics that influence how we earn, spend, save, and invest. They define what feels financially "normal," acceptable, or possible.

Consider the script "I'm bad with money." This belief, while common, is rarely questioned at its root. It may stem from early criticism, a lack of financial education, or a single failure that became overgeneralised. Regardless of its origin, the belief begins to direct behaviour. The person who holds it might avoid budgeting out of shame, miss bill deadlines because they freeze at the sight of numbers, or reject investment opportunities with the assumption they won't manage them well. The tragedy is not the lack of skill, but the internalised identity that prevents skill from developing. As Carol Dweck's research on mindset has shown, identity-based beliefs have a disproportionate influence on learning behaviour. If you believe financial competence is fixed, you will avoid the very activities that build competence.

Another insidious narrative is "Rich people are greedy." This belief may offer temporary psychological comfort—particularly in times of struggle—but it carries a corrosive long-term effect. If wealth is associated with moral failure, it creates an unconscious aversion to abundance. You may set income goals, but find yourself hesitating when success approaches. You might undercharge, overgive, or self-sabotage when financial expansion feels too close. This internal tension is not a lack of ambition—it is a moral dissonance between the desire for wealth and the fear of becoming someone you've been taught to despise. In behavioural economics, this is a classic *cognitive dissonance*, and the nervous system often resolves it not by changing the belief, but by suppressing the behaviour.

These narratives are not only personal—they are also *socially reinforced*. Media depictions of wealthy characters often portray them as villains: callous tycoons, tax dodgers, or emotionally bankrupt elites. Conversely, stories of working-class struggle are romanticised, reinforcing the idea that virtue lives in hardship. This dichotomy has historical roots. In many cultures, religious teachings have glorified poverty while vilifying material excess. Even in modern capitalist societies that outwardly reward success, subtle messages persist: that money changes people, corrupts intentions, or distances us from our roots. These cultural scripts shape our collective relationship with money, but unless made conscious, they also silently undermine individual progress.

There is also a gendered component to these narratives. Women, in particular, are socialised to see financial ambition as unseemly or selfish. The script "Nice girls don't talk about money" is still alive in professional settings, manifesting in lower salary negotiations, hesitancy to invest, and discomfort with financial visibility. For women entrepreneurs, this often results in chronic underpricing and burnout. Financial coach Barbara Stanny has written extensively on the *underearning complex*, which she defines as earning below one's potential due to internalised conditioning. Her research shows that shifting these beliefs is not merely about income—it's about identity, power, and permission.

The intersection of race and money scripts also warrants careful exploration. For many Black, Indigenous, and other marginalised communities, financial narratives are layered with historical trauma, systemic exclusion, and generational scarcity. The script "We don't do money like that" may carry both a protective warning and a constraint on possibility. Prosperity, in this context, is not just about breaking personal barriers—it involves untangling collective wounds and rewriting stories that were never written by choice. These narratives, while limiting, often contain resilience, cultural intelligence, and values that deserve to be honoured even as they evolve.

To rewrite these scripts, awareness is the first step—but not the last. We must ask not only *what* the belief is, but *whose voice* it carries. Is the belief "Money causes problems" a reflection of personal experience, or an echo of parental anxiety? Is "I'll never be rich" a realistic assessment, or an internalised cap from a teacher, partner, or peer? Distinguishing between internalised voices and authentic truth is a practice of psychological reclamation. It allows us to hold beliefs at a distance, to examine them without collapsing into them.

One powerful method for interrogating these scripts is narrative reframing. Drawing from therapeutic writing and cognitive behavioural techniques, this involves articulating the belief clearly, identifying its origins, and then consciously crafting a new version that is believable, grounded, and expansive. For instance, instead of "I'm not good with money," one might reframe: "I'm learning how to relate to money in a way that supports my goals." This is not blind optimism—it is a recalibration of identity that creates space for growth.

Real-world applications of this approach reveal its potency. Take the case of Jason, a freelance designer who had been stuck at the same income level for five years. His financial habits were inconsistent, and he avoided reviewing his income data. When he began exploring his money narratives, he identified a belief inherited from his father: "Success breeds enemies." His father, once laid off after a promotion made him "too visible," had internalised a deep distrust of advancement. Jason carried this belief without knowing it, subtly sabotaging growth to remain hidden. With coaching, he reframed the script to: "My visibility can create connection, not conflict." Over the next year, Jason doubled his client base—not through hustle, but through strategic visibility that aligned with his new belief system.

Changing internal narratives is not instantaneous. These scripts were not formed overnight, and they are rarely rewritten with a single affirmation or workshop. They require repeated engagement, emotional processing, and new evidence. The brain's reticular activating system, which filters what we perceive as relevant, will begin to register new cues when beliefs shift. You'll start noticing opportunities where you once saw threats. You'll begin to expect reciprocity, fairness, and ease—not because life has changed, but because *your lens has.*

This work also requires compassion. Many of our money narratives were once adaptive. They helped us survive, belong, or stay safe in unpredictable environments. Even the most limiting beliefs often had a protective intention. "Don't outshine others" may have preserved relationships. "Always save for a rainy day" may have buffered you from instability. The goal is not to shame these narratives, but to *update* them—to thank them for their service, and then release them if they no longer serve your current context.

Financial healing, then, is not merely about cash flow—it is about *narrative flow.* It is the capacity to examine the plot lines you've inherited and ask whether they reflect your true values, potential, and desires. It is the practice of moving from passive character to conscious author. From inherited script to chosen story.

Ultimately, the narratives we tell—and sell—about money are not trivial. They are cultural blueprints, identity markers, and behavioural cues. They shape whether we believe we can build wealth, hold it, share it, or grow it with integrity. The stories we accept become the ceilings we live beneath. But the good news is this: every narrative is editable. Every belief is revisable. And every sentence you speak about money can either reinforce a cage or unlock a new possibility.

It begins by listening. Then questioning. And finally, rewriting—one line, one belief, one empowered choice at a time.

Cognitive Reframing for Money Goals: Rewriting Limiting Beliefs Using Psychology-Backed Methods

The pursuit of financial growth is often framed in terms of behaviour: budgeting more effectively, investing consistently, or developing new income streams. But these outward actions are underpinned by a deeper, more powerful force—belief. The human brain is a meaning-making machine, and the beliefs we hold about money, often formed early in life, influence what we perceive as possible, safe, or desirable. When these beliefs are limiting—"I'll never get ahead," "Money always slips through my fingers," or "I'm just not wired for wealth"—they become internal ceilings that behavioural change alone cannot break. To truly transform our financial outcomes, we must first address the thoughts that shape them. This is where *cognitive reframing* becomes an indispensable tool.

Cognitive reframing, a technique rooted in cognitive behavioural therapy (CBT), involves identifying irrational or unhelpful beliefs and actively replacing them with thoughts that are more accurate, constructive, and empowering. At its core, it acknowledges that thoughts are not facts—they are interpretations. And when our interpretations about money are distorted by fear, shame, or inherited narratives, they can drive financial decisions that sabotage our goals.

The relevance of this to money goals cannot be overstated. Consider the belief, "I'm just not good with money." This common self-perception, often absorbed from childhood experiences or social comparison, creates a feedback loop. Because the individual believes they are incompetent, they avoid engaging with their finances. That avoidance leads to poor outcomes—missed payments, untracked spending, or neglected savings—which then reinforces the belief. It becomes a self-perpetuating cycle. Reframing begins with interrupting that loop.

The first step is awareness: identifying the limiting belief and recognising its emotional and behavioural consequences. This requires honest introspection. What assumptions do I carry about wealth? How do I explain financial failure or success? What stories have I told myself so often that I now treat them as truths? These questions form the foundation of reframing, and they must be approached with curiosity rather than criticism.

Once identified, the next phase is evaluation. Is this belief universally true? Is there evidence that contradicts it? What are the consequences of continuing to believe this? This process draws on *Socratic questioning*, a method used in CBT to challenge irrational thoughts. For instance, the belief "If I raise my prices, I'll lose all my clients" can be tested against reality. Have others raised their rates and retained clients? Is there evidence that clients value the service enough to pay more? What would be the impact of not raising rates in the long term? Through inquiry, the emotional charge behind the belief begins to diminish.

A powerful illustration of this process comes from Maya, a solopreneur who had plateaued financially for three years. Despite delivering high-quality work, she undercharged and overdelivered. Her core belief, uncovered through coaching, was "Asking for more makes me greedy." This belief had roots in childhood, where expressions of desire were met with reprimand. The reframing process began with identifying the belief, tracing its origin, and then gradually introducing a new perspective: "Charging what I'm worth allows me to serve from a sustainable place." Initially, this felt alien. But over time, and with reinforcement through affirmations and supportive experiences, the belief took root. Within a year, Maya had doubled her income—not because she learned a new strategy, but because she *changed the lens through which she saw herself and her value.*

This brings us to a crucial principle in cognitive reframing: *the replacement belief must feel believable.* Jumping from "I'm bad with money" to "I'm a financial genius" may feel disingenuous and backfire. The nervous system, already primed for scepticism, will reject the new narrative. The key is to create a *bridge belief*—one that is emotionally and cognitively accessible. For example, "I'm learning how to manage my money with more confidence each month" offers a middle path that affirms growth without demanding perfection.

Another effective method in the reframing process is visualisation. When paired with a new belief, mental imagery can anchor the shift by engaging the emotional and somatic systems. Neuroscience confirms that the brain does not differentiate strongly between vividly imagined experiences and real ones. Visualising oneself making empowered financial choices, confidently negotiating a contract, or calmly reviewing monthly accounts activates the same neural pathways that will later be used to carry out those actions. This primes the brain for follow-through and reinforces the restructured belief.

Language also plays a pivotal role in solidifying new frames. Our internal monologue—what psychologists call *self-talk*—is the environment in which beliefs are nurtured or dismantled. Shifting from self-flagellating language ("I always mess this up") to process-oriented language ("I'm experimenting with a new approach") changes not just how we think about ourselves, but how we *feel* about taking action. Psycholinguistic studies show that using present progressive tense ("I'm working on…") fosters a sense of agency and reduces resistance.

Importantly, reframing is not a one-time mental trick—it is a practice. Neural pathways do not change overnight. Beliefs, especially those linked to deep emotional experiences, require consistent exposure to new thoughts and repeated experiences that contradict the old frame. This is where accountability, journaling, and structured reflection come in. By returning to the reframe daily—through writing, speech, or embodiment—you reinforce the alternative narrative until it becomes default.

Real-world examples further affirm the efficacy of this approach. Consider Daniel, a mid-career professional who believed he could never be financially free because he "got a late start." Through reframing, he shifted to: "I bring life experience that helps me build wealth with intention." This reframed belief opened him to financial planning, property investment, and building an emergency fund—all actions he previously avoided due to resignation. His behavioural change was a byproduct of an identity shift.

From a psychological standpoint, this transformation aligns with *self-efficacy theory*, which posits that belief in one's capacity to achieve a goal is a critical predictor of whether that goal will be pursued or attained. By reframing beliefs about what is possible, cognitive reframing elevates self-efficacy and dismantles internal resistance. It turns abstract goals into attainable realities.

There are also broader cultural implications. In a society where financial status is often equated with worth, reframing becomes an act of resistance and redefinition. It allows individuals to detach self-esteem from net worth, and instead centre values like integrity, creativity, and purpose. This is especially powerful for individuals from communities where financial systems have historically excluded or marginalised them. Reframing shifts the locus of control from external structures to internal agency.

Cognitive reframing for money goals, then, is not about denial or false positivity. It is about choosing to think in ways that generate clarity, confidence, and possibility. It honours the past without being bound by it. It engages the brain's plasticity—the capacity to change—and the heart's longing to grow.

In the end, every financial goal is shaped not just by what we do, but by what we *believe is worth doing*. If we believe success is possible, action follows. If we believe it's futile, stagnation prevails. Reframing is the act of choosing the former—again and again—until belief becomes behaviour, and behaviour becomes reality.

The pen is in your hands. What will you write next?

The Archetypes of Wealth: Understanding Your Financial Persona Through Jungian Lenses

At the core of every financial decision lies more than logic, mathematics, or even opportunity. There is a deeper current—emotional, symbolic, and often unconscious—that drives how we relate to money. It explains why one person hoards while another overspends, why someone might sabotage a financial windfall, or why success is pursued with such ferocity it borders on self-erasure. These patterns often defy reason because they are not rooted in reason. They are rooted in archetypes—recurring psychological motifs that shape how we think, feel, and act in relation to wealth.

Carl Jung, the Swiss psychiatrist and pioneer of analytical psychology, introduced the concept of *archetypes* to describe universal symbols and behavioural patterns embedded in the collective unconscious. These archetypes are not static labels but dynamic energies that influence our motivations and identities. When applied to money, they help us decode the *emotional blueprints* behind our financial habits. By recognising our dominant archetype, we gain the insight necessary to shift from unconscious repetition to conscious choice.

In this subchapter, we explore several key wealth archetypes—The Martyr, The Magician, The Miser, The Monarch, and others—each representing a constellation of beliefs, strengths, and shadows. Understanding them is not about boxing yourself in, but about revealing the script you've been acting from, often without realising it. These archetypes offer language for what was previously intangible and provide a compass for growth.

Take The Martyr, for instance—a person who overextends themselves financially for the benefit of others, often at great personal cost. This archetype may be driven by a subconscious belief that their worth is tied to sacrifice. Their generosity is admirable, but when unexamined, it leads to depletion, resentment, and chronic under-earning. Consider the case of Leena, a 42-year-old nonprofit director who consistently dipped into her personal savings to supplement underfunded programmes. Despite working tirelessly, she was always financially strained. Through archetypal coaching, she recognised her Martyr tendencies, traced them back to early familial conditioning around being the "reliable one," and began rewriting her financial boundaries. The shift wasn't just behavioural—it was identity-level. She moved from self-sacrificial giving to *empowered stewardship*, increasing both her income and her impact.

Contrast this with The Magician—an archetype often found in creatives, visionaries, and entrepreneurs. The Magician sees money as energy, believes in synchronicity, and often trusts intuition over spreadsheets. At their best, Magicians are alchemists: they can turn ideas into income with fluidity. But in shadow, they may avoid structure, resist discipline, or use spiritual bypassing to justify financial disorganisation. Ravi, a sound healer and artist, exemplified this pattern. He manifested clients with ease, but couldn't sustain cash flow or plan for taxes. His resistance to "linear systems" kept him trapped in cycles of feast and famine. By integrating aspects of The Architect archetype—who thrives on structure and planning—Ravi didn't suppress his Magician energy; he *balanced* it. He maintained his creativity while introducing consistency, and as a result, stabilised his income for the first time in a decade.

Then there is The Miser—a persona often vilified but rarely understood. The Miser clings tightly to money, motivated by fear of loss or uncertainty. They may pride themselves on frugality, but underneath lies a nervous system attuned to scarcity. The Miser often has a backstory of instability, betrayal, or sudden financial loss. Anna, a successful consultant, found herself unable to enjoy her wealth. She drove a car ten years old, refused holidays, and panicked over minor expenses—even with a healthy bank balance. In therapy, she traced this behaviour to witnessing her father's bankruptcy during her adolescence. Her wealth hadn't changed her body's response to perceived threat. Through somatic work and archetypal exploration, Anna learned to engage with The Sovereign—an archetype grounded in trust, generosity, and long-term vision. As her internal security grew, so did her ability to circulate money with discernment rather than fear.

Jung's model also reminds us that archetypes are not destinies—they are *tendencies*. Most people are not dominated by a single archetype but express a constellation of them, depending on context and phase of life. Someone may embody The Warrior in business—driven, strategic, and relentless—while expressing The Orphan in personal finances, feeling helpless or dependent. The key is not to chase an ideal archetype, but to *integrate* the fragmented ones. Wholeness does not mean uniformity; it means balance.

From a practical perspective, working with money archetypes enhances financial literacy by adding emotional and psychological depth. Traditional financial education often fails because it addresses the "how" of money without the "who." Archetypes give form to the inner worlds that drive behaviour. They help explain why budgeting apps are abandoned, why financial plans are undercut by impulse decisions, and why advice that is rational on paper feels unreachable in real life. When you recognise that you're not bad with money, but perhaps stuck in The Innocent archetype—naïve, dependent, or overwhelmed—you can meet yourself with compassion rather than judgement. From there, you can begin to shift.

This insight is not only beneficial for individuals—it is equally transformative for couples, families, and teams. Financial conflict often arises when different archetypes collide. A Spender (aligned with The Lover or The Rebel) might clash with a Saver (The Guardian or The Architect), not because their values are wrong, but because their fears and desires are misaligned. Understanding each other's archetypal languages fosters empathy, negotiation, and shared vision. In wealth coaching, introducing archetypes often resolves long-standing tension more effectively than spreadsheets ever could.

Furthermore, archetypes are not fixed—they evolve as we do. A client who begins as The Orphan—dependent, overwhelmed, lacking trust—can grow into The Creator, developing a sense of agency and mastery. The key is intentional awareness. Without it, archetypes run us. With it, they serve us.

To support this process, readers are encouraged to engage with the interactive quiz provided later in this chapter. This tool is not diagnostic, but *revelatory*. It is designed to reflect back the patterns, narratives, and behaviours that define your current relationship with money. By answering honestly, you begin the process of financial individuation—moving from archetypal entanglement to conscious integration.

It's also worth noting that cultural and ancestral context plays a significant role in which archetypes dominate. In communities where survival has been precarious, The Guardian or The Survivor may reign—vigilant, resourceful, but resistant to risk. In upwardly mobile families, The Achiever may dominate—status-driven and image-conscious, yet internally insecure. Recognising the lineage of your archetype allows you to carry its strengths while releasing the limitations. You are not bound by inherited patterns. You are the author of their evolution.

Ultimately, working with the archetypes of wealth is not about performing personality tests or finding neat labels. It is about *developing an internal compass*—one that recognises the complexity of who you are and what you carry. It's about illuminating the hidden forces that shape your financial choices, and offering new pathways for expression, growth, and abundance.

In learning your archetype, you meet yourself. In integrating your archetypes, you reclaim power. And in choosing which archetypes to cultivate, you begin to embody wealth not as an external achievement, but as a reflection of inner wholeness.

Money doesn't change who we are—it *reveals* who we believe ourselves to be. Archetypes help us decode that belief, and reimagine what's possible.

Affirmations that Actually Work: How Psycholinguistics Rewires Financial Identity

Affirmations have long held a place in the lexicon of self-improvement, particularly in the worlds of manifestation, mindset, and positive psychology. They are widely promoted as simple tools for rewiring the subconscious mind—spoken or written declarations designed to reprogramme our beliefs and shift our reality. But for all their popularity, affirmations often elicit mixed reactions. For some, they catalyse profound change. For others, they feel forced, hollow, or performative. The difference, as research in psycholinguistics and cognitive neuroscience reveals, lies not in the concept of affirmations themselves, but in *how* they are constructed, delivered, and emotionally received.

To understand why affirmations can be powerful—when done correctly—we must first examine the psychological terrain they aim to influence: identity. Human beings are inherently narrative creatures. We interpret our experiences through language, and our self-concept is largely composed of internalised stories. These stories, repeated often enough, become beliefs. And beliefs, as behavioural economics and neuroplasticity research demonstrate, form the blueprint for behaviour. When we say, "I'm bad with money" or "Wealth is for other people," we are not describing objective truths—we are reinforcing linguistic scripts that govern action.

Affirmations, when grounded in psycholinguistic principles, provide an opportunity to *interrupt* those scripts and introduce new narratives that can eventually be internalised as identity. But they must do more than parrot empty slogans. They must *resonate*, *align*, and *evolve* with the speaker.

One of the critical findings in psycholinguistics—the study of how language shapes thought—is that the brain responds differently to statements perceived as *believable* versus those that feel incongruent with lived experience. When a person with deep-seated scarcity beliefs says, "I am wealthy and successful," their internal systems may reject the statement outright. Rather than building confidence, it triggers a stress response, increasing cognitive dissonance and reinforcing the original belief. In other words, affirmations that leap too far from current identity can backfire.

This insight has led many psychologists and coaches to recommend what are known as *bridge affirmations*—statements that gently nudge identity forward without provoking resistance. For example, instead of saying, "I'm financially free," one might affirm, "I am learning to feel more confident in managing my money." This framing leverages what psychologist Albert Bandura called *self-efficacy*—the belief in one's capacity to execute behaviours that produce desired outcomes. Affirmations that reflect a process, rather than a final state, are more likely to be internalised and acted upon.

Language structure also matters. Research shows that using the present progressive tense ("I'm becoming more…" or "I'm working on…") activates the brain's procedural systems, reinforcing habits and actions over time. It shifts focus from binary thinking (I am / I am not) to developmental thinking (I am becoming), which fosters resilience, especially when progress is non-linear.

Pronoun usage is another subtle but powerful factor. Studies conducted at the University of Michigan found that using *second-person* or one's own name in affirmations ("You've got this, Sarah" or "John is learning to trust himself with money") activates regions of the brain associated with emotion regulation and future planning. This linguistic distancing creates a psychological buffer, enabling individuals to step out of their habitual identity and speak to themselves as they would to a trusted friend or mentor.

Equally important is the *embodied delivery* of affirmations. Neuroscience confirms that beliefs are not housed purely in the neocortex; they are encoded throughout the nervous system. When affirmations are spoken aloud with breath awareness, posture alignment, and emotional presence, they activate somatic pathways that deepen their imprint. For instance, pairing a spoken affirmation with grounding practices—such as placing a hand on the heart, breathing deeply, or standing tall—sends safety signals to the vagus nerve, increasing the body's receptivity to new input. Over time, this practice builds what somatic therapists call *coherence*—a state in which thought, feeling, and physiology align.

Real-world case studies further illustrate these principles. Consider André, a tech entrepreneur who struggled with the belief that

"Money only comes with stress." This belief was reinforced by years of burnout, erratic cash flow, and cultural messaging around hustle. When he attempted to affirm, "Making money is easy," it rang false. But through guided coaching, he developed a new frame: "I am learning to create income with more ease and alignment." By repeating this affirmation during his morning walks—while consciously relaxing his shoulders and syncing his breath—he began to recondition not just his thoughts, but his *felt sense* of what financial success could mean. Within months, he reported a notable decrease in financial anxiety and a more stable client base.

Another example is Priya, a school teacher-turned-coach, who carried the subconscious belief that "Charging for my work is selfish." Her initial attempts at affirmations felt robotic. But when she reframed her statements to reflect her deeper values—"The more I receive, the more I can serve"—and paired this with journaling about past moments where her work made a difference, something shifted. Her affirmation became not just a sentence, but a *truth in motion*—anchored in evidence, aligned with purpose, and delivered with embodied trust.

To personalise affirmations effectively, one must first identify the limiting belief they wish to address. This requires honest reflection. What financial truths do you assume without question? What do you fear would happen if you reached your income goal? What emotions arise when you receive money, or when you think about wealth?

Once identified, the next step is to create an affirmation that *validates your growth*, honours your resistance, and gently points you forward. If a belief says, "I'll always struggle," an effective reframe might be, "I'm open to learning new ways of building security." If you believe, "Success will make me lonely," a reframe might be, "I'm attracting supportive people who celebrate my growth." These statements are not just linguistic tricks—they are new neural grooves, slowly deepening through repetition and feeling.

Affirmations also benefit from *repetition within context.* Saying an affirmation passively has limited impact. But integrating it into key moments—before a financial decision, after a difficult conversation, or at the start of a new venture—helps tether it to real-life change. Contextual affirmations create new memory associations, reinforcing the desired identity through action.

It is also helpful to regularly *revise* affirmations. As your self-concept expands, so too should the language that supports it. What felt aspirational three months ago may now feel authentic, even obvious. This evolution is not just a marker of progress—it is the mechanism of identity transformation. Your affirmations should grow as you do.

From a broader perspective, the practice of crafting affirmations that actually work reflects a deeper cultural shift: from performance to presence. Rather than using language to mask insecurity or chase unattainable ideals, we use language to build congruence between who we are and who we are becoming. This is not about pretending—it is about *practising*.

Ultimately, affirmations are not magic spells. They are linguistic cues that shape attention, energy, and possibility. When rooted in psychological truth, spoken with emotional presence, and paired with meaningful action, they do more than change our mindset—they *repattern our identity*. And from that place, all financial transformation becomes not only possible, but inevitable.

So the question is not whether affirmations work. It is whether we are willing to speak to ourselves with enough honesty, care, and clarity that our words become bridges—between the limitations of yesterday and the self we are choosing to believe in today.

Thought Experiment: Who Would You Be with Unlimited Money?

Ask someone what they would do with unlimited money, and you'll likely hear about travel, homes, charitable donations, or lifelong dreams finally pursued. But shift the question slightly—from *what would you do* to *who would you be*—and the conversation deepens. It becomes less about fantasy and more about identity. This subchapter invites readers to sit with this deceptively simple question not to indulge in financial escapism, but to excavate the assumptions, constraints, and identities we attach to money itself. It is a radical exercise in psychological excavation—an inquiry into how financial status has come to define self-concept, and what remains when that scaffolding is removed.

The premise of this thought experiment is straightforward: imagine that all your financial needs and desires—realistic or extravagant—are permanently met. You have access to any resource you could want. There are no debts to repay, no budgets to manage, no social comparisons to negotiate. Your material security is absolute. Now: *who are you?* How do you spend your time? How do you show up in relationships? What do you create, pursue, or let go of?

Initially, this exercise might evoke excitement, even giddiness. But for many, that feeling quickly gives way to discomfort. Without financial pressure, many of the behavioural patterns, goals, and obligations that once felt non-negotiable are revealed to be *contextual adaptations*. When survival or social acceptance is no longer the motivator, the scaffolding of identity can crumble, leaving behind an unsettling void—or, for some, an exhilarating space of possibility.

Psychologists call this phenomenon *identity foreclosure*—a state in which individuals adopt an identity based on external pressures or constraints without fully exploring alternative possibilities. Money, particularly in late-stage capitalism, is one of the most powerful forces shaping this foreclosure. It dictates career choices, defines status, influences relationships, and even colours morality. Many of us build lives not around intrinsic desires, but around strategies for economic safety. Asking "Who would you be with unlimited money?" confronts this foreclosure and cracks it open.

Take the case of Aaron, a corporate lawyer in his early forties who earned a seven-figure salary but felt chronically dissatisfied. When prompted with this thought experiment during a financial coaching session, his initial response was predictably material: travel the world, buy a second home, perhaps retire early. But when the facilitator pressed further—"And then what?"—Aaron hesitated.

"I don't know who I'd be without work," he admitted. Beneath his success was a tightly wound identity rooted in productivity, external validation, and scarcity conditioning. Even with wealth, he remained entangled in a belief system where *value equalled output.* It wasn't until he began exploring his non-monetised desires—mentoring young lawyers, returning to music, volunteering in prison reform—that a fuller picture of self began to emerge.

This shift—from *instrumental self* to *authentic self*—is the core invitation of the exercise. Money is so often used to compensate for a perceived lack: of freedom, of worth, of power. When we imagine ourselves beyond that lack, we begin to clarify which parts of our personality are truly ours, and which are adaptations to economic terrain. This is where the distinction between *extrinsic wealth* and *intrinsic abundance* becomes essential.

Intrinsic abundance is not the denial of wealth—it is the cultivation of fulfilment, purpose, and identity that are *not contingent on it.* It is what remains when status symbols are stripped away and validation is no longer currency. It is the version of yourself that pursues truth over performance, alignment over achievement. And paradoxically, those who begin to embody intrinsic abundance often find that material wealth becomes less strained and more sustainable, precisely because it is no longer charged with the task of filling emotional voids.

This is echoed in the work of psychologist Shira Taylor Gura, who found that when individuals detached their sense of self-worth from specific outcomes—whether income, recognition, or prestige—they became more psychologically resilient, more creative in problem-solving, and more open to risk. By visualising a life with unlimited money, people temporarily neutralise financial anxiety, allowing them to access this expansive mindset. The exercise serves as a cognitive disinhibition tool—it loosens the grip of internalised scarcity and allows the imagination to reorient around authenticity.

Real-world applications of this idea are visible across diverse fields. In entrepreneurship, founders who begin with intrinsic motivators—solving a problem, serving a mission, expressing a vision—tend to weather setbacks more effectively than those who are purely extrinsically driven. In career design, professionals who align their work with identity rather than income report higher levels of satisfaction, even when their earnings fluctuate. These outcomes are not coincidental—they are the fruits of psychological integration. When your sense of self is internally resourced, external volatility does not threaten your foundation.

The thought experiment also serves as a mirror for *value misalignment.* Many people discover, to their surprise or discomfort, that their current goals are not truly their own. An artist working in finance, a healer working in tech, a teacher dreaming of building a wellness retreat—all examples of people who pursued "safe" or socially sanctioned roles but feel increasingly estranged from themselves. Unlimited money removes the alibi. It reveals the suppressed desire not as indulgent, but as *truthful.* And the invitation is not necessarily to abandon one's current life, but to *reconcile* the gap between internal values and external expression.

There is also a communal dimension to this work. In societies shaped by systemic inequality, exploring identity without financial constraint is not merely personal—it is political. For individuals from marginalised backgrounds, this exercise can be both liberating and painful. It can surface generational grief, inherited financial trauma, or internalised beliefs about what is permissible to want. But it can also offer a radical reclamation: "If I were truly free, I would…." This imagining becomes a blueprint for reparation and redesign—not because it bypasses injustice, but because it affirms the legitimacy of joy, rest, and expansion as forms of resistance.

To engage meaningfully with this exercise, it is essential to approach it with sincerity and nuance. It is not a manifesting trick or a shallow indulgence in fantasy. It is a meditation on what drives you—and what might emerge when the fear of not having "enough" no longer governs your choices. Begin by writing a narrative: a day, a week, a year in your unlimited-money life. Observe the feelings that arise. What brings you alive? What fades into irrelevance? Which habits endure, and which dissolve? Then, reflect on this: which aspects of that life are truly dependent on money, and which are available now, in some form, through re-prioritisation or reframing?

This is not to dismiss the real and enduring material constraints many people face. Economic systems are not neutral, and not everyone has the privilege of contemplating identity detachment from financial status. But precisely because these systems are so dominant, thought experiments like this matter. They disrupt the automatic scripts. They reclaim the imaginative space colonised by fear and obligation. And they remind us that while money is a powerful tool, it is not the sole author of meaning, worth, or destiny.

Who would you be with unlimited money? Not just in action, but in essence? The answer is not fixed. It is a living inquiry—an invitation to design a life not dictated by status or scarcity, but guided by alignment, integrity, and inner abundance.

And perhaps, most profoundly, it is not about imagining a version of yourself far removed from the present. It is about discovering that the wisest, most expansive parts of you are already here—waiting not for wealth, but for permission.

Chapter 5
The Spiritual Science of Budgeting

For many, the very mention of a budget summons up images of austerity—a rigid ledger marked by limitation, a joyless tally of sacrifice and self-denial. Spreadsheets, scarcity, and the dull drum of restriction often spring to mind. But beneath this well-worn cultural shorthand lies something quite different, and far more potent: a deliberate, conscious allocation of energy and intention. Viewed through a spiritual or psychological lens, budgeting sheds its cloak of denial and becomes an act of reverence. It is not about denying life's pleasures; rather, it offers a framework through which life might be expressed more fully, with greater intention and closer alignment to what truly matters.

This chapter puts forward a bold proposition: budgeting is not simply a financial skill, but a spiritual discipline. It functions as a ritual, a sacred container that reveals not only the contours of our economic reality but also our values, wounds, priorities, and ability to be present. In that sense, budgeting shares kinship with meditation or prayer—any mindful act that invites a deeper connection with oneself. It acts as both mirror and map, showing us how we navigate the world, what we honour with our resources, and where we might be unconsciously leaking or avoiding responsibility.

And this isn't merely poetic thinking. Behavioural science tells us the ways we spend—and keep track of—our money are intricately tied to our identity and emotional regulation. When practiced with mindfulness, budgeting can calm the nervous system, ease anxiety, and bolster a sense of agency. It offers structure amid chaos, clarity within the bewildering complexities of modern life. Properly aligned with our deepest values, budgeting does not confine freedom—it magnifies it.

To grasp this shift, we must first understand the notion of sacred structure. Across spiritual traditions, structure is seldom viewed as a constraint; rather, it serves as a container. Consider the sacred geometry found in temples, the measured rhythm of breath in meditation, or the chant of a mantra—these are not burdens but liberations. They provide consistent vessels through which spirit flows. Approached with a similar reverence, budgeting becomes a practice of intentional design. It prompts the questions: What do I truly value? What am I building? What life am I stewarding with my time, energy, and money?

With this mindset, the monthly budget morphs from a chore into a living document of purpose. Instead of launching into categories and limits, we begin with values. This is the essence of values-based spending—a process that starts by identifying your core principles and ensuring your financial habits honour them. If connection ranks highest, does your spending nourish relationships? If creativity is key, do you allocate resources to support artistic expression? If peace is your priority, does your budget relieve stress or feed it?

Psychological research confirms the benefits of aligning behaviour with intrinsic values. Motivational theory tells us change sticks when it springs from who we are inside, not from external targets. Budgeting rooted in values becomes easier to maintain—not through sheer willpower, but because it coheres with identity. You're no longer tracking mere expenses; you're tending to what you cherish.

Still, even when values guide us, money has a sneaky way of slipping away—both practically and energetically. We spend out of habit, anxiety, avoidance, or impulse. Autopilot kicks in, and small purchases quietly snowball into significant consequences. Here, ancient wisdom meets pragmatic tradition in the envelope system. Historically, this meant physically placing cash into envelopes labelled for groceries, rent, leisure, spending only what the envelope contained.

Though digital banking has made actual envelopes somewhat quaint, the principle endures. Creating clear, intentional "containers" for spending anchors focus. Yet, this chapter extends the envelope metaphor, incorporating the idea of energy leaks—those unconscious drains like forgotten subscriptions, impulsive buys that leave regret, or social obligations that feel more like performance than nourishment. Pinpointing and sealing these leaks isn't about moral judgement; it's about conserving life force. Reclaiming your attention, and with it, your power.

Among the chapter's most innovative tools is the Gratitude Ledger. Unlike traditional accounting, which tends to reduce money to cold figures, this practice ties every transaction—income or expense—to a moment of reflection. Paying a bill becomes a pause to appreciate the service received. Receiving income prompts acknowledgement not just of the cash but of the value exchanged. It may sound simple, even quaint, but its psychological effects are profound. Studies in neuroplasticity demonstrate how gratitude reshapes the brain—boosting resilience, lowering stress, and improving decision-making. Linking money with gratitude shifts us from transactional thinking to relational awareness—cultivating abundance not by volume, but through presence.

Consider Saira, a graphic designer who once regarded budgeting as an ordeal of shame, a monthly reckoning filled with self-judgment. When she adopted the Gratitude Ledger, jotting down three things she was grateful for at each budget review, her attitude softened. What had felt rigid and punitive became spacious and reflective. She even found herself anticipating budget time—not as a dreaded audit, but as a monthly conversation with her intentions. The real transformation was not in numbers but in her nervous system's response.

Ultimately, this chapter guides you towards crafting your Aligned Budget—a monthly financial plan weaving together values, structure, mindfulness, and gratitude. This is no off-the-shelf template; it is a framework emerging from within you. It invites tracking not only dollars but stories—where your money flows, where your energy goes, and whether those currents align. Through practical exercises and concrete tools, you'll design a budgeting system that nurtures both your soul and your ambitions.

Most importantly, you will redefine what it means to "be good with money." Not as someone who slavishly follows rules, but as someone who listens, chooses, honours—and builds a financial life rooted not in fear, but in integrity.

Budgeting is not spiritual in spite of its structure—it is spiritual because of it. It is a modern ritual of alignment, an act of self-respect, and a map of what matters most. When embraced with reverence instead of resistance, budgeting stops being a limit and becomes a liberation—not a spreadsheet, but a sanctuary.

Sacred Structure: Why Budgeting is a Spiritual Practice

To the average person, the word *budget* may conjure images of spreadsheets, constraints, and a kind of financial penitence—a necessary evil invoked to contain overspending or to impose order upon economic chaos. Yet when approached through a deeper, more reflective lens, budgeting reveals itself as something far more meaningful: a sacred structure. One that, like meditation or prayer, holds space for intentional living. When reframed not as a tool of deprivation, but as an act of devotion, budgeting becomes a spiritual practice—one that honours what we value, what we steward, and ultimately, how we choose to express our lives through money.

At its essence, spirituality is about connection—between self and purpose, between values and action, between inner truth and outer expression. Budgeting, when approached consciously, facilitates precisely this connection. It is not merely about tracking transactions; it is about witnessing the energetic movement of value through our lives. It is a reflective practice that reveals whether our financial patterns are aligned with our ethics, our aspirations, and our wellbeing.

This perspective is not only philosophically compelling; it is supported by behavioural science. Studies in neuroeconomics have shown that financial anxiety decreases significantly when individuals use structured planning methods, not because they earn more money, but because they feel more *in control*. Control, in this context, is not synonymous with rigidity. Rather, it reflects *agency*—a felt sense that one's actions are congruent with one's intentions.

Budgeting, then, is not about limitation; it is about *liberation through intentionality.*

Consider the architecture of sacred spaces: a temple, a cathedral, a zendo. These are not haphazard or chaotic environments. They are structured by design—geometry, ritual, and rhythm—all working together to facilitate presence. This is precisely the function a budget serves within the spiritual life: it is a container. It offers rhythm to resource management, flow to intention, and boundaries that protect rather than punish. When designed with awareness, a budget becomes a living altar—one that reflects our evolving priorities and our deepest values.

For instance, let us consider the case of Miriam, a yoga teacher and holistic health practitioner. For years, Miriam resisted budgeting, associating it with scarcity and shame. She equated structure with control and feared that budgeting would rob her of the flow and creativity she prized. But her finances were inconsistent, and her anxiety around money was beginning to impact both her health and her work. At the suggestion of a coach, she began to approach budgeting not as a constraint, but as a *ritual.* Every Sunday, she would light a candle, sit in silence, and spend thirty minutes reviewing her finances—not mechanically, but contemplatively. She asked herself: *Where did my energy go this week? Did it reflect what I value? What needs to shift to support my wellbeing?*

This weekly ritual transformed Miriam's relationship with money. Her budget was no longer a cold ledger—it was a narrative. It told the story of her time, her priorities, her generosity, and her misalignments. Over time, she began to feel not only more financially stable but more integrated. She wasn't just managing money; she was *curating a life.*

What made the difference was not the system itself, but the *frame through which it was held.* This is where the language of the sacred becomes indispensable. When we regard budgeting as sacred, we elevate it from task to practice. We slow down. We infuse it with mindfulness. We ask not merely "What did I spend?" but "What did I honour?" We begin to see money not as neutral currency, but as *consecrated energy*—a manifestation of our labour, our choices, our relational commitments.

The significance of this shift is amplified when viewed through the lens of *value alignment.* According to research by Dr Sonja Lyubomirsky and her colleagues in positive psychology, people experience greater wellbeing when their daily actions align with their stated values. Budgeting, therefore, becomes a diagnostic tool: a way to assess whether your financial decisions are congruent with the life you claim to desire. If your budget shows high expenditure on things that exhaust you but little on what nourishes you—creative pursuits, rest, or community—then something essential is being neglected.

Importantly, sacred budgeting does not advocate for aesthetic minimalism or moralistic frugality. It is not about denying pleasure or retreating from material engagement. On the contrary, it invites *embodied abundance*: the practice of resourcing oneself in a way that sustains joy, supports growth, and upholds integrity. Whether that means investing in mentorship, saving for travel, or contributing to social causes, the sacred budget holds space for it—intentionally, respectfully, and with clear energetic boundaries.

Another dimension of budgeting as spiritual practice is *ritual rhythm.* Just as sacred traditions operate on cycles—daily prayers, sabbath rests, lunar observances—a budgeting rhythm creates predictability and trust. It teaches the body and the nervous system that attention to money is not a threat, but a support. Weekly or monthly reviews become rites of passage, marking time not by stress or avoidance, but by presence and renewal. When combined with sensory anchors—lighting incense, using a special journal, creating quietude—these reviews become somatic signals of safety. Over time, they recondition the emotional associations around money from fear and overwhelm to empowerment and clarity.

The shift from shame to sanctity is especially important for those who carry trauma or guilt around money. For many, financial planning triggers unresolved narratives: childhood scarcity, cultural conditioning, or fear of failure. Approaching budgeting as a sacred act softens the emotional charge. It replaces punitive accounting with compassionate awareness. And from this place, transformation becomes not only possible but inevitable.

Real-world examples underscore this shift. Consider José, a first-generation immigrant who had long internalised the belief that money was survival. Every penny was accounted for with fear, every expense evaluated through the lens of loss. When he reframed budgeting as a practice of dignity—a way to honour the sacrifices of his parents and build a future with intention—his financial habits shifted. He began saving not out of panic but out of pride. He invested not in status symbols, but in family experiences that reflected his values. The structure remained the same. What changed was the *soul within it.*

From a behavioural economics standpoint, this reframing also mitigates what is known as *present bias*—the tendency to overvalue immediate rewards at the expense of future gains. Sacred budgeting activates what Dr Hal Hershfield calls the "future self"—a mental construct that becomes more salient when we feel emotionally connected to our long-term wellbeing. By integrating spiritual reflection into financial planning, we foster empathy for our future selves and build habits that serve both the now and the not yet.

Ultimately, the sacred structure of budgeting is not about moralising or micro-managing. It is about *honouring.* It is about recognising that every pound you earn and spend is a thread in the fabric of your life—and that you have the power to weave that fabric with care. It is a spiritual discipline precisely because it requires presence, choice, and responsibility. It asks you to meet yourself in the numbers. Not with shame, but with curiosity. Not with perfectionism, but with reverence.

When you adopt this perspective, the spreadsheet becomes scripture—not because it tells you what to worship, but because it shows you what you already do. And in that awareness lies the power to choose again. To realign. To restructure not just your budget, but your life.

This is the sacred structure. Not rules. Not restriction. But a container for becoming. A living ritual of financial integrity and soulful stewardship—one transaction, one intention, one conscious breath at a time.

Values-Based Spending Plans: Aligning Your Finances with What Truly Matters

Most conventional advice on personal finance begins with categorisation—rent, groceries, transport, savings—as though the act of organising expenses is itself sufficient to foster wellbeing. Yet for many people, this approach produces a mechanical relationship with money, one that treats each transaction as a detached unit rather than part of a broader, more meaningful whole. What's missing from this framework is *intentionality*. Not just where money goes, but *why*—what it reflects, supports, and expresses. A values-based spending plan shifts the focus from external rules to internal resonance, offering a more nuanced, holistic, and sustainable approach to money management.

At its core, values-based spending is not merely about optimising finances. It's about *expressing identity* through economic behaviour. Every pound spent reflects a choice, and every choice is a declaration of priority. The goal, therefore, is not to restrict spending, but to align it with what you most deeply care about. In doing so, you move from reactive consumption to *conscious contribution*—to yourself, your relationships, and the world around you.

This concept draws from both psychological research and practical financial planning. The work of Edward Deci and Richard Ryan, developers of self-determination theory, underscores the importance of intrinsic motivation—behaviour that is aligned with one's values—as a driver of sustained wellbeing. When financial decisions reflect intrinsic values such as creativity, freedom, or connection, the resulting satisfaction is deeper and more enduring than when choices are based on external pressures or social comparison.

In a culture saturated with advertising, status-seeking, and scarcity conditioning, many individuals find themselves spending in ways that *numb*, rather than nourish. Emotional spending is often a compensatory strategy—an attempt to soothe anxiety, assert identity, or escape disconnection. But when money is used to support deeply held values, it ceases to be a trigger for shame or regret. Instead, it becomes a tool of alignment and empowerment.

The first step in building a values-based spending plan is clarifying what you actually value—not what you think you *should* value, but what genuinely animates and sustains you. This often requires looking beyond traditional financial goals like saving for retirement or paying down debt (though these remain important) and asking more existential questions. What brings meaning to your life? What makes you feel most alive, most connected, most whole? For some, the answer is family. For others, it's creative freedom, personal growth, community contribution, or adventure. Values are not abstract ideals—they are *lived orientations*.

Once these values are identified, the next step is translating them into categories of financial expression. If health is a core value, how does your spending reflect that—do you invest in nourishing food, movement, rest, or preventive care? If learning matters to you, are you budgeting for books, courses, or mentorship? If sustainability is central, does your spending pattern support that through local sourcing, ethical brands, or reduced waste?

Real-world examples illustrate the transformational potential of this approach. Consider Aisha, a software developer who was earning well but feeling chronically unfulfilled. Her budget showed high discretionary spending on takeaways, clothing, and streaming subscriptions—none of which aligned with her core values of creativity and social impact. Through coaching, she redesigned her spending plan to include a monthly donation to a literacy charity, a writing course, and a co-working space for creatives. Within months, her spending hadn't decreased dramatically, but its *effect on her wellbeing* had. Her purchases were no longer leaks—they were *investments in identity*.

This reorientation also has cognitive benefits. Research in behavioural finance shows that when people understand the *purpose* behind their spending, they are less likely to experience post-purchase regret. This phenomenon, often referred to as "value congruence," increases satisfaction and reduces the likelihood of emotional rebound spending. In other words, when your purchases match your principles, they continue to pay dividends—emotionally, psychologically, and socially—long after the transaction.

Values-based spending also challenges the idea that budgeting must be reductive. Traditional approaches often prioritise efficiency over meaning, urging individuals to cut "non-essential" expenses. But what is non-essential from one perspective may be sacred from another. For someone whose core value is aesthetic beauty, regular spending on art, clothing, or home design may be non-negotiable. For someone whose value is autonomy, allocating funds for outsourcing tasks or building a side hustle may be more important than saving for a traditional mortgage. The key is not to conform to an external standard, but to construct a budget that reflects a coherent internal compass.

This model also invites us to examine the *shadow side* of our spending. Sometimes, our financial patterns reflect distorted versions of our values. A person who values success may overspend on image-driven purchases in an attempt to feel credible. Someone who values generosity may give compulsively, neglecting their own needs. These are not flaws—they are invitations to deeper inquiry. By examining the difference between the *true value* and its distorted expression, we gain the clarity to recalibrate.

In practice, values-based spending can be implemented using a simple reflective framework. For each major category in your budget, ask: How does this spending support one of my core values? If it doesn't, what need is it trying to meet? Can that need be met in a more aligned way? Over time, this practice becomes habitual. You begin to evaluate not only cost, but *congruence.* Not only return on investment, but *return on alignment.*

This approach is also scalable. Families can use values-based frameworks to build collective financial plans that honour both shared and individual priorities. Organisations can design compensation and benefit schemes that reflect cultural values, not just market rates. Even community budgeting initiatives have begun to explore how public funds can be distributed according to participatory value frameworks, fostering civic trust and engagement.

Case studies in couples' financial counselling also show how this model can reduce conflict. When two people understand each other's values, they stop arguing about the *what* (the expense) and start negotiating around the *why*. A husband who values spontaneity and a wife who values stability can co-create a spending category called "flexible freedom"—a jointly agreed-upon fund that honours both needs. The focus shifts from compromise to *creative alignment.*

Importantly, values-based spending does not require wealth—it requires awareness. Even modest incomes can be managed with deep integrity. A person on a tight budget may choose to cook weekly meals with friends, valuing connection over convenience. Another may allocate their limited funds toward an education savings plan, honouring the value of legacy. These choices are powerful not because they involve large sums, but because they reflect agency and meaning.

Ultimately, a values-based spending plan is not just a tool for managing money—it is a philosophy for living. It asks us to treat our finances not as a burden to control or a resource to accumulate, but as a canvas upon which our values are painted. It bridges the abstract and the concrete, the soulful and the strategic. It affirms that money, like language, tells a story. And we get to decide what kind of story that is.

When your money reflects what matters most, you are no longer merely surviving or striving—you are *living in alignment.* You are no longer reacting to financial pressure, but responding with presence. And in that shift, budgeting becomes less about discipline and more about devotion. Less about what you have, and more about *who you are* becoming.

Envelope Systems and Energy Leaks: Merging Practical Budgeting with Energetic Awareness

In the age of financial apps and algorithmic automation, the simplicity of envelope budgeting might seem like an outdated relic. Yet this traditional system, which involves allocating cash into physical envelopes labelled with specific spending categories, endures because of one fundamental truth: *clarity creates intention.* By offering visual and tactile awareness of limits and choices, the envelope method provides an elegant solution to impulsive or unconscious spending. But what happens when we go a step further—not only mapping where our money goes, but also tracking where our *energy* flows? In merging envelope budgeting with principles of somatic awareness and emotional regulation, we arrive at a modern financial practice that is as strategic as it is soulful.

To understand this evolution, we must first revisit what made the envelope system so effective in the first place. Originally popularised during the era of physical cash management, the envelope system created psychological boundaries by design. You would take your pay, divide it into categories—groceries, rent, entertainment, fuel—and place the designated cash into individual envelopes. When an envelope emptied, so did your spending in that area. The discipline didn't come from restriction—it came from transparency. You could see, feel, and respect the container of your financial intention.

Even as we move into digital environments, the *psychology of containment* remains potent. Behavioural economists like Richard Thaler have long discussed the concept of "mental accounting"—the way humans instinctively divide money into categories even when all funds come from a single source. By creating compartments, we make abstract flows tangible. The envelope method amplifies this instinct and gives it form. In doing so, it counters the numbing effect of frictionless spending—tap, swipe, subscribe—that characterises modern consumer culture.

But envelope budgeting in its traditional form addresses only half the picture. While it tracks where money is going externally, it often overlooks the *internal economy*—the emotional, cognitive, and energetic dynamics that underpin our financial behaviours. This is where the concept of *energy leaks* enters with force.

An energy leak is not just a metaphor. It is a real phenomenon observable through patterns of fatigue, decision fatigue, anxiety, avoidance, or overextension in relation to financial tasks and transactions. These leaks often manifest in the invisible domains: subscriptions forgotten, underused services maintained out of guilt, or emotional spending that provides fleeting relief but long-term depletion. The cost is not just monetary—it is psychological and physiological. You may feel drained not because of how much you're spending, but *how* and *why* you're spending.

Integrating energy awareness into envelope budgeting invites a radical shift in perspective. Instead of merely categorising spending by function—"food," "bills," "entertainment"—we begin to categorise it by *energetic impact*. Which expenses feel light, aligned, nourishing? Which feel heavy, obligatory, or avoidant? Which transactions support your vitality and creativity, and which deplete your sense of presence and autonomy?

Take the case of Danika, a freelance writer who used a digital version of envelope budgeting but constantly felt overwhelmed by her finances. Though her system was technically in order, her experience of money remained emotionally chaotic. She noticed that certain expenses, though minor, created disproportionate stress: a professional membership she no longer used but couldn't bring herself to cancel; a donation subscription she felt guilty letting go of; a growing list of online courses she hadn't completed. Each of these was an energy leak—not because they were objectively unaffordable, but because they carried an invisible load of guilt, indecision, or misalignment.

With coaching, Danika created a new envelope category: *Energetic Integrity*. Into this she placed funds only for those expenses that made her feel both resourced and respected—like a therapist she saw monthly, a co-working space that uplifted her, and a creative mentorship programme that reconnected her with her purpose. She also began conducting monthly *energy audits* alongside her financial reviews, asking not only "What did I spend?" but "Where did I leak?" and "Where did I thrive?" This dual awareness transformed budgeting from a mechanical process to a sacred check-in with her lived reality.

The envelope system, when layered with energetic awareness, becomes not only a tool for financial clarity, but also a mirror for *emotional congruence.* It highlights the dissonance between what we say we value and how we act. A person may claim to value peace but spend excessively on high-maintenance products or social obligations. Another may claim to value health but allocate nothing towards rest or wellness. These discrepancies are not moral failings; they are invitations. When brought into awareness, they allow for recalibration—not just of budgets, but of identity.

From a neurobiological standpoint, this integration also enhances regulation. According to polyvagal theory, our nervous systems respond to environments of predictability with increased safety and coherence. When budgeting is structured and paired with emotional checking-in, it creates a *co-regulated loop* between mind, body, and finance. We are no longer outsourcing our financial state to spreadsheets alone—we are listening to what our bodies already know. That impulse purchase didn't just affect the balance; it spiked cortisol. That monthly expense isn't just a line item—it's a micro-exchange of life force. When we honour this awareness, we begin to design lives not just of solvency, but of sovereignty.

This practice also counters what financial therapist Bari Tessler calls "money fog"—the dissociative state that many people enter when facing money matters. The envelope system brings visibility. Energetic auditing brings embodiment. Together, they cultivate *financial intimacy.* You begin to see your money not as a problem to solve or a puzzle to optimise, but as an expression of how you live, love, and lead.

The implications are both personal and collective. On a personal level, this approach allows you to build a budget that feels not only sustainable, but *soulful.* On a relational level, it offers a new language for discussing money with partners or family—not just in terms of how much is being spent, but how spending *feels.* On a societal level, it encourages a shift from unconscious consumerism to intentional stewardship—where every transaction is a vote for the kind of world, relationship, and self we want to nurture.

Practical implementation may vary. Some may continue using physical envelopes; others will use digital tools with labelling features. The key is not the method, but the *mindset.* Label your envelopes not just by function, but by *felt experience*: "Nourishment," "Expansion," "Security," "Play," "Obligation (Review Monthly)." These labels turn budgeting into a conversation with the self—dynamic, honest, and alive.

In merging envelope systems with energetic awareness, we bring together the old and the new, the structured and the intuitive, the measurable and the felt. We begin to see that financial discipline is not at odds with emotional freedom—in fact, it is the very foundation for it. We are not just managing money; we are tending to energy. We are not just controlling expense; we are cultivating *alignment.*

And in that practice, something radical unfolds. Budgeting stops being an exercise in fear or control and becomes a map of devotion. Each envelope, each choice, each check-in becomes an act of reclaiming your power—not just over your finances, but over the rhythm and integrity of your life.

The Gratitude Ledger: Rewiring Your Financial Nervous System Through Daily Appreciation

In contemporary culture, money is often a trigger—of stress, fear, comparison, or self-judgement. For many, engaging with finances means encountering shame, scarcity, or pressure. Yet what if the act of tracking your money could become a tool for healing rather than anxiety? What if a financial ledger could serve not only as a record of transactions, but as a mirror for your blessings—a place where each expenditure, income, or investment becomes an opportunity to honour, reflect, and rewire? This is the core idea behind the *Gratitude Ledger*, a deceptively simple yet profoundly transformative practice that links financial activity with emotional regulation and neuroplasticity.

The Gratitude Ledger is more than journaling. It is a conscious act of *repatterning*—a practice that invites you to interrupt the autopilot of financial stress and replace it with awareness, appreciation, and choice. Drawing from fields as diverse as behavioural finance, neuropsychology, somatic therapy, and positive psychology, this method proposes a radical yet accessible shift: attach a gratitude reflection to every financial transaction, however small. By doing so, you not only track your money—you rewire your *relationship* with it.

To understand the impact of this, we must consider the biological and emotional context in which most people engage with money. Neuroscientific research confirms that the amygdala—our brain's threat detection system—is frequently activated during financial decision-making, especially under conditions of uncertainty. This can result in chronic dysregulation: heightened cortisol, tightened muscles, scattered attention, and reactive behaviour. When someone opens their banking app and feels a spike of panic, this is not irrational—it is a conditioned nervous system response rooted in past experiences and perceived threat.

Gratitude, by contrast, activates the parasympathetic nervous system—the rest-and-digest branch that promotes calm, presence, and integration. Studies by researchers such as Robert Emmons and Martin Seligman have consistently shown that gratitude increases psychological resilience, improves sleep quality, reduces depression, and fosters a stronger sense of control. When paired with financial awareness, gratitude becomes more than a pleasant emotion—it becomes *a neurological antidote to financial fear.*

The Gratitude Ledger works by making this pairing systematic. After each financial action—whether it's paying a bill, receiving income, buying a meal, or making a donation—you pause to reflect: What did this transaction enable? What value did it create or honour? What need did it meet? Even in moments of frustration or expense, the practice invites a reframing. A dental bill becomes an opportunity to be grateful for access to healthcare. A rent payment becomes a ritual of honouring shelter and stability. A cancelled subscription becomes a celebration of reclaiming alignment.

This is not toxic positivity. It is not about denying the reality of financial hardship or pretending every transaction is joyful. Rather, it is a practice of *emotional integration*—making space for the full experience while training the nervous system to notice sufficiency rather than just lack. Over time, this repeated linking of gratitude and finance creates a new neural pattern: instead of money being associated with threat, it becomes associated with empowerment and presence.

Real-world stories illustrate how profound this shift can be. Take the case of Helena, a school administrator with a long-standing pattern of anxiety around bills. Every month, she would avoid opening emails from utility providers or banks until she was forced to act. Through guided coaching, she began using the Gratitude Ledger method. At first, her reflections were perfunctory—"Paid power bill. Grateful for electricity." But as the practice deepened, so did her presence. She began to connect her payments with the comfort of warm meals, the ability to read at night, the safety of her children. The act of noting these connections created a subtle shift—not just in how she felt about paying bills, but in how she experienced her role as a provider. Within three months, she was opening financial correspondence without fear and had automated most of her bill payments. The psychological weight had lifted, not because the numbers changed, but because *her relationship to them had.*

The Gratitude Ledger is also effective in reshaping spending patterns. Behavioural research shows that mindfulness-based practices reduce compulsive and emotionally reactive behaviours by increasing the time between impulse and action. When gratitude is built into spending, it creates a pause point—an opportunity to check in with your values. Is this transaction aligned? Does it support who I want to become? Does it reflect respect for my resources? When these questions are anchored not in judgement, but in appreciation, they create space for discernment.

Another key benefit of this practice is that it builds *financial intimacy.* For couples, families, or even business partners, a shared Gratitude Ledger can foster trust and transparency. Instead of discussing budgets in terms of limitations or errors, the conversation can centre around shared values, appreciation for contributions, and mutual goals. A family that reviews their monthly spending by noting what each transaction brought to the household—education, nourishment, connection—will naturally develop a more cohesive and resilient financial culture than one that focuses only on cost-cutting.

Practically speaking, the Gratitude Ledger can take many forms. Some prefer a physical notebook, dedicating a line to each transaction and its associated reflection. Others use a digital spreadsheet or a notes app, pairing budget categories with weekly gratitude entries. The format matters less than the *consistency and sincerity* of the practice. The key is to make gratitude habitual—not a fleeting thought, but a muscle exercised in tandem with financial engagement.

One powerful adaptation of the Gratitude Ledger is to reflect not only on *outflows*, but also on *inflows*. Many people receive money—salary, refunds, gifts, or passive income—without pause, immediately moving to the next obligation. This normalises a state of financial disconnection, where receiving becomes unconscious and undervalued. By pausing to give thanks for income, however small, we reconnect with the truth that money is more than a number—it is energy, relationship, and exchange. This reinforces what positive psychology refers to as a "receiving orientation"—the capacity to welcome abundance without guilt, deflection, or contraction.

Gratitude also expands our capacity to experience sufficiency. As Lynne Twist explores in her seminal work *The Soul of Money*, the greatest poverty is not material—it is the belief that there is never enough. The Gratitude Ledger gently counters this belief by highlighting what is already present, already flowing, already available. It trains the mind to notice not only the gap between current and desired reality, but the *fullness of the now.*

Of course, resistance will arise. Some days the reflection may feel rote or forced. At times, the ledger may reveal uncomfortable truths—patterns of overspending, unaligned choices, or neglected priorities. This is part of the process. Gratitude is not a bypass—it is a bridge. It allows you to meet discomfort with compassion and to respond from a place of wholeness rather than shame.

In the long term, the Gratitude Ledger cultivates what psychologists call *cognitive coherence*—the alignment between beliefs, values, and actions. When your financial behaviour reflects your values, and your values are consciously honoured through gratitude, a sense of internal congruence emerges. This congruence is not only satisfying—it is *stabilising*. It calms the nervous system, sharpens decision-making, and enhances long-term motivation.

The Gratitude Ledger may seem simple, but its implications are profound. It reframes the act of financial management as a sacred dialogue between the practical and the profound. It honours the truth that every transaction is not just economic—it is emotional, energetic, and existential.

And in a world that often treats money as either a measure of worth or a source of shame, this practice offers something rare: *reverence*. Not for money itself, but for what money *makes possible*. For what it reflects about how we love, how we live, and how we honour the abundance already flowing through our lives.

In the end, the Gratitude Ledger is not just about changing how you feel about money. It's about *changing what money means*—from burden to blessing, from trigger to teacher, from scarcity to sacred stewardship.

Interactive Tool: Create Your Aligned Budget

Budgeting has long been treated as a dry exercise in arithmetic—a necessary, often dreaded task tethered to discipline, deprivation, and spreadsheets. Yet in a more conscious paradigm, budgeting is neither punishment nor perfectionism. It is an intimate act of self-leadership: a mirror for your values, a blueprint for your priorities, and a ritual of intentional living. To budget well is not simply to control spending. It is to *design flow*—a rhythm that supports both your material needs and your soulful aspirations. An *aligned budget*, then, is more than a financial tool; it is a practice of congruence. It ensures that where your money moves, your meaning follows.

Creating such a budget requires moving beyond abstract goals and into grounded embodiment. It demands a clear-eyed look at your actual financial landscape—income, fixed costs, savings, and discretionary spending—paired with a deeper inquiry into your values, desires, and lived emotional experience with money. This is not an either-or scenario between logic and intuition, but a conscious fusion of both. The aligned budget integrates spreadsheets and soulwork, structure and spirit, numbers and nervous system cues.

The first step is to anchor in awareness. Begin by understanding your current cash flow—what comes in, what goes out, and where leaks might be occurring. This may sound obvious, but many people operate from estimations or assumptions. They believe they "roughly know" their expenses, only to be surprised each month by the unconscious accumulation of spending. The aligned budget begins with clarity. Not for the sake of judgement, but for empowerment. As Carl Jung once observed, "Until you make the unconscious conscious, it will direct your life and you will call it fate." The same applies to money.

Once clarity is established, the next move is to map your values. This requires more than listing virtues. It involves naming the lived experiences you most cherish and want to prioritise. For one person, this may be adventure, expressed through travel or novel experiences. For another, it might be health, requiring investments in quality food, movement, and restorative practices. Someone else may prioritise creativity or service, needing funds for education, mentorship, or community contribution. The key is specificity. Values must be translated into actionable categories to meaningfully shape the budget.

This is where the interactive nature of this tool comes into play. Rather than beginning with generic budgeting categories, start by creating categories rooted in your *why*. You are not merely assigning money to "transport" or "groceries." You are assigning it to *mobility*, *nourishment*, *belonging*, or *growth*. This subtle linguistic shift reorients your relationship with spending. It becomes less transactional and more relational.

Consider the case of Rafael, a consultant who was earning well but felt perpetually disconnected from his money. Despite budgeting diligently, he often felt resentful about fixed expenses and guilty about discretionary ones. Through values clarification, Rafael realised that autonomy, adventure, and generosity were core drivers for him. He restructured his budget to include categories such as "Spontaneous Generosity," "Creative Exploration," and "Freedom Fund." These names weren't gimmicks—they reflected real emotional priorities. The result? He didn't spend more, but he felt *better* about what he spent. His budget became a living document, not a constraint.

After values have been clarified and categories renamed, the aligned budget invites you to allocate funds with *presence*. Begin with fixed obligations—rent, utilities, debt repayments—and ask: are these aligned with my current life and future direction? Are they proportionate? Are there contracts, subscriptions, or agreements I've outgrown? This step is not about immediate overhauls, but about honest evaluation. Are your current obligations serving your evolution?

Next, move to discretionary spending. Here, rather than defaulting to last month's pattern, imagine starting from zero. If you had a blank canvas, how would you distribute your available funds across your values-based categories? What would feel generous but not excessive? Sufficient but not stingy? This process is less about precision and more about resonance. It requires you to listen inwardly: Where does your money *want* to go? Where does your energy feel most respected?

This process often reveals underinvestment in meaningful areas. You might discover that you deeply value rest, yet allocate nothing to holidays or downtime. Or that you crave creative expression but haven't funded any tools, lessons, or spaces to support it. The aligned budget does not shame you for these gaps—it illuminates them so they can be addressed. It invites you to move from unconscious avoidance to conscious design.

The emotional layer of the aligned budget cannot be overstated. Neuroscience shows that habits change most effectively when supported by emotion. When your budget is not just functional but *felt*, you are more likely to sustain it. That's why this method encourages journaling as part of the monthly review. Ask: How did my spending align with my values this month? Where did I overspend, and why? What gave me the most joy per pound spent? What patterns are emerging—not just financially, but emotionally?

One client, Meena, integrated this practice and discovered a recurring theme. Each time she under-allocated for self-care, her spending on food delivery increased. The convenience was not about hunger; it was about fatigue and unmet emotional needs. By increasing her self-care budget—even modestly—she reduced her overall discretionary spending and felt more regulated throughout the week. The numbers didn't change dramatically, but the alignment did. Her body felt the shift. Her nervous system relaxed. Her financial anxiety diminished.

This points to a core truth: budgeting is not just intellectual—it is somatic. Your body carries financial memory. Stress, guilt, scarcity—all of these leave imprints. The aligned budget, especially when created with monthly or weekly reviews, helps recondition those imprints. It says: *You are safe to look. You are worthy of design. You are trusted to choose again.*

Of course, the aligned budget must also include space for spontaneity and the unknown. Too much rigidity leads to rebellion. That's why categories like "Serendipity" or "Magic Money" can be both playful and essential. They allow for improvisation without derailing structure. They honour the unpredictability of life while maintaining the integrity of intention.

From a behavioural standpoint, what makes the aligned budget effective is that it satisfies both system one and system two thinking—the fast, emotional, intuitive brain, and the slow, analytical, rational brain. It creates enough structure to support executive function, while also allowing enough emotional expression to engage intrinsic motivation. It's budgeting for *whole humans*, not robots.

The final phase of this practice is calibration. Each month, the aligned budget should be reviewed—not just for numerical accuracy, but for energetic resonance. Where was the flow easeful? Where was it tight? What surprised you? What no longer feels true? Like any good system, the aligned budget is living. It evolves as you do.

In sum, the aligned budget is not a prescriptive formula—it is a *conscious conversation* with your money, your identity, and your values. It is the bridge between your inner world and your outer world. A reflection of what you stand for, and a container for what you're becoming.

Creating one doesn't require perfection. It requires honesty, attention, and care. And in return, it offers something extraordinary—not just better finances, but a more integrated life. A life where your soul and your spreadsheet are not in opposition, but in harmony. Where your goals support your spirit, and your spirit fuels your goals.

This is the future of money management—not sterile, not fear-based, but soulful, embodied, and deeply, irrevocably *you*.

Chapter 6
Investing with Intuition and Intellect

Investment, as it is usually framed, is a matter of cold logic—a domain of analysis, risk assessment, and long-term strategising. It's the realm where charts and ratios reign supreme, and feelings are treated like troublesome distractions. But, beneath the familiar language of returns and diversification, there lies a subtler truth: decisions around investing rarely unfold in a vacuum of pure reason. Instead, they are invariably shaped by our beliefs, values, and experiences, as well as that elusive inner compass we call intuition. The most adept investors don't pit intellect against instinct; they blend the two. This chapter delves into that potent fusion between financial acumen and energetic attunement, demonstrating how investing can be both shrewd and deeply grounded in spirit.

Today's investment world stretches far beyond the confines of Wall Street. With real estate platforms, peer-to-peer lending, ethical funds, cryptocurrencies, and fractional shares now widely accessible, individuals find themselves not just empowered to invest but compelled to question how and why they do so. This widening of choice brings with it a more profound inquiry: What kind of investor are you? Do you lean on rigorous research, historical data, and technical signals? Or do you tune into momentum, follow your gut, and read emotion as meaningful data? These aren't polar opposites but rather facets of ourselves that can coexist—if only we learn to recognise and honour them both.

Understanding your investing style begins with self-awareness. The analytical investor craves structure—values due diligence, prefers facts over guesswork, and usually approaches risk with caution unless backed by solid evidence. Their forte is consistency and risk mitigation, though sometimes they get caught in paralysis by analysis, missing moments that call for swift, instinctive action. On the flip side, the intuitive investor rides the currents of energy. They sense patterns, catch timing signals, and feel drawn to ventures that defy easy explanation. Agile and visionary, yes—but sometimes erratic or overly confident. The savvy investor does not shoehorn themselves into one camp but cultivates both faculties, learning when to trust the ledger and when to heed the whisperings of intuition.

Investing is far from a neutral act. Money always carries intention, and every allocation sends out energetic ripples toward a specific outcome. This is where the notion of energetic resonance comes into play. If you put your funds into companies whose ethics clash with your own, that dissonance can gnaw away at your peace of mind, disrupting your flow. Conversely, investments that align with your values—be they sustainability, innovation, community, or fairness—become an extension of your purpose. Ethical investing is no mere marketing ploy; it's an energetic pact, a declaration of what you believe deserves to flourish.

Empirical evidence supports this too. Research from the Global Impact Investing Network reveals that values-driven portfolios frequently match, if not exceed, the performance of conventional ones. Yet, even if returns were identical, the emotional and spiritual dividends of aligned investment are incomparable. There's a satisfaction that goes beyond profit—a profound contentment found not just in what rises, but in why it rises.

One of the chapter's most compelling frameworks is the pairing of compound interest with the Law of Gestation. Financially, compound interest represents the exponential growth that comes from reinvesting earnings—rewarding patience, steady contributions, and time. Metaphysically, the Law of Gestation reminds us that all creation requires incubation; a crop cannot be hurried to harvest, nor can ideas be rushed before they're ready. Together, these principles offer a powerful metaphor for wealth: trust the timing of your seeds. Investing wisely is not a pursuit of quick wins but a commitment over time, even when progress isn't immediately visible.

This patience proves especially crucial when investing in yourself—through education, entrepreneurship, skill-building, or wellbeing. These forms of investment seldom produce immediate financial returns but generate exponential rewards over the long haul in confidence, capacity, and earning potential. They demand faith, resilience, and a tolerance for uncertainty. Honour the gestational rhythm of growth, and you free yourself from the tyranny of instant gratification, moving toward lasting wealth instead.

Distinguishing between money moves and money momentum is critical here. A money move might be a single transaction—buying stock, acquiring property, or trading cryptocurrency. Such moves can be thrilling, bold, even lucrative, but they remain isolated acts. Money momentum, by contrast, is the cumulative force of aligned choices sustained over time. It is energetic consistency, an unseen current building as you make decisions that honour your values, respect your tolerance for risk, and expand your potential. The momentum-builder may not be flashy, but their wealth deepens through congruence.

Take, for example, Devan, a creative entrepreneur with no financial training. For years, he avoided investing, convinced it was too complex, risky, or simply "not for someone like him." Yet, after exploring his money mindset through somatic therapy and coaching, he began to notice intuitive nudges. Drawn to a start-up focused on mental health technology, he sensed integrity in its leadership and a resonance with his own healing journey. With some basic research under his belt, he made a modest investment and let it rest. Over four years, the company grew steadily, yielding not just financial gain but a deep sense of meaningful participation. His choice was neither blind faith nor cold calculation but a synthesis of gut feeling, values, and grounded action. Slowly, he saw himself less as a passive investor and more as a steward of positive change.

This, then, is investing as a dance between intuition and intellect—a dynamic interplay between logic and embodied knowing, spreadsheets and subtlety. It doesn't ask you to abandon critical thinking in favour of wishful thinking, nor to silence your inner wisdom for the sake of abstract numbers. Instead, it invites you to listen—to the data and your nervous system alike. To realise that the best investments nourish not only your bank balance but your identity. Who do you become through this choice? What does this investment cultivate within you?

As you work through this chapter, you will be encouraged to explore your investing style, clarify your values, evaluate your portfolio through an energetic lens, and experiment with decisions that honour both your strategic mind and intuitive heart. Remember, investing is not merely an external pursuit of accumulation—it's an internal journey of expansion.

In an age obsessed with volatility, speed, and spectacle, this integrated approach is at once radical and rooted. It dares to suggest that your money is more than a resource—it is a signal. A signpost pointing towards what you deem possible, what you hold worthy, and who you believe yourself to be.

When that signal grows clear—when your investments are guided by both data and dignity, timing and trust—your wealth will do more than increase. It will resonate, compound, and multiply, not just in figures, but in meaning.

Beyond Wall Street: What Kind of Investor Are You?

The archetype of the investor has long been shaped by Wall Street: sharp suits, ticker symbols, and cold rationality. In this traditional model, investing is an exercise in data-driven decision-making, where the ideal investor is unemotional, highly analytical, and perpetually detached from the outcome. But the world of investing has shifted—and continues to evolve. No longer confined to institutional trading floors or elite hedge funds, investing today is accessible, diverse, and deeply personal. The question is no longer just *what* you invest in, but *how* you invest—and more importantly, *who* you are as an investor.

Understanding your investing style is not a trivial matter of preference; it is a foundational act of financial self-awareness. It helps you filter out noise, clarify your approach, and avoid strategies that may appear profitable on paper but feel incongruent in practice. At the heart of this self-inquiry lies a powerful distinction: the analytical investor and the intuitive investor. These two approaches are not binary opposites but expressions of different cognitive strengths and decision-making preferences. Recognising where you naturally lean—and where you may benefit from balance—can transform not only your financial outcomes, but your entire relationship with money.

Analytical investors are methodical and research-oriented. They thrive on due diligence, trend analysis, and macroeconomic indicators. Their decisions are driven by facts, projections, and quantifiable models. This approach is grounded in the principles of rational choice theory, which assumes that individuals make decisions by systematically evaluating all available information to maximise expected utility. While this model has been widely critiqued—particularly in behavioural economics—it continues to inform much of conventional investment education and strategy. The analytical investor is often disciplined, risk-aware, and consistent. But their potential blind spot lies in over-analysis, scepticism of instinct, and the occasional paralysis that comes from waiting for "perfect" conditions that never arrive.

By contrast, intuitive investors operate more from an internal compass than a spreadsheet. They are attuned to subtle cues—emotional resonance, timing, gut feeling—and often make decisions quickly, guided by a sense of alignment rather than pure logic. Cognitive neuroscience offers insight into this style: intuition is not guesswork or mysticism. It is the rapid processing of experiential knowledge, stored in the unconscious brain and delivered as a felt sense. The somatic markers hypothesis, introduced by neuroscientist Antonio Damasio, explains how emotional signals from the body influence decision-making, often more effectively than rational deliberation in uncertain or complex environments. Intuitive investors tend to be agile, bold, and creative—but they may be prone to inconsistency, overconfidence, or insufficient due diligence if they do not temper instinct with inquiry.

The most effective investors—especially in the evolving landscape of ethical, impact, and conscious investing—blend both styles. They honour the precision of logic and the wisdom of emotion. They know when to run the numbers and when to trust a subtle pull. But such integration begins with awareness: knowing your default setting, understanding its strengths and limitations, and choosing when to expand or lean in.

Take the story of Anita, a social entrepreneur with no formal finance background who entered the investment space through crowdfunding platforms. Initially, she relied solely on instinct, investing in ventures that felt aligned with her values. While this created a strong emotional connection to her portfolio, it also led to uneven results—some investments thrived, others failed due to structural weaknesses she had not investigated. Through mentorship, she began layering in analytical practices: evaluating business models, reading financial statements, and checking track records. Her returns improved, but more importantly, she felt *empowered.* She had not abandoned her intuitive strength—she had *strengthened its context.*

Compare this with Jordan, a quantitative analyst who had long managed his portfolio through algorithmic trading and market models. Despite steady returns, he began to feel detached and uninspired. Investing had become mechanical. He started exploring ESG (Environmental, Social, Governance) funds, first with scepticism, then with curiosity. He discovered that allocating capital toward causes he believed in—clean energy, education, equitable tech—infused his financial strategy with meaning. His overall returns remained solid, but his engagement and satisfaction increased significantly. He didn't give up analysis; he layered in resonance.

These examples illustrate the emerging paradigm of self-honouring investing—a practice that does not demand conformity to one method, but instead invites a conscious blending of strengths. Financial advisor and author Carl Richards speaks to this balance with his concept of "the behaviour gap"—the difference between investment performance and investor performance, caused by emotionally driven decisions in reaction to markets. When intuition and intellect are seen as partners, rather than adversaries, this gap narrows. The investor becomes less reactive and more responsive.

This responsiveness is especially crucial in today's complex financial ecosystem. With the rise of cryptocurrency, decentralised finance, AI-led trading, and global volatility, the future of investing demands more than rigid models. It requires adaptability, emotional intelligence, and ethical clarity. It asks investors to cultivate both competence and conscience, both acuity and agility. It is no longer enough to chase returns—you must define what *a return means to you.* Is it capital appreciation? Is it impact? Is it sovereignty?

Practical tools can support this inquiry. Journalling after investment decisions to explore what felt clear or misaligned. Creating a decision matrix that includes both financial metrics and emotional resonance. Tracking not only ROI but what we might call "ROE"—*return on energy.* Which investments energise you? Which drain you? Where do you feel pride, peace, or growth? This is not indulgence. It is *due diligence for the soul.*

Furthermore, integrating intuition into your investment process does not mean ignoring risk. Rather, it invites a different relationship with risk—one where uncertainty is not a trigger for fear, but an invitation to deepen your discernment. The intuitive investor does not predict markets—they sense *readiness.* The analytical investor does not chase hunches—they evaluate *feasibility.* Together, these approaches create a model of investing that is resilient, reflective, and rooted.

Ultimately, identifying what kind of investor you are is not about finding a label. It is about cultivating a lens. It is about building a practice that reflects both your financial intelligence and your personal evolution. It is an invitation to move beyond Wall Street dogma and into your own wisdom—to remember that investing is not just a tool for accumulation, but a mirror for who you are and who you are becoming.

The question, then, is not just *what's in your portfolio?* It's *who are you as the steward of that portfolio?* When your investing reflects not only your analysis but your essence, you don't just build wealth—you build coherence. You create a strategy that makes sense on paper and feels right in your bones. That is the essence of investing in alignment. And that is where your truest returns begin.

The Energy Behind Investments: Aligning Capital with Consciousness

In the conventional investment world, success is largely measured by financial return—percentages gained, portfolios diversified, capital appreciated. This framework, while financially sound, often bypasses a more subtle and potent dimension of investing: the *energy* behind the money we move. Every investment is not merely a transaction; it is a transmission of belief, intention, and influence. When we allocate money—whether into stocks, businesses, real estate, or causes—we are not only seeking return, we are *endorsing a direction of growth*. The question then becomes not simply, "Will this make money?" but "What is this investment *energising*, and does that resonate with who I am?"

The concept of energetic resonance in investing invites us to re-evaluate the conventional wisdom that treats money as neutral. While money itself may be inert in form, its *function* is always energetic—it flows toward, accelerates, and amplifies whatever it is connected to. When we invest without considering the energetic consequences—ethical, environmental, emotional—we risk amplifying systems, industries, and narratives that contradict our deeper values. But when we invest with conscious intent, our money becomes more than a tool for personal gain; it becomes an agent of integrity.

This is the heart of ethical investing, a movement that has gained significant traction in recent years under various names—ESG (Environmental, Social and Governance) investing, socially responsible investing (SRI), impact investing. These frameworks allow investors to consider not only profitability but also sustainability, social justice, and governance transparency. What is often overlooked, however, is the inner alignment required to truly practise ethical investing. It is not enough to select a green mutual fund or avoid certain industries. One must ask: *Do I feel congruent with this investment? Does it amplify the world I want to live in? Does it honour both my intellect and intuition?*

Research supports the viability of ethical investments from a performance standpoint. A 2021 meta-analysis published in the

Journal of Sustainable Finance & Investment reviewed over 1,000 empirical studies and found that ESG investing typically yields comparable or better financial performance than traditional portfolios. But beyond performance, ethical investments often generate *psychological dividends*: a sense of purpose, peace, and pride that cannot be quantified by spreadsheets but is acutely felt in the body and psyche.

This energetic clarity creates what we might call *portfolio coherence*—a state in which your investments are not just financially diversified but philosophically integrated. Consider the story of Marcus, a former oil executive turned investor. After years of accumulating wealth in extractive industries, Marcus experienced what he later described as a "values dislocation." His financial life was growing, but his sense of personal fulfilment and social responsibility was in decline. After a sabbatical and period of self-inquiry, he redirected his capital into clean energy start-ups, regenerative agriculture, and educational equity platforms. While his overall returns remained stable, Marcus reported a dramatic decrease in financial stress and an increased sense of meaningful contribution. His money, he said, was finally "pointed in the right direction."

This concept—pointing your money—requires sensitivity to energetic feedback. Just as we can walk into a room and sense harmony or dissonance, we can engage with an investment opportunity and feel alignment or contraction. This is not about mysticism; it's about neuroception—the body's ability to detect safety, congruence, or risk below the level of conscious thought. An investor who ignores these cues may profit materially but feel drained, distracted, or ethically conflicted. An investor who honours them is more likely to experience what Mihaly Csikszentmihalyi called "flow"—a state of effortlessness, clarity, and purpose.

Practical integration of energetic awareness into investing begins with inquiry. What are the implicit values of the companies or projects you're funding? Who benefits from their growth? Who may be harmed? Are there supply chain practices, labour policies, or environmental impacts that matter to you? Do you trust the leadership team? Does the business model promote resilience or exploitation? These questions do not replace financial due diligence—they *enhance it.* They add a moral and emotional layer that deepens understanding and guards against blind spots.

For instance, investing in a fast-growing tech company may look attractive on paper, but what if its core revenue comes from data mining practices you consider invasive? Conversely, a small local business with modest returns may offer profound energetic alignment—circulating money within your community, supporting ethical employment, and resonating with your commitment to relational economies. One is not objectively superior; the question is which one *aligns with your frequency of purpose.*

Energetic investing also reframes the concept of *return on investment.* Financial return is important, but it is not the only form of return. There is return on energy, return on impact, return on alignment. When these are in harmony, financial returns often follow—not because of magical thinking, but because coherence attracts flow. A coherent investor is less likely to self-sabotage, more likely to stay committed through volatility, and more resilient in the face of uncertainty. The body does not fight the decision; it supports it.

Consider the case of Leila, a millennial investor who began her financial journey with robo-advisors and index funds. As her income grew, she became increasingly uneasy with the blind automation of her portfolio. A review revealed holdings in industries she found ethically troubling—arms manufacturing, tobacco, exploitative real estate trusts. Rather than divest immediately, Leila took six months to educate herself on ESG metrics, energy economics, and stakeholder capitalism. She rebuilt her portfolio with a blend of green bonds, community-lending platforms, and climate tech funds. While her new strategy required more engagement, Leila described the process as "a financial reclamation." Her investments were no longer abstract—they were extensions of her identity.

This kind of energetic clarity can also influence timing. Investors often focus exclusively on *what* to invest in, but *when* to invest can be equally significant. Intuition plays a powerful role here. A deal may look solid but feel rushed. A market may be down, but your body may signal readiness. Energetic investing trains you to listen for these cues—not as a substitute for market trends, but as an additional layer of intelligence. It invites you to ask, "Is now the time?" and to wait if the answer isn't clear.

Importantly, energetic investing does not require saintliness or perfection. It is not about moral absolutism or the eradication of financial ambition. It is about *integration*—ensuring that your investments reflect the world you want to shape and the self you want to express. It is about recognising that money is a frequency, and you are its transmitter. The more attuned you are, the more aligned your wealth-building process becomes.

This chapter has implications beyond the individual. As collective capital increasingly shifts toward values-driven frameworks, markets themselves begin to change. Companies that uphold transparency, sustainability, and human-centred design are attracting more funding. Shareholder activism is reshaping corporate agendas. Crowdfunding platforms are enabling grassroots movements to gain economic traction. When enough individuals invest with energetic integrity, the system begins to evolve—not through revolution, but through recalibration.

In a financial world that still often prioritises speed, scale, and speculation, the practice of energetic investing offers something profoundly needed: *depth.* It reminds us that investing is not a neutral act, but a creative one. Every pound we place into the world is a seed. What grows from that seed depends not only on the market, but on the intention, clarity, and consciousness with which it was planted.

To invest energetically is to invest as a whole person—mind sharp, heart open, values alive. It is to recognise that your money is not separate from your spirit, and that wealth, when aligned with purpose, becomes not only a resource, but a ripple. And that ripple, once set in motion, can move markets—not just in numbers, but in meaning.

Compound Interest and the Law of Gestation: The Alchemy of Time, Intention, and Trust

The brilliance of compound interest is often described as one of the most powerful forces in finance. Quiet, consistent, and exponential by nature, it defies the expectations of linear growth. Albert Einstein reportedly referred to it as the eighth wonder of the world—not merely for its numerical impact, but for its embodiment of a principle far older and more universal than modern economics: the *law of gestation*. In the spiritual context of manifestation, this law reminds us that all creation—whether a financial goal, a business, or a dream—requires time to take form. It must be nurtured in its unseen phase before it is visible in the world. Together, compound interest and the law of gestation offer a framework that transcends transactional thinking and invites us into a deeper partnership with time, patience, and trust.

To grasp their integration, we must first explore each on its own terms. Compound interest is the process by which the earnings on an investment are reinvested, generating additional earnings over time. It is a self-reinforcing loop of growth. The longer capital is left untouched and allowed to accrue, the more powerful the effect. A £10,000 investment with an average annual return of 7%, for example, will grow to over £38,000 in twenty years without any further contributions. But the power is not just in the return rate—it lies in *time*, and in the consistency of *non-interference*. The moment an investor prematurely withdraws or interrupts the compounding cycle, they forfeit its most potent rewards.

This dynamic mirrors the spiritual principle of gestation, which holds that every intention, once planted, requires its own sacred unfolding. A farmer does not tug on seedlings to force their growth; a pregnant mother does not hasten the birth before the due date. Similarly, when we set a financial intention—or any manifestation—we must allow for its incubation. The timing is not always under our control. What *is* within our domain is the clarity of the seed, the consistency of nourishment, and the faith to wait without abandoning the process midway.

Too often, modern culture's obsession with immediacy disrupts both financial strategy and spiritual trust. We chase short-term returns, pivot erratically in the face of discomfort, and judge ourselves by metrics designed for urgency rather than depth. In doing so, we lose not only money but a deeper kind of momentum: the energetic confidence that builds when one commits, aligns, and allows time to do its part. The investor who understands both compound interest and gestation does not merely calculate—they *cultivate.*

Consider the story of Priya, an educator who began investing later in life. With modest income and little prior exposure to finance, she started small—£200 a month into a global index fund. At first, progress seemed slow. In year two, her portfolio had only grown by a few hundred pounds beyond her contributions. Doubt crept in. Was this even worth it? But instead of withdrawing or changing course, Priya decided to pair her strategy with spiritual reflection. She treated each investment as a sacred act of faith. She journaled her vision for financial sovereignty, practised gratitude for each monthly contribution, and reminded herself that results follow rhythm, not rush. By year ten, her investment had not only grown significantly but had begun to provide a sense of security she never thought possible. "The numbers were only part of it," she reflected. "What really changed was my relationship with *time.*"

This is the essence of pairing compound interest with the law of gestation. It is not passive. It is not idle. It is *intentional non-interference.* It is the discipline of staying the course without micromanaging the unfolding. Financially, this looks like consistent contributions, low-fee diversified portfolios, and refraining from panic during market fluctuations. Energetically, it means tending to your mindset, releasing attachment to outcomes, and deepening into trust—trust in your strategy, trust in your timing, and trust in yourself.

This perspective challenges the dominant narrative of wealth-building as conquest. Instead of pursuing outcomes, we become stewards. We create environments in which growth can occur, and we respect the invisible mechanics of incubation. This does not mean we avoid all intervention—there are seasons for rebalancing portfolios, updating intentions, or learning new tools. But these actions come from alignment, not fear. From responsiveness, not reactivity.

The intersection of these principles also offers insight into goal-setting. Traditional financial advice often stresses SMART goals—specific, measurable, achievable, relevant, and time-bound. While useful, this framework can fall short when applied to goals that require *gestational unpredictability*. A dream to create a multi-income investment portfolio, start a purpose-driven business, or fund a charitable trust may not conform neatly to a 12-month timeline. Applying gestational awareness means holding the goal with clarity while relinquishing rigid control over its exact unfolding. It invites a *co-creative stance* with life.

This is where manifestation intersects with strategic patience. Manifestation is not mere wishful thinking; it is the act of aligning belief, emotion, and action toward a desired outcome. But even the most aligned manifestations require *maturity*. The law of gestation protects us from premature outcomes. It ensures that what we receive is truly ours to hold. Just as compound interest ensures that returns are earned over time, gestation ensures that manifestations arrive when we are ready to receive them—not only financially, but emotionally and spiritually.

The impatience that leads many investors to over-trade, abandon solid strategies, or chase hype is mirrored in spiritual impatience—doubting one's worthiness, questioning divine timing, or trying to force manifestations into being. Both forms of impatience reveal an underlying lack of trust. When we understand that both money and miracles require time, we begin to move differently. We stop measuring worth by immediacy and start honouring *rhythm*.

Importantly, integrating these principles doesn't mean avoiding ambition. It means anchoring ambition in a broader context. A well-structured financial plan based on compound interest can still accommodate bold goals. A manifestation practice grounded in gestation can still hold high vision. The integration is not about limitation—it's about *liberation from misalignment*. It allows us to pursue wealth and purpose without becoming slaves to urgency.

Another layer of this integration is emotional regulation. Both investing and manifestation require navigating uncertainty. There will be dips—in markets, in mood, in momentum. The nervous system, if untrained, interprets these dips as danger. The ungrounded investor reacts by selling. The ungrounded manifester reacts by spiralling into doubt. But those who practise alignment with gestation and compound growth understand these dips differently. They are fluctuations in an overall upward trajectory. They are contractions before the next expansion.

This understanding builds what behavioural finance calls *time perspective maturity*—the ability to delay gratification for greater future reward. It also builds spiritual maturity—the willingness to trust in unseen progress. Together, they create what might be called *compound faith*—a layered trust that, when invested regularly, deepens and expands with time.

To cultivate this in practice, consider adopting a dual review process. Each quarter, review your financial metrics: growth, contributions, adjustments. Simultaneously, reflect on your energetic posture: Are you trusting the process? Are you staying aligned with your values? Are you allowing the space for your goals to unfold without anxious interference? When these reviews are done consistently, they reinforce each other. Financial progress becomes a mirror for spiritual evolution. Spiritual trust becomes a foundation for financial resilience.

In this way, the concept of wealth is transformed. It is no longer just about what you accumulate. It is about what you *become* in the process. A person who masters compound interest and the law of gestation is not merely building assets—they are building *character*. They are cultivating the qualities of patience, discernment, trust, and vision—qualities that outlast markets, surpass monetary value, and ripple outward into every area of life.

This is the alchemy of time and intention. This is the true return on investment. When you align the logic of compound growth with the wisdom of divine timing, you stop chasing wealth and begin *receiving it*—not all at once, but in rhythm, with grace, in fullness.

And that is the kind of wealth that compounds far beyond the balance sheet.

Money Moves vs Money Momentum: Strategy Meets Energetic Sustainability in Wealth Creation

In the ever-evolving landscape of financial advice, the allure of the "money move" is omnipresent. Social media is flooded with strategies promising quick gains—day trading secrets, cryptocurrency tips, lucrative side hustles, and real estate flips. These tactics, often presented as urgent and essential, can certainly create shifts in one's financial position. But when we zoom out and take a more integrated perspective, a different truth emerges: not all movement creates *momentum*. There is a fundamental distinction between tactical financial activity and the deeper, sustained force that builds enduring wealth. That force is money momentum—a combination of intentional strategy, energetic alignment, and inner congruence that compounds not only capital but *coherence*.

Money moves are by nature acute. They are decisions made in a moment of opportunity or necessity—a new investment, a career change, a shift in pricing strategy, or a budget overhaul. They can be pivotal, even life-changing. However, they are only as effective as the foundation they're built upon. Without a stable energetic and strategic base, a money move can become reactive rather than responsive, externally impressive but internally dissonant. This is where the concept of momentum enters—not as a substitute for strategy, but as its deeper substrate.

Money momentum refers to the energetic and behavioural consistency that underlies sustainable wealth. It is not about speed; it is about *direction and endurance*. It is not about dramatic shifts; it is about sustained alignment. Think of momentum as the difference between a flash of movement and a river's flow—slow, deliberate, and powerful enough to shape landscapes over time. In financial terms, momentum is created when your earning, spending, saving, and investing behaviours are all anchored in your values, guided by intentionality, and repeated with discipline.

To understand this interplay, let's consider the example of Karim, a graphic designer who decided to freelance full-time. His initial "money move" was bold: quitting his job to start his own business. He launched quickly, gathered clients, and hit several five-figure months within his first year. From the outside, it looked like success. But beneath the surface, Karim felt anxious, overworked, and creatively depleted. His rates were inconsistent, his clients didn't reflect his ideal audience, and his pricing was driven more by scarcity than sovereignty. What he had created was activity—not momentum. His business had moved, but not in a direction that was sustainable.

After working with a financial and mindset coach, Karim began to rebuild. He re-evaluated his niche, restructured his offerings, aligned his pricing with his values, and implemented systems to support recurring income. He also began practising regular financial embodiment work—using breathwork, journalling, and somatic awareness to understand his internal money narratives. Slowly, a new rhythm emerged. He no longer needed to chase income—it began to flow with less resistance. His nervous system settled. Clients came through referrals. Cash flow stabilised. His business now had momentum—less visible perhaps, but exponentially more resilient.

This kind of transformation is only possible when we move beyond a surface-level relationship with money. Most conventional financial advice is built around accumulation, optimisation, and execution. While these are important, they often overlook the inner architecture of wealth—the beliefs, emotions, and energetic patterns that either amplify or block momentum. A money move that conflicts with your nervous system's capacity, your values, or your sense of worth may create short-term results but eventually collapses under its own weight. In contrast, a momentum-based approach builds gradually but carries *integrity*—it feels true, sustainable, and expansive.

Energetically, momentum is created when your actions are congruent with your identity. This is supported by research from behavioural economics and identity theory, which shows that people are more likely to maintain habits and financial behaviours that are consistent with how they see themselves. If you identify as someone who is "bad with money," no amount of tactical advice will stick. The behaviour will eventually revert to match the identity. But when the identity begins to shift—when you begin to *see yourself* as financially wise, generous, or intentional—then even small actions, repeated consistently, generate compounding results.

This brings us to the nervous system's role in building momentum. Money is one of the most emotionally charged topics in modern life. Financial decisions often activate the stress response, especially in individuals with histories of scarcity, debt trauma, or financial instability. The fight-or-flight response hijacks the prefrontal cortex—the part of the brain responsible for long-term planning and critical thinking. In this state, short-term tactics are tempting. The brain wants relief, and a money move—like making a high-risk investment, enrolling in an expensive programme, or cutting all expenses—offers the illusion of immediate control. But such decisions, made under pressure, often lack sustainability. Momentum cannot be built from a place of contraction.

This is why practices like somatic regulation, mindfulness, and values-based budgeting are not luxuries—they are necessities. They create the internal conditions for consistent financial behaviour. They allow your system to stay regulated enough to make decisions from your higher self rather than your survival brain. When you feel safe in your body, you stop chasing financial dopamine hits and start building *rhythms*. That rhythm is the engine of momentum.

Let's look at another case—Talia, a corporate employee who wanted to become a financial coach. Her initial "move" was to build an online course. She spent thousands on branding and software but struggled to enrol clients. The external infrastructure was there, but the internal clarity was not. She wasn't clear on who she wanted to serve, what results she promised, or how her own money story shaped her messaging. It wasn't until she spent six months refining her own financial boundaries, rewriting limiting beliefs, and coaching a small cohort for free that things began to shift. She built confidence, testimonials, and systems organically. When she relaunched her programme, enrolments flowed effortlessly. She hadn't just made a move—she had built momentum. Her business was no longer just a strategy; it was a living reflection of her integrity.

The broader cultural context also plays a role. In a system that rewards speed and spectacle, momentum is often misunderstood. We are told that wealth is built by seizing opportunities, acting fast, and pushing harder. But many of the world's most enduring fortunes were built quietly—through long-term vision, relational capital, ethical alignment, and patient reinvestment. Warren Buffett famously attributed his wealth not to complexity, but to *patience.* Oprah Winfrey credits her financial success to deep alignment with purpose and consistency. These are not just money moves—they are momentum manifest.

From a practical standpoint, momentum is about *systems.* A values-aligned spending plan that repeats monthly. An investment strategy that compounds quietly over years. A content schedule that grows a loyal audience. A weekly CEO day where you review finances and recalibrate. These are not glamorous. They are rarely shared virally. But over time, they create conditions in which wealth can take root—not as a spike, but as an *ecosystem.*

To differentiate between a move and momentum, ask yourself: Is this action rooted in clarity or reactivity? Does it expand my capacity or deplete it? Am I repeating this with consistency, or am I starting over every few months? Most importantly, does this path feel *true* to who I am becoming? If the answer to these questions is "yes," then you are likely building something that will endure.

The invitation, then, is not to abandon strategy, but to infuse it with soul. To understand that the most powerful wealth isn't built in frenzied bursts, but in sustained alignment. That the most enduring legacies aren't forged through hustle, but through harmony. Money moves can change your life. But money momentum can *transform your reality.*

In the final analysis, the difference between those who stay stuck and those who build wealth is not merely intelligence, resources, or opportunity. It is the cultivation of aligned momentum—where every decision becomes a vote for your future self. That self does not need to rush. It moves with purpose. It builds with patience. And eventually, it arrives—not by accident, but by *alignment sustained over time.*

Case Study: The Gut-Driven Investor

The narrative surrounding investment has long leaned on the premise of rationality. Classical economic theory posits that individuals make decisions grounded in logic, risk analysis, and empirical data. Yet, in practice, the act of investing is rarely that sterile. Emotion, intuition, and subconscious pattern recognition often precede—or even override—purely analytical thought. While the mainstream still frames intuition as speculative or naïve, growing research in cognitive neuroscience, along with countless real-world stories, reveals that when paired with fundamental financial principles, intuitive investing can be not only effective but deeply transformative. This case study explores the journey of Maya Patel, a 42-year-old London-based former corporate project manager turned full-time passive income investor, whose wealth-building approach was guided not by traditional formulas, but by an uncommon trust in her internal compass.

Maya's financial life began conventionally enough. Educated in economics and employed in a structured corporate environment for over fifteen years, she was, by all appearances, financially competent. She managed her salary prudently, avoided consumer debt, and maintained a modest ISA. But despite her discipline, Maya felt unfulfilled and increasingly disconnected from the systems she was part of. Her investments in index funds and retirement accounts grew steadily, but her enthusiasm for the process waned. "It felt like I was outsourcing not just my money," she later recalled, "but my soul."

The turning point came not through a financial crisis but through a deeply personal reckoning. After a close friend passed away unexpectedly, Maya found herself questioning the assumptions she had held about safety, time, and success. She began meditating regularly, exploring somatic therapy, and journaling—not to improve her finances, but to reconnect with a sense of vitality she felt she had lost. Unexpectedly, this inner work began to influence how she related to money. She became acutely aware of the energetic tension she felt when reviewing her investments. "It wasn't that they were wrong," she said. "They were just emotionally dead to me."

Around the same time, she stumbled across an online forum discussing peer-to-peer property lending. The thread itself was uninspiring—charts, yield percentages, default risk projections—but something about the underlying model sparked an embodied response. She felt a surge of warmth in her solar plexus, a sense of intrigue that went beyond logic. She researched further, cross-referencing platform reviews, regulatory policies, and risk disclosures. Still, the numbers didn't tell the full story. Her mind was cautiously sceptical, but her body said yes.

Rather than dismissing this signal, Maya paused. She gave herself permission to explore—not with recklessness, but with respect. She decided to allocate a modest portion of her investment capital—just under £5,000—to a diversified basket of P2P lending platforms, focusing on those funding ethical housing developments and community regeneration projects. It wasn't just a financial decision; it was a values-aligned move. She wanted her capital to build more than returns—she wanted it to build *something she could feel proud of.*

In the first year, the returns were modest—around 4.8% annualised—but the emotional return was immense. For the first time, she was excited to log in and review her dashboard. She began tracking not only performance but energetic congruence. Did this platform feel aligned? Did the project resonate? Were the communications transparent? She noticed that the more she honoured her intuitive cues—staying with platforms that felt coherent, withdrawing from those that felt "off"—the more confident she became. This wasn't gambling. It was discernment.

With growing confidence, Maya expanded into direct investments in small-scale real estate projects through a socially conscious investment club. One opportunity—a co-living space for single mothers in Birmingham—initially made her nervous. It was unconventional, and some of her financial peers dismissed it as high risk. But Maya felt a deep emotional pull and a strange sense of calm when visiting the project site. She reviewed the financials, found the fundamentals reasonable, and invested. That decision became one of her most rewarding—yielding not only an 8% return but a profound sense of contribution.

Maya's approach was not without challenge. Intuition, she found, could be clouded by fear, excitement, or social influence. To manage this, she began developing what she called her "alignment filter"—a three-part system grounded in nervous system awareness, value congruence, and rational scrutiny. Before making any investment, she would check in with her body (Did this feel expansive or contracting?), her values (Did this honour who she was becoming?), and the data (Were the basics sound?). If all three aligned, she proceeded. If even one was off, she waited or declined.

Over the next five years, Maya built a diversified portfolio of passive income streams: ethical property investments, dividend-yielding shares in sustainable energy companies, micro-lending to women-led enterprises in developing economies, and royalties from a co-authored wellness e-book. Her passive income eventually surpassed her corporate salary. But what's notable is not just the financial success—it's how she *arrived there*: not through maximum optimisation, but through maximum *resonance*.

Psychologists and neuroscientists have begun to catch up with what Maya and others have intuited for years. Studies in embodied cognition show that the gut-brain axis plays a pivotal role in decision-making. The vagus nerve, which connects the gut to the brain, carries a wealth of sensory data that informs subconscious assessments of safety, risk, and trust. What we often call "a gut feeling" is, in fact, a form of fast, embodied intelligence—particularly useful in complex, uncertain environments like investing, where data may be incomplete or contextually ambiguous.

Moreover, behavioural finance teaches us that even the most rational investors are deeply influenced by emotion—fear of loss, greed, herd mentality. The difference with intuitive investors like

Maya is not that they have fewer emotions—it's that they are *in dialogue* with them. They don't ignore signals. They investigate them. They honour their knowing without being hijacked by it.

Maya's journey is not a blueprint, but a case study in the power of internal coherence. Her path challenges the binary of logic versus instinct. It shows that when financial knowledge is paired with self-awareness, when strategy is supported by somatic sensitivity, and when intuition is cross-checked by data, a powerful synergy emerges.

In teaching others, Maya now helps clients develop what she calls a "financial resonance map." It includes traditional tools—risk assessment, diversification principles, time horizon planning—but overlays them with reflective prompts: How does this investment feel in your body? What values does it express? What role does it play in your legacy? For many, this opens a new dimension of investing—one where money is not just managed, but *embodied.*

The gut-driven investor is not reckless, nor are they mystical. They are relational. They treat money not as a sterile object to be controlled, but as an energetic force to be partnered with. They ask deeper questions. They honour nuance. They recognise that wealth, at its highest expression, is not just about accumulation—it's about *alignment.*

In a financial culture dominated by speed, noise, and constant novelty, Maya's story reminds us that the most powerful investing tool may not be a strategy, platform, or spreadsheet. It may be something quieter, deeper, and far more ancient: the wisdom within. When cultivated with care, that wisdom doesn't just guide us to the right investments—it guides us to the right relationship with wealth itself.

Chapter 7
Income Flow and Identity Expansion

Most conversations about increasing income tend to zero in on skills, tactics, or opportunities—rarely do they venture into the deeper terrain of how income intertwines with identity. Yet, it's precisely this internal landscape—our sense of worth, the roles we accept or reject, the limitations we internalise—that often dictates not only how much we earn but also how steadily that income flows and whether it grows sustainably over time. To truly transform one's financial situation, mastering external strategies won't suffice. Instead, it demands a recalibration of the inner framework that shapes our earning identity. This chapter explores the psychological, emotional, and energetic layers behind income generation, offering a guide not just to increasing financial flow, but to becoming the kind of person who can receive and expand it naturally.

We start by unpacking the idea of earning identity. Many people carry an invisible ceiling on their income, but this limit usually stems less from market realities than from deep-seated self-perceptions. Perhaps you grew up in a household where financial hardship was the norm, or where wealth was regarded with distrust or disdain. Maybe the messages you absorbed were along the lines of "I'm not the kind of person who earns more than this," or "People like me don't get rich." These inherited narratives quietly set the boundaries within which your income moves. Psychologists call this phenomenon self-concept congruence—the tendency to act in ways that align with our internal identity. Translated to finances, it means we tend to earn in harmony with who we believe ourselves to be, not necessarily who we might objectively become.

Escaping these internal scripts begins with awareness. Here, narrative work proves indispensable. What story have you been telling yourself about your capacity to earn? Did your parents' views, cultural conditioning, or past setbacks cement this story? Rewriting it isn't about wishful thinking; it's about reclaiming authorship of your financial journey. It acknowledges that earning potential isn't fixed—it evolves alongside your self-concept.

Real-life stories illuminate this process. Take Alina, a massage therapist who for almost a decade capped her earnings at around £30,000 a year. Despite loyal clients and glowing reviews, she resisted raising prices or broadening her offerings. Coaching revealed that she carried a heavy guilt about out-earning her mother, who had worked tirelessly with little financial reward. Alina was unknowingly bound by a loyalty that limited her growth. Once she reframed her success as a tribute rather than a betrayal of her lineage, she adjusted her pricing and launched digital products. Within a year, her income doubled—not through aggressive salesmanship, but through expanding her identity.

With this refreshed self-view, the next step is diversification—but not simply scattering efforts everywhere. This chapter advocates a model of multiple income streams united by singular purpose. The aim isn't to chase every shiny opportunity, but to ensure each stream resonates with your core values and vision. When income sources are fragmented, misaligned, or opportunistic, they drain your energy. Conversely, when anchored in a clear purpose—be it healing, teaching, building, or leading—they become synergistic. Your presence deepens, your reputation flourishes, and momentum builds through coherence rather than chaos.

Consider Jordan, a former corporate strategist who shifted into holistic coaching. Initially, he juggled an array of side gigs—consulting, yoga instruction, affiliate marketing—but none tied back to a unified mission. Busy yet energetically scattered, he eventually realigned around his central goal: helping professionals reconnect with their bodies. This clarity birthed a cohesive suite of offerings—somatic workshops, an online breathwork course, and a subscription podcast. His income stabilised and became easier to sustain. This wasn't just a tactical adjustment; it was existential. Jordan stopped earning as a hustler trying to prove himself and began earning as a creator aligned with his true essence.

Supporting this growth is the idea of the money-receiving muscle. Many excel at hard work, but stumble when it comes to receiving.

They might set ambitious income targets, but when money arrives—whether a raise, a client payment, or a surprise windfall—anxiety, guilt, or self-sabotage often follow. This isn't a failure of ambition; it's a matter of capacity. Just as the body must be conditioned to lift heavier weights, the nervous system needs training to hold larger sums of money without retreating into contraction.

Strengthening this capacity calls for nervous system regulation, embodiment practices, and emotional processing. Exercises such as accepting compliments without deflecting, receiving support without guilt, and practising gratitude ahead of achievement can slowly rewire the circuitry that otherwise associates abundance with threat. The money-receiving muscle must develop not only in the bank account but in the body itself. When the body feels safe to hold more, it stops pushing away what it has consciously invited.

Yet, there's another layer often neglected in the pursuit of financial growth: the shadow. Many earning blocks have little to do with strategy or self-worth; they arise from unconscious emotional conflicts—envy (resentment of others' success), guilt (desiring more than those around you), or superiority (believing money is beneath your spiritual or intellectual standing). These shadows act as energetic anchors, tugging you backward no matter how fiercely you strive forward.

Shadow work around income means bringing these hidden forces into the light, free of judgment. If you look down on "rich people," becoming one might feel unsafe. If you envy a friend's success, you could be unconsciously sabotaging your own to preserve connection or moral high ground. Facing these tensions isn't about condemning yourself, but about integration. When the shadow is embraced, your energy aligns, and earning flows without internal conflict.

To weave these threads together, the chapter closes with a powerful reflective tool: your financial origin story. This journaling exercise invites you to trace the formative moments shaping your relationship with money—from childhood impressions and early jobs to financial highs and lows, alongside the emotions each phase carried. Mapping your income narrative grants clarity on the beliefs you have inherited and the identities you have adopted, while empowering you to author a new script—not one of default, but of deliberate design.

Ultimately, income flow transcends mere numbers—it is an energetic signature. It narrates how much life force you permit yourself to express, receive, and circulate. Identity expansion isn't a luxury in wealth creation; it is the very mechanism by which wealth manifests. As you evolve who you believe yourself to be, you expand what you welcome into your life—not only money, but meaning, ease, and sovereignty.

This chapter offers more than a fresh perspective on earning; it proposes a new paradigm. One where income is not wrested from struggle but cultivated through alignment. Where receiving is not accidental but embodied. And where wealth is not a status symbol but a mirror reflecting who you have become.

Decoding Your Earning Identity: The Psychology of Worth, Wealth, and Income Potential

For many, the act of earning is approached as a functional equation—skills plus opportunity equals income. But beneath the surface of professional strategy and financial planning lies a far more complex and influential force: your earning identity. This invisible template, shaped by a lifetime of experiences, beliefs, and subconscious associations, governs not only how much you earn, but how you feel about earning, how you respond to financial growth, and whether you can sustainably hold and expand your wealth over time. To understand income in its truest context, we must look beyond external variables and turn inward—into the architecture of identity itself.

Your earning identity is the internal blueprint that defines what you believe is possible, appropriate, or available to you when it comes to making money. It operates like an internal thermostat, maintaining a set financial "temperature" based on your self-concept, emotional comfort zone, and unconscious loyalty to past narratives. Raise the external temperature—perhaps through a raise, promotion, or new business—and if it exceeds the identity's set point, self-sabotage or discomfort often follows. This is not simply a mindset issue; it is an identity issue. Until that thermostat is adjusted, no amount of skill development or strategic action will create lasting change.

At the heart of earning identity is self-worth. Not in the abstract, self-esteem sense, but in a deeply practical, embodied sense of *what you believe you are allowed to receive.* If you subconsciously associate high income with exploitation, abandonment, or excessive responsibility, you may unconsciously limit your earnings to avoid those perceived risks. Similarly, if your sense of worth has been tied to struggle or self-sacrifice—as is common among those raised in environments where hard work was valued above all else—you may resist easeful earning, even when it's available.

Consider the case of Raj, a senior consultant who consistently undercharged for his freelance work. Despite accolades from clients and years of experience, Raj struggled to invoice at market rates. When he explored his earning identity through coaching, he discovered an early association between wealth and emotional disconnection. His father, a financially successful executive, had been distant and emotionally unavailable. Raj had unconsciously equated higher income with disconnection from love and presence. To preserve his sense of integrity and relational closeness, he kept his fees low—ensuring that he remained approachable, overworked, and underpaid. This was not irrational behaviour; it was *identity congruent.* Only by disentangling money from abandonment could Raj begin to expand his financial ceiling.

This phenomenon is echoed in psychological research on identity-based motivation. According to the work of Oyserman and Destin (2010), individuals are more likely to engage in behaviours that align with their salient identity narratives. If someone sees themselves as a creative but not business-minded, they may avoid actions that could expand their income, such as pitching, marketing, or negotiating—because those actions feel out of sync with their perceived self. Similarly, if someone identifies as spiritual but not materialistic, they may cap their earning potential out of fear that financial success would compromise their authenticity.

The challenge, then, is not to change what you do first, but to evolve who you *think you are* in relation to money.

This evolution often requires a deeper inquiry into the origin of your financial story. Childhood experiences are particularly formative. Perhaps you witnessed a parent hustle tirelessly with little reward, subtly teaching you that money requires sacrifice. Or maybe financial success in your family came with emotional cost—divorce, jealousy, or distance—embedding the idea that more income equals more problems. These experiences don't just sit in memory; they become the scaffolding for your adult beliefs. Without reflection, these stories calcify into limits. With awareness, they can be rewritten.

Sara, a non-profit executive, offers a powerful example of this process. After receiving a substantial promotion, she began experiencing intense anxiety and imposter syndrome. Despite her qualifications, she felt undeserving of the role—and, more specifically, the salary increase. In sessions with a therapist, Sara traced her discomfort back to a childhood memory of her mother, who had been laid off and subsequently struggled financially. Her mother had often remarked, "People like us don't get lucky. We have to work for everything." Sara had internalised the idea that windfalls—or seemingly easy success—were untrustworthy. By reframing this belief and honouring both her mother's resilience and her own capacity, she began to accept her new financial reality with greater ease. Her anxiety subsided, and her performance improved—not because her competence changed, but because her *identity expanded.*

To evolve your earning identity is to challenge the stories that no longer serve your highest financial self. But this is not merely a cognitive exercise. The body must be brought into the process. Somatic practices—such as breathwork, visualisation, or EFT (Emotional Freedom Techniques)—can help regulate the nervous system, particularly when encountering the edges of financial comfort. These practices are essential because identity shifts often trigger discomfort. When you raise your rates, ask for a raise, or step into a new role, you are disrupting the status quo. Your nervous system may interpret this as threat—even when the change is positive.

This is where support and integration become vital. Working with coaches, therapists, or peer groups who reinforce your expanded identity can anchor your new earning set point. So can creating rituals of affirmation, celebration, and embodiment that remind your system: "It is safe to grow. It is safe to earn more. It is safe to become more visible." These messages, repeated over time, begin to rewire the emotional circuitry around money.

Yet identity expansion is not about chasing arbitrary income goals or adopting someone else's definition of success. It is about *alignment.* The most powerful earning identity is not the one that makes the most money, but the one that allows you to express your full self without internal conflict. When your income reflects your values, your service, and your self-concept, earning becomes less effortful and more authentic. You stop contorting yourself into strategies that don't fit. You stop undercharging to feel safe. You stop overworking to feel worthy.

One of the most effective tools for reprogramming your earning identity is storytelling—not fiction, but autobiographical narrative. Reflecting on the pivotal moments in your financial history, noticing the emotional tone of each chapter, and intentionally rewriting the arc can have profound effects. What if, instead of seeing your past as a series of financial mistakes or limitations, you saw it as the exact terrain that has prepared you to be a steward of conscious wealth? What if the setbacks were not signs of failure, but invitations to grow your capacity?

The truth is, no financial tactic will stick if it conflicts with your identity. You may implement a new pricing model, adopt a budgeting system, or invest in a business strategy—but if the underlying self-concept remains small, scared, or ashamed, the tactic will eventually collapse. Sustainable financial growth, therefore, is not a matter of tools. It is a matter of *who you are when you use them.*

In this way, decoding your earning identity is not just about making more money. It is about reclaiming authorship over the story that shapes your financial life. It is about choosing worth over shame, sovereignty over survival, and expansion over contraction. When your identity shifts, your income doesn't just increase—it stabilises. It integrates. It reflects not just what you do, but who you have become. And that, in the end, is the deepest form of wealth.

Multiple Streams, Singular Purpose: Redefining Side Hustles Through Alignment

The idea of creating multiple streams of income is no longer reserved for ambitious entrepreneurs or financial independence devotees. It has become a central tenet of modern wealth-building advice, reflecting a world in which economic volatility, automation, and evolving career models demand agility and diversification. But somewhere along the way, the multiple streams concept lost its soul. In chasing breadth—more platforms, more gigs, more passive income—we often sacrifice depth. Time fractures. Energy splinters. Passion dilutes. The result is not freedom but fatigue.

This subchapter offers a different paradigm: one that does not dismiss multiplicity, but grounds it in coherence. At its heart is a deceptively simple but radical question—*what if every stream of income flowed from the same source: your purpose?* What if your various income activities were not disconnected hustles, but extensions of a singular identity, each reinforcing the other? This is the essence of building multiple streams with singular purpose—a model of income generation that is not only strategic but soulful, not just profitable but integrative.

To understand this model, we must first confront the problem with how side hustles are typically approached. In many cases, they are reactive: a response to financial pressure, career dissatisfaction, or a desire for greater autonomy. While these motivations are valid, they often lead people to bolt on income projects that lack any real connection to their long-term vision. An accountant becomes a ride-share driver on weekends. A coach sells drop-shipped gadgets on the side. A creative builds a digital product that bears no resemblance to their deeper calling. These hustles may generate revenue, but they rarely generate *resonance.* Over time, they can create energetic drag, pulling the individual further from alignment rather than closer to fulfilment.

The alternative is to cultivate a *purpose-centred income ecosystem*—one in which every stream, while functionally distinct, is thematically integrated. Your offerings, products, partnerships, and platforms all speak to the same core intention, reinforcing your authority, deepening your brand, and expanding your impact. You become known for something—not just as someone who does a lot.

Take the example of Renée, a former schoolteacher turned literacy advocate. When she left the classroom, she didn't abandon her purpose—she expanded its expression. She began tutoring online, consulting for curriculum developers, and creating digital products to support parents of struggling readers. Eventually, she launched a podcast, a subscription-based book club, and co-authored a book on literacy equity. Each income stream stood on its own, but all reinforced her singular purpose: democratising reading for underserved children. The result was not just financial diversification, but identity integration. Her work felt meaningful, her message consistent, and her audience deeply loyal.

This approach is also supported by psychological research. According to the *self-determination theory* developed by Deci and Ryan, human motivation thrives on autonomy, competence, and relatedness. Side hustles that emerge from disconnected or purely extrinsic motives often lead to burnout or disengagement. But when income-generating activities align with intrinsic goals—such as creativity, contribution, or growth—they become self-sustaining. Purpose, then, is not a luxury. It is a structural necessity for long-term engagement and coherence.

Moreover, the idea of singular purpose does not mean singular expression. On the contrary, diversity is encouraged—so long as it is anchored. A purpose can be expressed through coaching, writing, teaching, building, mentoring, facilitating, or innovating. What matters is that each stream feels like a limb of the same body—not an appendage from a different organism. This is the difference between being a fragmented freelancer and being a mission-driven creator. One chases income. The other cultivates *impact pathways.*

To begin this process, it helps to articulate your purpose clearly—not as a slogan, but as a functional directive. What is the transformation you are here to facilitate? Who do you serve? Why does it matter? From this clarity, you can audit existing or potential income streams through the lens of resonance. Does this activity amplify my message? Does it deepen my credibility? Does it allow me to operate in integrity? If the answer is yes, it becomes a candidate for inclusion. If not, it is better left behind—even if it pays well in the short term.

Case studies continue to affirm this model. Consider the story of Marcus, a chef with a deep passion for ancestral foodways. Instead of launching a generic catering business, he began offering cultural storytelling dinners, online courses on traditional fermentation, and authored a memoir on the spiritual significance of food in diasporic communities. His streams included events, royalties, merchandise, and consulting—but all were bound together by a singular thread: reclaiming ancestral nourishment. The effect was powerful. His business grew, his reputation deepened, and he experienced a sense of vocational joy that transcended income alone.

This alignment also creates *brand gravity*. In a crowded market, coherence becomes a differentiator. Audiences are drawn to those whose offerings feel intentional and interconnected. They trust you more. They refer you more. They are willing to pay more. As your ecosystem grows, opportunities become synergistic. A podcast drives book sales. A workshop feeds into a membership. A keynote unlocks a consulting retainer. You're no longer building silos—you're building a *field.*

Practical frameworks can support this process. Mapping your income ecosystem visually, for instance, allows you to see connections and gaps. You may notice that your content is disconnected from your services, or that your highest-income stream lacks long-term scalability. From there, you can refine—tightening your message, developing complementary products, or phasing out income that feels extractive. Over time, your financial landscape begins to mirror your internal clarity.

Still, it is essential to acknowledge that purpose-aligned diversification is not a fast track. It is a strategic garden, not a cash crop. The early stages may require slower growth, deeper listening, and more intentionality than a scattershot hustle model. But the long-term yield is not only more sustainable—it is more satisfying. You don't just earn more. You *become more*—more visible, more grounded, more sovereign.

And it is precisely this integration that transforms the meaning of financial freedom. It is not merely about earning from multiple sources. It is about expressing yourself fully through multiple modes. It is about creating a business—or a life—that doesn't require you to fragment your identity to pay your bills. It is about reclaiming the idea that work can be a sacred extension of who you are, rather than a compromise of what you need.

In the end, multiple streams of income are not inherently liberating. Without intention, they can become a golden cage. But when those streams flow from a unified source—a purpose that resonates deeply within you—they become something else entirely. They become a current of coherence, carrying you not just toward wealth, but toward *wholeness*. And in a world that often asks us to choose between passion and practicality, that may be the most radical financial move of all.

The Money-Receiving Muscle: Expanding Your Capacity to Ask For, Receive, and Sustain Greater Income

Despite decades of financial literacy education and entrepreneurial advice, one topic remains noticeably underexplored in traditional discourse: the ability to *receive* money. Not just earn it, negotiate for it, or budget it, but to genuinely and sustainably *let it in.* For many people, particularly those with complex relationships to self-worth, visibility, or control, this act is far from passive. It requires skill, awareness, and deep inner work. Like any other muscle, the money-receiving muscle must be trained—consciously and consistently—so that when greater wealth flows in, it can be welcomed, held, and multiplied without energetic collapse.

The idea that we each have a set "capacity" to receive income is not theoretical—it is observable in behaviour. People routinely hit income plateaus that are not the result of market limitations or skill deficits, but internal set points. They raise their prices and then over-deliver. They receive a financial windfall and unconsciously spend it down. They experience a successful launch and immediately feel guilt or imposter syndrome. These are not failures in strategy—they are symptoms of *nervous system mismatch.* When what you receive exceeds what your body believes it is safe or right to hold, sabotage follows—not out of malice, but out of unconscious regulation.

This dynamic is well-documented in trauma psychology and somatic studies. The body seeks homeostasis—familiarity—even when that familiarity includes scarcity. Financial expansion that is not accompanied by *capacity expansion* becomes unsustainable. Just as a runner must train their lungs and heart to handle longer distances, an entrepreneur or professional must train their system to handle more money, more attention, and more opportunity without overwhelm. The capacity to receive is not fixed. It can be grown. And the training begins within.

Consider the example of Eliza, a wellness coach who had been earning between £3,000 and £4,000 a month for several years. After working intensively on her marketing and packaging, she launched a group programme that netted £18,000 in a single month—more than four times her previous high. What followed was not celebration, but paralysis. Eliza struggled to respond to emails, delayed delivering modules, and began questioning her pricing. She told herself it was burnout, but beneath the fatigue was fear: "What if I can't deliver? What if I'm found out? What if I lose it all?" Her body had interpreted the sudden income spike as a threat. Until she did the deeper work of regulating her receiving capacity, growth felt unsafe.

The act of receiving requires more than a mindset shift—it demands a reorganisation of belief, identity, and embodied experience. For many, this begins with unlearning the idea that receiving is selfish, greedy, or transactional. Especially among those raised in cultures that glorify self-sacrifice or emotional labour, the notion of being *given to* without having to endlessly justify or earn it can feel almost heretical. Yet without the capacity to receive, even the best income strategies will fall flat—or worse, succeed in ways that produce internal conflict.

Exercises to build the money-receiving muscle are rooted in both psychology and physiology. One foundational practice is to develop *tolerance to being seen.* Visibility is often the precursor to income—whether you're launching a product, negotiating a raise, or pitching your work. But for many, being seen is inherently uncomfortable, especially if it was once associated with criticism, exclusion, or vulnerability. The nervous system interprets visibility as exposure. The receiving muscle, therefore, must include exercises in being witnessed with acceptance. This could be as simple as allowing yourself to be celebrated without deflection, accepting compliments without minimising, or sharing your achievements publicly without apology. These small practices accustom the body to standing in its value.

Another critical dimension is *asking.* Many people unconsciously expect money to find them, while simultaneously fearing what it means to articulate their worth. Whether it's quoting a higher fee, asking for overdue payment, or renegotiating a contract, the act of asking is emotionally charged. It surfaces stories of rejection, unworthiness, or scarcity. Training the money-receiving muscle means practising the ask—not just when you're "ready," but as a deliberate expansion exercise. One method is to engage in micro-asks: requesting support, feedback, or resources in low-stakes environments to build familiarity and reduce charge. Over time, the threshold for discomfort shifts. The ask becomes an act of service, not intrusion.

Receiving also means *holding.* It is one thing to earn more money—it is another to keep it, allocate it wisely, and grow it without fear or dissociation. This is where practices like financial intimacy and energetic hygiene become essential. Do you look at your accounts regularly, or avoid them? Do you feel calm when reviewing your income, or tense? Holding money is about relationship, not just retention. People who are uncomfortable with money's presence often unconsciously push it away—not through lack of effort, but through lack of *familiarity*. Just as holding a relationship requires presence and attention, so does holding wealth.

Sofia's story illustrates this well. A graphic designer who experienced a sudden influx of high-paying clients, she found her bank balance higher than it had ever been. But instead of feeling secure, she felt restless. She booked an unnecessary holiday, bought high-ticket items she didn't truly want, and within months her savings had dwindled. In therapy, she uncovered a belief that money creates distance—that having more would make her unlikeable or disconnected from her friends. Once she began unpacking that story and redefining money as a tool for deeper connection, she was able to hold and grow her income without emotional sabotage.

It's important to note that none of this is about greed or accumulation for its own sake. Building your receiving muscle is about *resilience*. It is about creating internal spaciousness for abundance so that you can steward wealth in a way that is aligned, generous, and grounded. When you can receive without guilt, ask without shame, and hold without fear, you become a channel—not just for personal prosperity, but for collective impact. Your income becomes a mirror of your capacity to honour your worth and serve with integrity.

From a broader societal lens, expanding the collective money-receiving muscle is also a form of economic healing. Many historically marginalised groups carry inherited trauma around money—whether through colonisation, systemic disenfranchisement, or cultural narratives that equate wealth with corruption. To receive, for these groups, is not just personal—it is revolutionary. It requires rewriting generations of internalised limitation. In this way, financial capacity-building becomes a form of liberation work.

Practically, developing this muscle includes rituals of affirmation, embodiment, and reflection. Simple but consistent practices—like tracking income with gratitude, spending from a place of intention, or visualising the energetic act of receiving—can shift the neural and emotional baseline. Over time, what once felt foreign becomes familiar. What once felt unsafe becomes easeful. The body catches up with the soul's ambition.

Ultimately, the money-receiving muscle is not about performance. It is about *permission.* Permission to feel deserving. Permission to expand. Permission to be seen in your fullness and to have that fullness met with reciprocal value. Income, then, is no longer a fight. It is a flow—one that you are structurally, emotionally, and spiritually prepared to sustain. And from that readiness, new possibilities emerge—not because you've worked harder, but because you've learned how to *let it in.*

Shadow Work for Wealth Expansion: Transforming Envy, Guilt, and Superiority into Financial Maturity

While many wealth-building frameworks focus on mindset, strategy, and skill acquisition, few delve into the subterranean psychological forces that quietly shape, constrain, or sabotage our financial potential. Shadow work—the process of confronting the repressed, disowned, or unconscious aspects of the self—is one of the most potent yet overlooked tools in wealth expansion. Not because it teaches us how to earn or invest, but because it liberates us from the hidden emotional contracts and identity distortions that quietly limit what we allow ourselves to receive and sustain. Envy, guilt, and superiority are not just moral failings or personality quirks; they are energetic blocks that shape our relationship to income, success, and visibility. Left unexamined, they form a glass ceiling. Brought into awareness, they become the raw material for transformation.

To understand shadow work's relevance to financial growth, we must first clarify what is meant by "the shadow." Popularised by Carl Jung, the shadow represents the parts of ourselves we disown because they do not fit our self-image or the image we want to project to others. These can be undesirable traits—rage, arrogance, greed—but also positive ones that threaten belonging or perceived safety, such as ambition, power, or confidence. When these traits are repressed, they do not vanish. Instead, they are projected outward or expressed sideways, distorting our relationships, decisions, and self-concept. In the context of money, shadow traits often manifest as self-sabotage, judgement of others, emotional spending, or chronic under-earning.

Envy is one of the clearest signals that shadow work is needed. In a culture that shames this emotion, we often dismiss it or intellectualise it away. Yet envy contains profound intelligence. It reveals a split between who we are and who we believe we are allowed to be. If you envy someone's wealth, visibility, or lifestyle, it is not necessarily because you are shallow or greedy. It is because some part of you recognises a disowned desire—one that has been buried beneath shame, conditioning, or protective narratives. Envy says, "That could be me, but I'm not allowed to want it." Shadow work invites us to sit with that envy, not as a defect to purge, but as a doorway to integration. When we can admit, "I want that, too," we begin to collapse the distance between ourselves and the abundance we project onto others.

A powerful case study is Ana, a holistic practitioner who struggled to raise her rates despite an overflowing waitlist. She found herself feeling resentful of peers who charged more and marketed themselves confidently. At first, she dismissed these feelings as evidence that she was "more grounded" or "less commercial." But upon deeper reflection, Ana recognised that her disdain masked envy—and that beneath that envy was a disowned desire for financial ease and recognition. She had internalised the belief that being spiritual meant rejecting material comfort. By bringing this conflict into the light, Ana was able to renegotiate her relationship with money. She restructured her offerings, doubled her income within six months, and, more importantly, felt *authentic* doing so. Her success was not a betrayal of her values, but an expansion of them.

Guilt is another common shadow that quietly erodes financial sovereignty. Many people carry guilt around earning "too much," especially if they come from modest backgrounds, work in helping professions, or have internalised narratives that equate wealth with harm. Guilt may also arise from surviving or thriving when others close to us are struggling. This is often unconscious, but it shows up in behavioural patterns: undercharging, over-delivering, sabotaging windfalls, or giving away money in ways that bypass genuine discernment. The guilt says, "If I have more, someone else will have less." It reflects a zero-sum perception of value, rooted in scarcity and often reinforced by early family dynamics or cultural beliefs.

Working with guilt requires both intellectual reframing and emotional processing. Intellectually, we must understand that wealth is not finite, and that our financial expansion can be generative rather than extractive. Emotionally, we must process the grief and fear that often accompany separation from old identities or belonging systems. This may mean grieving the loss of simplicity, of shared struggle, or of the narratives that once kept us safe. Guilt cannot be transcended through logic alone. It must be *felt*, metabolised, and released. Only then can we earn and receive from a place of integrity, rather than apology.

Superiority, though less discussed, can be just as limiting. It often hides behind humility or detachment, especially in intellectual, academic, or creative communities where financial success is viewed with suspicion. Superiority says, "I'm above all that," or "I don't need much." It may sound virtuous, but often it masks fear—fear of being judged, of becoming corrupted, or of having to confront our own power. Superiority creates a false moral hierarchy, in which being broke or modest is equated with being good, and being wealthy is equated with being compromised. This belief system is not only inaccurate, it is corrosive. It divides us internally and externally, reinforcing shame around visibility, desire, and leadership.

Shadow work here involves reclaiming the parts of ourselves we've buried in the name of virtue. Can we acknowledge our desire for influence, ease, or recognition without collapsing into ego or defensiveness? Can we respect wealth without idolising or demonising it? When we integrate the shadow of superiority, we develop *financial humility*—the ability to grow without grandiosity, to succeed without needing to dominate or hide. This allows for a more mature, relational form of wealth—one that is grounded, accountable, and transparent.

One practical way to begin this shadow integration process is through triggered reflection. When you feel discomfort, judgement, or resentment in relation to someone else's success, pause. Ask yourself: What part of me is being mirrored? What desire or fear is being exposed? What belief am I holding about money, power, or worth? Then, trace that belief back to its source. Is it yours? Or was it inherited, conditioned, or adopted for survival? This kind of inquiry is not always comfortable—but it is profoundly liberating. It shifts the locus of control from external circumstances to internal clarity.

Another method is expressive shadow dialogue—a journalling technique in which you allow the disowned part of you to speak freely. Let envy, guilt, or superiority have a voice. What does it want? What is it afraid of? What is it protecting you from? By allowing these parts to express themselves without censorship, we dissolve their grip. We humanise them. And in doing so, we reclaim the energy they were holding hostage.

Ultimately, shadow work for wealth expansion is not about purging darkness. It is about *bringing light*—the light of awareness, compassion, and integration. It is about recognising that our limitations are not just technical or circumstantial; they are often psychic contracts we've made with our past. When we renegotiate those contracts, we unlock not only more income, but more coherence. We stop leaking energy into avoidance, projection, or performance. We become whole.

In a society obsessed with optics—where financial success is measured in public display—shadow work offers a quieter, deeper path. It invites us to meet the parts of ourselves we've hidden and to understand that our relationship with money is never just about money. It is about *self-permission*, *truth-telling*, and *emotional maturity*. And from that foundation, wealth becomes not a mask or a weapon, but a natural expression of who we are becoming.

When envy becomes clarity, guilt becomes discernment, and superiority becomes humility, the path to financial expansion is no longer blocked. It opens—not through force, but through *integration.* And in that opening, we discover not just more money, but more of ourselves.

Interactive Exercise: Your Financial Origin Story

Every financial decision you make today is, in part, an echo of a story you began writing long before you were aware you were the author. This story—your financial origin story—is not simply about numbers, accounts, or transactions. It is a complex psychological narrative shaped by early experiences, inherited beliefs, cultural programming, and emotional imprints. It governs your attitudes towards earning, saving, spending, giving, and receiving. And until you consciously unearth, examine, and revise this story, it remains the unchallenged script of your financial life.

The idea of a financial origin story borrows from narrative therapy and depth psychology, which hold that the stories we unconsciously tell ourselves become self-fulfilling prophecies. These narratives shape our identity, influence our choices, and determine what we believe is possible. In the realm of money, this can mean the difference between chronic under-earning and confident wealth-building; between unconscious sabotage and intentional stewardship.

This subchapter invites you into a guided process of deep financial reflection. Not to judge the past, but to understand it. Not to glorify trauma or hardship, but to reclaim agency. And not to bypass the complexity of your financial evolution, but to explore it with precision, curiosity, and compassion.

To begin, it is essential to recognise that your financial beliefs were not born in adulthood. They were absorbed in the most formative years—long before you earned your first paycheque. Childhood is where the financial blueprint is drafted. Not through explicit lessons, but through observation, emotional atmosphere, and patterned responses. Perhaps your parents argued about money in hushed voices behind closed doors. Or maybe money was talked about constantly, but always with stress, urgency, or shame. Perhaps abundance was present, but love was not—and so wealth became associated with coldness or distance. Conversely, perhaps your family struggled, but offered warmth and connection—linking scarcity with safety and emotional intimacy.

One client, Malcolm, shared how his father—an accountant by profession—rarely spoke about money, yet radiated anxiety whenever bills arrived. Malcolm, though well-educated and skilled, found himself resisting financial success well into his thirties. Despite multiple job offers with higher pay, he gravitated towards roles with minimal responsibility and modest salaries. Through guided journalling and therapeutic dialogue, he uncovered a deep-seated belief that more money meant more pressure—and pressure meant becoming emotionally unavailable like his father. Once that link was made conscious, Malcolm was able to disentangle income from stress and gradually accept roles aligned with both his talents and his values.

This is the power of the financial origin story. It reveals how your present is often an unconscious homage to your past. By bringing these patterns into awareness, you create the space to choose differently. Not by rejecting where you came from, but by updating the operating system.

Journalling, in this context, becomes more than self-expression—it becomes a method of memory excavation and belief transformation. The process involves identifying key scenes, characters, and messages from your early life that shaped your views on money. These memories might include witnessing a parent receive a promotion, experiencing the loss of a home, hearing a teacher comment on your economic background, or observing how wealthier peers were treated. Each vignette contains emotional data. Not just what happened, but how it made you feel. Safe? Ashamed? Envious? Invisible? Those emotions are not incidental—they are the glue that binds belief to behaviour.

Consider the case of Lianne, a visual artist who struggled to monetise her work. Her art was celebrated, but she habitually gave it away or sold it at below-market prices. Through the origin story process, she revisited a childhood memory of her mother telling her that "art is a gift to the world, not something you charge for." This well-meaning sentiment had lodged in Lianne's psyche as a directive: to monetise her art would be to betray its purity. Once she surfaced this belief, she was able to examine it critically and reframe it. She created a new mantra: "My art is a gift—and gifts deserve to be received with value." Within six months, she had launched a profitable online shop, all while maintaining the integrity of her creative work.

Importantly, your origin story is not just about what you internalised. It's also about what you *rejected.* Some people construct their financial identity as a rebellion—consciously doing the opposite of what they witnessed. If your parents hoarded money, you might overspend to prove your generosity. If wealth was flaunted in ways that felt shallow, you might under-earn to maintain moral superiority. While rebellion can feel empowering, it still leaves you tethered to the very story you're trying to escape. True sovereignty comes not from opposition, but from integration—from choosing what to keep, what to discard, and what to reauthor.

This exercise also invites you to examine the cast of characters who populated your early financial life. Who modelled wealth? Who modelled lack? Who spoke openly, and who avoided the subject entirely? What lessons were taught explicitly—and what messages were absorbed implicitly, through tone, absence, or contradiction? By naming these figures and their influence, you begin to understand the ancestral and cultural lineage that informs your current financial behaviours. This is particularly powerful for those from marginalised communities, where economic trauma and generational survival strategies are often passed down without reflection or repair. Naming these inherited patterns is the first step towards breaking them.

Once the raw material of your origin story has been explored, the next phase is reauthoring. This involves crafting a new narrative—one that honours your past but is no longer dictated by it. Instead of "I'm bad with money," you might write, "I was never taught financial skills, but I am learning now." Instead of "People like me don't get rich," you might declare, "My wealth serves a higher purpose, and I am safe to expand." This is not about delusional positivity. It's about narrative sovereignty. You are no longer the passive recipient of a script—you are the writer, editor, and director of your financial life.

Rewriting your origin story also means acknowledging your growth. What beliefs have you already challenged? What evidence do you now have that contradicts the old script? These validations matter. They create emotional ballast for your new trajectory. If you once thought you couldn't raise your rates, but did—record it. If you feared investing and now hold a portfolio—own it. Transformation is not always dramatic. Often, it is a quiet accumulation of small rebellions against old stories.

To support this process, you may wish to create a ritual around your journalling. Light a candle. Play music that grounds you. Set aside time when you are unhurried. Treat the exercise not as a task, but as a conversation—with yourself, your lineage, and your future. You might begin with prompts such as:

What is my earliest memory involving money?

What did I learn about people who had more than us? Less?

What unspoken rules about money did my family live by?

What role did I take on financially—as a child, a teenager, an adult?

How do those early experiences still shape my financial decisions today?

By the end of the exercise, your origin story will no longer be a mystery. It will be a map—a living document that helps you navigate where you've been and where you are capable of going. More than that, it becomes a portal to reclaim your power. Because when you can name your story, you are no longer owned by it.

Ultimately, understanding your financial origin story is not about fixing what is broken. It is about illuminating what has been hidden. It is about recognising that every fear, resistance, or blind spot has an origin—and therefore, an opportunity for resolution. As you unearth, reflect, and reauthor, you transform money from a source of confusion or constraint into a mirror of your personal evolution. In doing so, you don't just change your income. You change the consciousness with which you create, receive, and steward your wealth. And that, more than any number in a bank account, is the true measure of prosperity.

Chapter 8
Navigating Setbacks and Staying in Flow

Financial growth is often portrayed as a tidy, upward climb—a staircase, steady and predictable. But anyone who's actually walked the path knows it rarely unfolds so neatly. More often, it resembles a spiral: looping back, sidestepping, pausing, sometimes dipping before rising again. Those bumps along the way—the setbacks—aren't mere detours; they're catalysts, revealing what smooth sailing never could. They expose hidden beliefs, unveil structural weaknesses, and grant us the chance to rebuild with deeper alignment. This chapter explores what it truly means to remain in flow when the current unexpectedly turns against you.

Setbacks are an unavoidable part of the journey. Whether caused by economic recessions, job losses, business collapses, sudden health crises, or market upheavals, everyone faces moments when external finances falter despite a clear internal vision. The question isn't if difficulty will arise, but how we interpret and respond to it. Conventional financial advice tends to focus on emergency funds and contingency plans, seldom addressing the psychological or spiritual terrain that disruption unsettles. Yet it is precisely within this inner realm that the difference lies—whether a setback becomes a source of shame or a gateway to newfound strength.

Financial hardship often acts like a mirror, reflecting not only our practical preparedness but also the beliefs we hold about value, resilience, and self-worth. When income dries up or dwindles, the reaction isn't always just fear—it's often wrapped in a sense of failure. Identity, security, and adequacy begin to feel shaky. This response is hardly irrational; in societies where money equates with success, losing income can feel indistinguishable from losing status, safety, even selfhood. But these moments of contraction also invite a radical shift in perspective—challenging us to see prosperity not as a fixed state, but as a flowing rhythm.

The idea of Prosperity Through Uncertainty introduces a mindset untethered from external stability. True prosperity, it suggests, is measured by one's capacity to adapt, recalibrate, and stay tethered to purpose even when the numbers sag or circumstances shake loose. Neuroscience lends support here: flexible thinking correlates with enhanced creativity and emotional regulation. Those who flourish amid setbacks often share one trait—not necessarily greater resources, but greater resourcefulness.

Consider Dev, a marketing executive laid off in the midst of a major corporate restructure. Initially, he was devastated, tumbling into self-doubt and interpreting the layoff as proof his success was merely circumstantial. Yet through therapeutic reflection and mindfulness practices, Dev began to unravel this belief. He reframed the layoff, not as personal failure, but as a forced invitation to pivot toward deeper meaning. Within a year, he had launched a consultancy focused on ethical branding—earning less at first, but gaining far more alignment and autonomy. His prosperity hadn't vanished; it had simply reshaped. The setback didn't stop him. It redirected him.

This brings us to the essence of The Spiral Path. Authentic, sustainable progress rarely travels in a straight line. Setbacks are not regressions but moments ripe for integration. Each return to a familiar challenge arrives from a higher vantage point. It's not about going in circles, but spiralling upward, even when it feels like retracing steps. This perspective dismantles the toxic myth of constant forward momentum and invites a gentler, cyclical understanding of financial evolution.

Beyond metaphor, the neuroscience of transformation offers insight into why breakdown often precedes breakthrough. The brain's plasticity—the capacity to forge new neural pathways—is at its peak during times of uncertainty and disruption. When routine patterns are broken, the brain becomes more open to novel ideas and associations. Hence, major life upheavals often trigger profound insights or radical changes. Financial setbacks are not merely inconvenient; they are fertile ground for rewiring beliefs, habits, and identity.

This fusion of spiritual insight and scientific validation is captured in the notion that The Detour is Destiny. What feels like a delay or derailment may, in hindsight, be the very disruption needed to spark overdue transformation. This isn't about romanticising hardship or passively surrendering to it. Rather, it's an invitation to engage hardship consciously—to ask not just "How do I fix this?" but also "What is this revealing to me?" Through this, we reclaim authorship even amidst instability.

Practical tools back this philosophical shift. The Flow Recovery Toolkit, introduced here, offers concrete practices designed to help individuals re-centre during and after financial upheaval. These include nervous system resets, gratitude-based focus exercises, and micro-alignment techniques intended to restore a sense of agency. Take, for instance, the "5-Second Reset," a somatic grounding method that nudges the nervous system away from fight-or-flight, or the "Mini Gratitude Audit," which gently shifts the mind from scarcity to sufficiency. These tools don't bypass challenges; they create the internal steadiness needed to navigate them with clarity.

Aisha's story, a restaurateur who lost her business amid a global health crisis, exemplifies these principles in motion. Overwhelmed by the collapse of what she'd painstakingly built over a decade, she initially sank into grief and paralysis. Yet instead of rushing to rebuild or forcing a pivot, she allowed herself to pause. During this liminal period, she began writing—processing the emotional and psychological fallout. Those journal entries evolved into a book proposal, which was published. Today, Aisha works as a speaker and coach for food entrepreneurs, blending her prior expertise with her newfound voice. She didn't retrace her old path; she carved a new one—richer, more aligned, born from loss's ashes.

Her journey embodies The Comeback Curve—a concept reframing recovery not as returning to a former place, but emerging from disruption with deeper integration and insight. It rejects the productivity culture's "bounce back" myth, honouring instead the slow, layered, multidimensional nature of true comeback. Rebuilding is not merely about external measures—income, assets, growth—but about internal alignment, clarity, and readiness.

Ultimately, this chapter invites a more mature relationship with flow—one that embraces contraction, delay, and recalibration as essential rhythms in the creative cycle. Flow is not some peak state to clutch at desperately; it's a dynamic cadence to observe, engage with, and trust. When we accept this, setbacks cease to feel like threats. They become teachers. We cultivate an identity that is supple, not brittle; responsive, not reactive; shaped not by outside events, but by inner coherence.

Financial resilience, therefore, is less about mere preparation and more about perspective. When we learn to meet uncertainty with insight and disruption with depth, we don't just stay in flow—we become it. From that vantage, setbacks stop defining us. Instead, they refine us, forging a wealth that is as mental and emotional as it is material. And that kind of wealth, once claimed, is never truly lost.

Prosperity Through Uncertainty: Mindset Shifts and Tools for Staying Empowered During Financial Disruption

True prosperity is often imagined as a destination—a stable point marked by predictability, security, and abundance. Yet, the lived reality of financial growth is far more volatile. Economic upheaval, job loss, business contraction, and personal emergencies routinely upend even the most carefully laid plans. In these moments, conventional financial advice tends to focus on damage control: cut spending, liquidate assets, seek employment. While these steps may be necessary, they do little to address the internal disorientation, fear, and loss of agency that often accompany financial disruption. To cultivate prosperity through uncertainty requires more than strategy; it demands a radical shift in mindset and the development of tools that address the psychological, emotional, and energetic dimensions of instability.

Uncertainty, particularly in financial matters, often triggers a primal response. The human nervous system, attuned to threats against survival, can quickly default to fight, flight, freeze, or fawn responses when income is threatened. This is not a failure of discipline or resilience—it is biology. But the danger lies not in the stress response itself, but in how long we remain in it, and whether we allow it to dictate our decisions. Neuroscience tells us that chronic stress diminishes our ability to access the prefrontal cortex—the seat of rational thought, creativity, and long-term planning. When our survival brain takes over, we may make reactive choices: clinging to the familiar, rejecting support, or internalising shame. These reactions perpetuate the very scarcity we fear.

Prosperity through uncertainty begins by decoupling abundance from circumstance. This is not to deny the material reality of job loss or economic contraction, but to create an inner foundation that remains intact even when external conditions shift. At its core, this mindset invites us to redefine prosperity as *capacity*—our ability to adapt, relate, and reimagine, not just accumulate. It challenges the idea that wealth is solely about what we have and repositions it as how we relate to change.

Take the example of Jordan, a mid-level manager who was made redundant during a company merger. The initial response was panic and self-recrimination. Despite glowing performance reviews, Jordan interpreted the redundancy as a sign of personal inadequacy. But after engaging in structured reflection and somatic grounding practices, he recognised the situation not as a verdict on his value, but as a structural shift unrelated to his worth. This reframing allowed him to approach his next steps not from desperation, but from discernment. He identified latent interests in the sustainability sector, upskilled through a short online course, and within five months was consulting for a green tech start-up—at a higher salary than before. The shift wasn't just logistical—it was *ontological.* Jordan didn't just find a job. He redefined his economic identity.

This kind of turnaround does not happen by chance. It requires specific mindset disciplines, the first of which is *emotional sovereignty.* In times of financial instability, it is easy to collapse into external narratives—market panic, peer comparison, or inherited fears. Emotional sovereignty means staying anchored in your own inner compass, even amid noise. It means feeling your fear, but not outsourcing your decision-making to it. Practices such as breathwork, body scanning, and reflective journalling are not luxuries—they are essential technologies for restoring psychological agency. They allow us to observe our reactions rather than be governed by them.

Another vital reframe is understanding setbacks not as regressions but as recalibrations. This shift draws from both spiritual traditions and systems theory. In many indigenous and cyclical worldviews, breakdown precedes rebirth. In systems thinking, chaos is often the precursor to reorganisation. What looks like collapse may in fact be the shedding of what is no longer aligned, clearing space for innovation. This is not a call for passivity, but for presence. When you view financial disruption through this lens, you are more likely to ask expansive questions—What is this moment asking of me? What wants to emerge?—rather than reductive ones like, What went wrong?

The COVID-19 pandemic offers fertile ground for such reflections. During this period of mass economic instability, countless individuals were forced to pivot. Some experienced loss beyond measure. Others uncovered dormant talents, reconnected with purpose, or restructured their work lives in ways that brought them greater alignment. One such individual, Amina, a London-based events planner, lost nearly all her income in the early months of lockdown. After an initial period of despair, she began hosting virtual mindfulness retreats—a passion she had long sidelined. Within a year, she had built a thriving online community and diversified her income through digital courses and partnerships. The pivot was not linear, but it was transformative. Her new model not only generated income—it reflected her values.

This kind of resilience is not innate; it is cultivated. One practice that supports this cultivation is *contextual zooming*—a reflective tool that invites you to alternate between micro and macro perspectives. In the micro view, you engage with the immediate practicalities: What expenses can be renegotiated? What support can I access? In the macro view, you ask: What does this moment mean in the broader arc of my life? How might it serve my long-term alignment? This oscillation keeps you grounded while preventing tunnel vision. It is both strategic and soulful.

Another essential practice is *financial transparency with yourself.* In uncertainty, the temptation is often to avoid—bank statements, overdue invoices, or unreturned calls. But avoidance breeds anxiety. Transparency, on the other hand, creates clarity. Creating a simple "emergency clarity sheet"—a one-page summary of your current income, liabilities, and essential expenses—can restore a sense of agency. When paired with a daily practice of emotional check-ins, it helps ensure that your financial decisions are not driven by dissociation, but by grounded awareness.

Equally important is the capacity to receive. Financial disruptions often invite support—through severance, unemployment benefits, mutual aid, or community goodwill. But many people struggle to accept help due to internalised shame or hyper-independence. Yet, the refusal to receive is not strength—it is scarcity dressed as stoicism. True prosperity requires the humility to be held when needed. It also requires the willingness to give from overflow when the roles reverse. This reciprocity is the root of resilient economies, especially in times of instability.

Finally, we must speak to the role of meaning. Without a sense of purpose or coherence, financial uncertainty can feel existentially destabilising. But when disruption is placed within a context of meaning—growth, recalibration, contribution—it becomes not just tolerable, but transformational. Viktor Frankl, the Austrian neurologist and Holocaust survivor, argued that meaning is the single most important driver of resilience. When people have a "why," they can survive almost any "how." The same applies financially. Those who link their income to values, relationships, and creative expression are more likely to adapt with grace than those who chase security for its own sake.

In closing—though not to conclude, as the work is ongoing—prosperity through uncertainty is not about ignoring risk or bypassing pain. It is about cultivating an inner structure strong enough to hold you through turbulence. It is about developing mindset agility, emotional regulation, and strategic clarity. And it is about refusing to let fear become your compass.

In doing so, you don't just weather the storm. You become the still point within it. And from that place, you can rebuild—not as you were, but as who you were always capable of becoming.

The Spiral Path: Progress Is Not Linear

Financial growth is frequently depicted as a line—straight, upward, incremental. The dominant narrative in economics, entrepreneurship, and even personal development hinges on this model: save more each month, scale predictably, accumulate steadily. It is a worldview rooted in linearity, inherited from industrial-age systems of control, measurement, and productivity. Yet for many people—especially those building conscious wealth—this model bears little resemblance to their lived experience. Income fluctuates. Confidence ebbs and flows. Breakthroughs are often preceded by breakdowns. Progress stalls, reverses, and resurfaces. Rather than a staircase, financial evolution often looks like a spiral—circling back to similar lessons, revisiting old fears with new insight, and advancing through cycles rather than straight lines.

The spiral path is not failure masked in metaphor. It is a more honest—and more regenerative—way of understanding growth. It aligns not only with the psychology of transformation, but with patterns found across nature, biology, and even quantum physics. From the Fibonacci sequence in shells to the synaptic rewiring of the brain, growth is rarely linear. It loops, integrates, and revisits. When applied to finances, this perspective does not weaken discipline or undermine structure. Instead, it offers a framework for understanding setbacks, consolidating gains, and maintaining momentum in a way that honours the human psyche.

Linear thinking creates unrealistic expectations. It tells us that once we "get it"—a raise, a windfall, a six-figure year—we should never have to struggle again. But real life rarely complies. A therapist might double their income and then panic when tax season exposes their lack of systems. A coach might book out their programme only to burn out mid-launch. A corporate leader might leave their job to start a purpose-driven venture and earn far less than expected for a season. These are not signs of regression. They are signs of *integration*—the natural recalibration that occurs as our identity catches up with our reality.

The spiral path allows for the coexistence of expansion and contraction. In cyclical models, contraction is not regression—it is consolidation. It is the moment when growth turns inward to strengthen before re-emerging. This mirrors the natural seasons: winter is not death, but dormancy. The fields lie fallow not because they have failed, but because they are preparing for renewed fertility. Similarly, a financial lull does not necessarily indicate a problem. It may be an incubation period—where systems are being refined, strategies are maturing, and the nervous system is adjusting to new levels of visibility or responsibility.

Neuroscience supports this view. Learning and behaviour change occur through repetition, reflection, and integration—not linear acquisition. The brain forms new neural pathways not in a continuous upward slope, but in loops, with each revisit deepening the imprint. This is why old money fears resurface even after external success. It is not weakness. It is the brain revisiting an old map to redraw it with better tools. Each cycle becomes more conscious, less reactive. What once paralysed you may still appear—but now, you respond with discernment instead of panic. That is *progress*, even if the external numbers stay the same.

This concept is particularly liberating for those healing financial trauma. The linear model demands constant improvement, punishes backslides, and rarely allows space for emotional integration. The spiral model, by contrast, honours the messiness of real transformation. It creates room for relapse without shame, for hesitation without judgment. It recognises that healing does not happen in a straight line—and neither does prosperity.

Consider the story of Leila, a freelance writer who, after years of undercharging and overdelivering, finally broke through a long-standing income plateau. She landed a high-paying retainer client, started saving consistently, and felt, for the first time, financially empowered. Yet six months later, she found herself cancelling pitches, procrastinating on invoices, and avoiding her financial tracker. Old avoidance patterns had resurfaced. But instead of spiralling into self-blame, Leila paused. She reviewed her journals, revisited her original money affirmations, and realised that her nervous system had not yet adjusted to holding this new level of income and visibility. She returned to breathwork, spoke to her coach, and re-grounded herself—not by forcing forward, but by circling inward. That inward turn allowed her to break through again—but this time with deeper resilience.

Spiral growth also challenges the binary of success and failure. In a linear model, you are either progressing or regressing. In a spiral model, you are always in motion—even if the motion brings you back to an old wound. The key difference is that you return with new tools, new perspective, and new capacity. The same issue—fear of charging more, guilt around abundance, discomfort with visibility—may reappear. But your relationship to it has changed. You are not repeating—you are refining. This distinction is essential. It replaces the shame of recurrence with the insight of evolution.

One of the practical applications of spiral thinking in financial life is the *tracking of emotional milestones*, not just numerical ones. Instead of measuring only income growth or asset accumulation, track moments of courage, boundary-setting, or new levels of financial intimacy. Did you negotiate a rate for the first time? Did you say no to a misaligned client? Did you calmly review your expenses even during a low-income month? These are markers of maturity. They signify movement on the spiral—movement that may not yet show up in your bank balance, but is already rewiring your capacity to hold and grow wealth.

Another implication of the spiral path is the necessity of pause. In linear models, pauses are seen as weaknesses or delays. In spiral growth, they are strategic. A pause is where integration happens. It is where insight crystallises and new structures emerge. Without pause, growth becomes brittle. We build fast, but not deep. We succeed, but cannot sustain. The spiral reminds us that every upward phase needs a corresponding rest—not as indulgence, but as infrastructure.

This model also fosters a deeper kind of confidence. Not the bravado of perpetual winning, but the quiet assurance that you can meet whatever arises. You trust the spiral. You no longer panic when progress plateaus, because you understand the terrain. You can locate yourself within the cycle, knowing that contraction precedes expansion, and that revisiting old patterns does not negate your growth—it proves it.

From a cultural standpoint, embracing the spiral path invites a move away from hustle mythology. In a society that worships acceleration, the spiral offers a counter-narrative: that slow is not stagnant, that deep is not inefficient, and that returning is not regressing. This is particularly healing for creatives, healers, and entrepreneurs whose work defies conventional metrics. When your wealth is rooted in service, story, or soul, your financial path may be nonlinear by design. The spiral honours that.

Ultimately, the spiral path redefines what it means to be on track. It tells us that growth is not about how far you've come in a straight line, but how deeply you've evolved through each return. It invites us to track not only how much we've earned, but how much we've *integrated*. Not only what we've built, but how much of ourselves we've reclaimed in the process.

To walk the spiral path is to walk with grace. It is to meet financial life not as a ladder to climb, but as a rhythm to dance. A rhythm that includes expansion, contraction, pause, and renewal. A rhythm that makes space for your whole self—messy, brilliant, evolving—to participate in your prosperity.

And from that rhythm, something profound emerges: not just more wealth, but a more *intelligent* wealth—one that reflects who you truly are and what you are truly ready to hold. That kind of wealth does not simply rise. It spirals—deeper, wider, fuller—with every turn.

The Detour is the Destiny: Spiritual Insights and Neuroscience on Why Breakdowns Often Precede Breakthroughs in Wealth

In our collective mythology of success, we are trained to revere the straight path: the clear plan, the upward climb, the incremental victories. But financial transformation—especially when it involves deep inner rewiring—is rarely linear. It often arrives disguised as chaos. For many, the most significant breakthroughs in wealth consciousness follow a period of disorientation, loss, or failure. These moments are commonly dismissed as setbacks or missteps. Yet viewed through a more nuanced lens—one informed by both spiritual wisdom and neuroscience—these so-called detours often reveal themselves as the very terrain required for the emergence of lasting prosperity.

Breakdowns, particularly in the realm of money, often evoke shame, fear, and self-blame. Whether it's a failed investment, an unexpected redundancy, a cash flow crisis, or a sudden plunge in income, the experience can feel like a collapse not just of finances, but of identity. The reason for this lies in the psychological attachment most people have to financial stability. Money, in modern society, is rarely just a medium of exchange; it is a proxy for safety, competence, and social legitimacy. When that structure falters, it can catalyse an existential crisis. But herein lies the opportunity. What feels like falling apart may in fact be falling into place—albeit along a path we did not plan.

In spiritual traditions across the world, the motif of dissolution as precursor to revelation is well established. In Buddhist philosophy, the principle of *sunyata*—emptiness or void—is not a nihilistic absence but a fertile space from which new form can arise. In mystical Christianity, the concept of "the dark night of the soul" represents a necessary phase of spiritual disintegration before union with deeper truth. In indigenous rites of passage, initiates are often led through symbolic or literal "deaths" before being reborn into a new role within the community. Across these traditions, breakdown is not a deviation—it is an initiation.

In the context of wealth, these breakdowns can function as sacred interruptions. They rupture the ego's attachment to control, certainty, and identity. They expose unsustainable habits, outdated beliefs, and inherited scripts. And crucially, they create the psychological and energetic space for something new to emerge—something more aligned, resilient, and whole.

Contemporary neuroscience adds an empirical layer to this understanding. The human brain is a predictive organ. It constructs internal models of the world based on past experience and uses these models to interpret new input. When our lived reality suddenly deviates from our expectations—say, a lucrative client cancels, or an economic downturn wipes out our savings—the brain initially registers this as a threat. This can activate the amygdala, triggering a cascade of stress responses: increased cortisol, narrowed focus, and emotional reactivity. But—and this is key—when these disruptions are met with awareness rather than panic, they also open up a neurobiological window for change.

During such periods of uncertainty, the brain becomes more plastic. Neuroplasticity, the brain's ability to form and reorganise synaptic connections, increases when familiar patterns are interrupted. In other words, crises dislodge the default settings. They destabilise the autopilot. And this destabilisation—if navigated consciously—can lead to more adaptive, creative, and integrative patterns of thought and behaviour. From a neuroscientific perspective, the detour is not only a spiritual initiation—it is a biological imperative for transformation.

One illustrative case is that of Arun, a successful product designer in the tech industry who, after years of steady income and predictable career growth, was abruptly made redundant due to a company merger. The initial aftermath was emotionally disorienting. Arun found himself questioning not just his employability, but his entire sense of worth. Yet during the forced pause, he began exploring long-ignored creative pursuits—particularly sustainable design. What began as a side project evolved into a full-fledged consultancy serving eco-conscious brands. A year later, Arun's income had not only recovered but surpassed previous levels—and for the first time in his professional life, it was deeply tied to his values. The layoff was not a detour from his path. It was the path.

This pattern echoes a deeper spiritual truth: that evolution often requires disruption. Not because pain is noble or struggle is romantic, but because old forms must be dismantled before new ones can be embodied. In financial terms, this may mean that the breakdown of a business model, the collapse of a revenue stream, or the disillusionment with a once-coveted goal is not the failure we fear—but the liberation we need.

The danger lies not in the detour itself, but in how we interpret it. If we internalise the breakdown as a personal defect, we may spiral into paralysis or cynicism. If, however, we approach it as a revelatory pause—as a teacher rather than a threat—we open the door to profound recalibration. This is where mindset practices such as metacognition, somatic regulation, and spiritual reflection become vital. They enable us to *stay with the rupture* long enough to mine its intelligence.

One of the most powerful reframes during these periods is the question, "What is this breakdown making possible that stability never could?" This is not a bypass—it is a reorientation. It shifts the focus from loss to revelation. From what is ending to what is *wanting to begin*. Such reframes are not merely mental gymnastics. They create measurable shifts in the nervous system. Studies in affective neuroscience have shown that meaning-making in the face of adversity reduces the impact of trauma and accelerates post-crisis growth. Meaning is not a luxury. It is a technology for resilience.

In practice, this might look like creating space to grieve what has been lost while simultaneously holding curiosity about what might be gained. It might mean using mindfulness to sit with discomfort, rather than rushing to fix or replace it. It might involve rituals of release, dialogue with trusted mentors, or journalling prompts that bring unconscious fears to the surface. All of these are tools not to escape the detour, but to *enter it fully*, armed with presence and trust.

Importantly, the detour is also relational. It often forces a renegotiation of boundaries, roles, and support systems. As income fluctuates, so too may one's dynamics with partners, family members, or colleagues. These are not side effects. They are integral to the process. A financial crisis often reveals where codependency, avoidance, or silence have masked deeper truths. Addressing these patterns is not just emotionally healing—it is economically strategic. True wealth is relational, and crises expose the relational scaffolding that sustains or sabotages our prosperity.

At the collective level, detours can catalyse systemic insight. Entire industries, economies, and communities undergo ruptures that expose inequality, inefficiency, or unsustainability. These breakdowns, while painful, are also invitations to reimagine. The 2008 financial crash birthed new movements in ethical investing and decentralised finance. The COVID-19 pandemic prompted widespread reevaluation of work-life balance, remote labour, and economic justice. Just as individuals face initiatory detours, so too do societies. And the question remains the same: Will we cling to the old story—or write a new one?

To embrace the detour as destiny is not to glorify hardship or advocate chaos. It is to recognise that transformation is often nonlinear, non-consensual, and non-negotiable. It comes when we least expect it, disrupts what we thought was permanent, and demands a deeper level of alignment than we previously knew how to access.

But if we meet the detour with courage, inquiry, and grace, it reveals itself not as a departure from our path, but as the *deepening* of it. The road may bend, crumble, or vanish altogether. But something else appears—something truer, stronger, and more uniquely ours. Not despite the breakdown. Because of it.

And when that new path emerges—when the pieces reconfigure and the insight crystallises—we do not just return to wealth. We return to ourselves, more whole than we were before. That is the real breakthrough. That is the destiny we never could have planned, but were always being prepared for.

Flow Recovery Toolkit: Actionable Tools to Reconnect with Financial Flow After Setbacks

Setbacks can feel like a sudden rupture in the current of one's life—especially when they involve money. Whether triggered by a job loss, an unexpected expense, or a failed investment, these disruptions can arrest our momentum and sever our connection to what felt like financial "flow." In such moments, even those who are typically grounded and resilient can find themselves paralysed—emotionally reactive, cognitively foggy, or spiritually disoriented. The human nervous system, hardwired to interpret uncertainty as threat, often responds by contracting. And in this contracted state, we tend to default to patterns of avoidance, shame, or compulsive action. The work, then, is not simply to fix the finances—but to restore the conditions in which flow can be felt and reactivated.

To recover financial flow is not to bypass the reality of difficulty. It is to intentionally reengage with your power of perception, physiology, and focus—so that you can meet disruption with agency rather than collapse. This is where tools like the *5-Second Reset* and *Mini Gratitude Audit* become profoundly relevant. These are not merely techniques; they are recalibrations of awareness. They allow you to shift from survival mode into a space of receptivity, presence, and intelligent action. And unlike large-scale financial strategies, these tools work at the micro-level—precisely where stuckness begins.

The first principle of flow recovery is recognising that *flow is a state, not a circumstance.* You can be in flow while unemployed and out of flow while fully employed. You can feel abundant with minimal cash on hand, and simultaneously feel scarcity while flush with assets. This is because flow is not defined by external metrics but by internal coherence—when your mind, body, and values are aligned in the present moment. Neuroscience calls this "neurointegration." It's a state in which different parts of the brain communicate fluidly, especially the prefrontal cortex (executive function), the amygdala (emotional processing), and the insular cortex (interoception). In lay terms, you think clearly, feel calmly, and act congruently.

Yet during financial upheaval, this integration often breaks down. The sympathetic nervous system activates a fight-or-flight response. Blood flow is redirected away from the brain's rational centres toward survival functions. This is when a late bill feels catastrophic, a minor expense triggers panic, or future planning becomes impossible. To re-enter flow, then, one must *downshift the nervous system* before attempting to make significant financial decisions. This is where the *5-Second Reset* proves invaluable.

The 5-Second Reset is a somatic-interrupt technique designed to arrest the stress cascade before it hijacks your cognition. The method is simple but neurologically potent. As soon as you notice the telltale signs of financial overwhelm—tight chest, spiralling thoughts, reactive impulses—pause. Inhale deeply for five seconds, hold for two, and exhale slowly. As you do, anchor your attention to a single sensory detail: the texture of your clothing, the sound of your breath, the weight of your feet on the ground. This interrupts the amygdala's overactivation and brings your awareness back to the *now*—the only place from which intelligent action can arise. One breath cycle may not erase the problem, but it *creates a pocket of clarity* within which better choices can be made.

Another critical tool in the Flow Recovery Toolkit is the *Mini Gratitude Audit.* Gratitude is often misunderstood as a feel-good accessory—nice to have, but non-essential. Yet research in positive psychology reveals that gratitude activates brain regions associated with emotional regulation, reward processing, and resilience. In moments of financial strain, this practice is not sentimental; it is strategic. The Mini Gratitude Audit involves identifying three small, specific things related to your financial life that you appreciate right now. Not abstract ideals, but immediate realities: a helpful conversation, a resource you still have access to, a payment that cleared, a skill that can be monetised. The act of naming what is still intact—even amidst disruption—counters the brain's negativity bias and helps restore cognitive flexibility.

Consider the experience of Devika, a freelance editor who faced an abrupt income gap when two major clients simultaneously ended their contracts. Initially, she spiralled into despair, interpreting the loss as a verdict on her value. But through the practice of the 5-Second Reset and a daily Mini Gratitude Audit, she began to regulate her nervous system and reclaim perspective. She remembered a dormant contact in her network, whom she reached out to with a spirit of service rather than desperation. That single conversation led to a retainer contract that, while smaller than before, allowed her to stabilise—and eventually rebuild with more aligned clients.

What Devika's experience illustrates is a broader truth: flow does not return through force. It returns through presence. Presence allows us to discern where energy is leaking, where stories are distorting perception, and where small shifts can create disproportionate impact. Flow recovery is therefore about *sensitivity*—learning to read the body's signals, listen to intuitive nudges, and respond from inner alignment rather than fear.

Another powerful yet underutilised recovery tool is *context switching with intention.* When stuck in financial worry, many people either ruminate endlessly or distract themselves compulsively. Neither approach truly interrupts the feedback loop. Intentional context switching, by contrast, involves shifting your physical environment or focus to trigger a different neural network. This might mean stepping outside, changing posture, speaking aloud your next step, or engaging in a brief creative act. These micro-interventions activate the default mode network—a system linked to self-reflection and future planning—and can help initiate mental reorganisation after overwhelm.

In the longer term, recovering financial flow also involves recalibrating your *relationship with setbacks.* This is where narrative framing becomes essential. If you view every disruption as a verdict on your competence, you are likely to stay in a constricted loop. If instead you interpret the setback as part of a larger pattern—an initiation, a refinement, a re-routing—then even the most difficult experiences can yield insight. Psychologist Dan McAdams' work on narrative identity shows that people who frame adversity as redemptive rather than defeating are more likely to report post-traumatic growth. What this means in financial terms is simple: how you *story* the setback affects how you *recover* from it.

The Flow Recovery Toolkit, then, is not a one-time fix but a modular set of practices—each designed to bring you back to centre, restore coherence, and reignite movement. Its power lies in its adaptability. You don't need perfect conditions to implement it. You don't need clarity about your five-year plan or even your next client. All you need is a willingness to pause, re-regulate, and choose your next best step *from alignment.*

This toolkit is not a replacement for financial literacy or long-term planning. It complements those by ensuring that your mindset and physiology are prepared to *use* the tools of budgeting, saving, or investing effectively. After all, no spreadsheet can help you if you're paralysed by fear. No wealth strategy works if your nervous system is in chronic shutdown. By integrating somatic intelligence, mindset tools, and micro-practices into your recovery process, you not only bounce back—you bounce forward, with greater insight and emotional resilience than before.

Financial flow, at its core, is a state of receptivity and responsiveness. It does not mean constant upward motion or uninterrupted abundance. It means staying *available* to life—to adapt, to adjust, to receive, to give. When setbacks occur, the real work is not in fixing everything immediately. It is in *returning* to that availability. The Flow Recovery Toolkit is your compass in that return—not to where you were, but to who you are becoming. And from that place, flow becomes not something to chase, but something you learn to *trust* again.

Case Study: The Comeback Curve — Rebuilding from a Deeper, More Aligned Place

Every compelling financial transformation shares one common trait: at some point, the protagonist hits the ground. Not figuratively, but undeniably. They lose what they built, the confidence they carried, or the illusion they clung to—and in that fall, the real ascent begins. This arc is what we call the *Comeback Curve.* It is not simply about regaining material wealth or career status. It's about rebuilding from a more rooted sense of self, integrating past mistakes with new insight, and aligning future growth with values previously ignored. The curve does not arc neatly upwards. It dips, twists, and at times flatlines. But it ultimately bends towards coherence, agency, and authentic prosperity.

Consider the story of Marcus, a thirty-seven-year-old entrepreneur who built—and lost—a seven-figure wellness business before finding his way back, not just financially, but existentially. Marcus' story isn't unique because he failed. Failure is common. What makes it significant is how he used the collapse as a portal to reclaim his purpose, rethink his identity, and redefine wealth on his own terms.

At the height of his success, Marcus embodied the influencer economy: charismatic, strategic, and publicly revered. His company offered a range of high-ticket coaching programmes, wellness products, and corporate retreats. From the outside, it looked like a conscious empire. But behind the branding was a business model running on burnout. Decisions were driven by scaling targets, not service impact. Hires were reactive. Systems were patchworked. And Marcus, privately, was running on caffeine, imposter syndrome, and a mounting sense of misalignment.

The unravelling began subtly: a few missed targets, a key team member departure, a scandal involving a marketing claim that, while technically defensible, felt ethically grey. Then came the pandemic. Retreats were cancelled. Clients pulled out. Within six months, Marcus had depleted his reserves trying to stay afloat. He let go of his team, dissolved the company, and moved out of his flat into a friend's spare room. His identity—CEO, thought leader, provider—collapsed alongside the enterprise he had built.

For weeks, Marcus alternated between shame and numbness. He found it difficult to explain what had happened, even to himself. Friends offered platitudes, but few understood the complexity of losing not just money, but a persona. In coaching circles, he had been the golden boy. Now he felt like a cautionary tale. Yet it was in this groundless space that the real work began.

Unable to distract himself with productivity, Marcus turned inward. He began daily breathwork and journalling, not to optimise his next move, but to *feel*. To sit with the grief of having lost something he once loved, and the relief of having escaped a machine he had grown to resent. In these quiet confrontations, he realised that much of his earlier drive had been fuelled by scarcity narratives inherited from childhood. Growing up in a working-class household, financial security had always felt precarious. Building a business was, in part, his way of ensuring he'd never have to feel small again.

But the empire he built was never anchored in nervous system safety. It was a house of glass—beautiful, impressive, and fundamentally fragile.

Over the next year, Marcus reframed his relationship to work. He enrolled in a trauma-informed coaching certification—not to rebrand, but to understand the somatic patterns he had been ignoring. He took on freelance strategy work, not for ego, but to stay grounded. He lived simply. Quietly. He read less business theory and more philosophy, returning often to the words of Viktor Frankl and bell hooks. And in this space, a new vision emerged—not for a company, but for a conversation.

Rather than rebuild the same structure, Marcus decided to start again from the inside out. He launched a podcast focused on honest, unglamorous stories of rebuilding. Not the highlight reels, but the real arcs—the Comeback Curves. He began writing essays about shame, identity collapse, and financial trauma. And instead of targeting elite clients, he offered affordable group sessions for early-stage creators navigating transitions. Within a year, he had a modest but engaged community, a portfolio of aligned partnerships, and a business that, while smaller on paper, felt exponentially richer.

Marcus' comeback was not dramatic. It wasn't fuelled by viral posts or sudden windfalls. It was incremental, integrated, and deeply intentional. His income today is steady but not explosive. His nervous system is regulated. His work feels expressive rather than performative. He's built savings again—not to silence fear, but to honour sustainability. Most importantly, he no longer equates money with safety or visibility with value. His self-worth is no longer contingent on metrics he cannot control.

The lessons embedded in Marcus' arc offer a profound alternative to the dominant narrative of success and recovery. First, they highlight that loss is not always a deviation. Sometimes it's the only thing strong enough to interrupt a trajectory that was unconsciously self-betraying. What Marcus experienced wasn't just financial failure—it was an existential clearing. A disruption that made space for authenticity.

Second, his story illustrates that the comeback curve is less about acceleration and more about *attunement*. He didn't rush to rebuild. He paused to integrate. He didn't return to what worked before; he examined why it had stopped working. And in doing so, he broke the cycle of repeating the same errors in new disguises.

Third, Marcus' experience reveals the power of embodiment. While he had all the mindset tools from his previous work, what shifted his trajectory was regulating his body. Breathwork. Slowness. Stillness. These practices restored his capacity to feel safety without external validation. From that place, wiser decisions became not just possible but *inevitable*.

In coaching, there's a term called "returning to zero." It refers to the process of deconstructing everything you thought you knew to rebuild from a more truthful place. Marcus didn't just visit zero. He lived there. And in doing so, he realised that the real wealth was not in the product launches or the client rosters—it was in the clarity, connection, and courage he cultivated when no one was watching.

His comeback was not a redemption story. It was a reintegration story. A descent into the underworld of identity, followed by a re-emergence—more whole, more human, more sovereign.

The broader implication of the Comeback Curve is that it invites a redefinition of what success looks like after loss. It challenges the idea that recovery must be rapid or impressive. It encourages us to measure growth not only by external outcomes but by internal coherence. It reminds us that setbacks strip away what is unsustainable—not to punish us, but to prepare us for deeper alignment.

For anyone currently navigating their own fall—from income, status, structure, or self—the Comeback Curve offers both hope and challenge. Hope that what you're losing may be making space for something truer. Challenge to sit with the discomfort long enough to hear what it's trying to teach.

Marcus' story is not unique. Many rebuild after collapse. But few do it consciously. Few resist the pressure to rush back to market. Few take the time to untangle the patterns that created the fragility in the first place. When they do, their comeback is more than economic. It's evolutionary.

The next time life knocks you off course, ask yourself: What if this detour isn't ruining my path, but *revealing* it? What if your fall isn't the end of your story, but the moment your real story finally begins?

That is the promise of the Comeback Curve—not just to recover what was lost, but to discover who you are when nothing else is left to prove.

Chapter 9
The Legacy Frequency

Legacy—it's a word we hear often, a concept tossed around in wills and wealth seminars, yet so rarely do we confront its deeper truth. For many, it brings to mind the tangible: money, property, a family name etched into a brass plaque. But real legacy is far less material, and far more intimate. It's not only about what we bequeath, but what we embed—in people, in communities, in culture. Legacy lives in the choices we make, the energy we carry, the values we model, and the questions we leave unfinished. It's not merely about accumulation, but about transmission. Not just wealth, but wisdom. This chapter shifts us beyond the mechanics of financial planning, guiding us into the soulful architecture of generational influence.

Enter the idea of the Legacy Frequency—the subtle yet potent energy of our impact. Just as sound moves in waves, so too does wealth, in all its forms—emotional, material, spiritual. The decisions we make with money ripple forward, influencing lives well beyond our own. For many, particularly those who are the first in their family to generate sustainable prosperity, this is more than personal work. It is ancestral. It means breaking inherited patterns of scarcity, rewriting the silent scripts passed down through generations, and consciously planting new patterns into the soil of the family system. This isn't just financial literacy—it's the healing of a lineage.

To shift generational momentum, one must first understand the stories they've inherited—stories about money, success, and self-worth. These narratives may be loud, or they may be subtle, woven into the everyday fabric of how one's family approached life. Perhaps yours is a lineage where wealth was always just out of reach, viewed with suspicion, or earned only through overwork and sacrifice. Or maybe money was present, but always entangled in guilt, power, or silence. Regardless of the particulars, this work asks more than personal responsibility. It demands the digestion of generational residue—both emotional and financial.

Doing this work with presence and purpose means becoming a kind of energetic fulcrum—respecting the past, yet choosing not to be bound by it. It's the quiet but radical act of saying, "It ends here. And something new begins." But resolve alone won't sustain that choice. It requires structure, tools, and a supportive ecosystem. This chapter isn't just about ideas; it's about anchoring those ideas in practice, and viewing this role not as a burden, but as a calling. We'll explore how to create not from pressure, but from purpose—how to move resources with discernment, and how to plan for something far greater than mere financial security.

One essential principle in this journey is soul-aligned generosity. Too often, giving is reduced to optics or obligation—we give because we feel we must, or because it proves something about who we are. But generosity born of guilt or identity maintenance seldom yields true abundance. It drains. In contrast, soul-aligned giving arises from overflow. It stems from a deep recognition that we *are* abundance—and what we share is an extension of that fullness. It's less about the amount given, and more about the energy behind it. Does it expand the giver and the receiver alike? If not, perhaps it's worth a pause.

Take Alma, for instance—a software architect who amassed substantial wealth in her thirties. Her early philanthropic choices were traditional: large donations to established charities. But something felt off. Her giving, though well-intended, lacked resonance. It was too clean, too expected. So she stepped back. Reflected. Then began funding grassroots initiatives in her grandparents' homeland—projects aimed at education and digital access for girls. Suddenly, her generosity wasn't about generosity. It was about legacy. It wasn't spare change—it was a seed. The impact deepened. So did her connection to it.

From here, we move into the notion of the Impact Blueprint—a living map of how one's resources, skills, and presence might ripple meaningfully through the world. Legacy, after all, needn't be deferred until death. Why wait? What causes ignite your spirit? What wisdom do you hold that others might need—especially the younger ones coming up behind you? What do you want your presence to *do*, beyond earning and saving? These aren't abstract musings. They're deeply practical prompts—calls to align your money with your mission.

In this light, legacy is no longer a static document stored in a drawer. It becomes a living, breathing system. You might mentor budding changemakers, fund environmental projects, support artists, or simply model emotional maturity in a household that never had that before. The specifics matter less than the intent. And when intention is anchored in strategy, real change takes root.

That strategy, of course, includes the financial instruments—wills, trusts, insurance, end-of-life planning. But legacy isn't only legal. There's also the matter of energetic closure. Facing our mortality may be uncomfortable, but it is essential. When we die without tending to the emotional and spiritual dimensions of departure, we leave behind confusion, silence, and conflict. That's not legacy—that's residue. But rituals—letters, voice recordings, family conversations—can soften that edge. They transform the end from a rupture into a rite of passage.

It is this weaving together of the pragmatic and the poetic that turns legacy into initiation. And to help you bring that vision into being, there's a tool: The Legacy Map. Unlike a standard estate plan, this interactive visual framework invites you to plot not just your assets, but your intentions. Your values. Your hopes. Your frequency. It doesn't just ask, "What will they inherit?" It asks, "Who might they become through what I leave behind?" It is part map, part mirror—part ledger, part love letter.

As we move through the chapter, you'll encounter stories of individuals who altered the arc of their family's future—not by chasing fame or fortune, but by anchoring clarity and coherence. Entrepreneurs who created mission-driven businesses that spanned generations. Teachers who redirected modest earnings into scholarships for students who reminded them of themselves. These are not tales of excess. They are stories of resonance. Of choosing depth over volume.

You'll also find guided exercises to help articulate your own legacy—reflections on ancestral patterns, core values, and the imprint you want to leave. Don't rush them. They are meant to unfold slowly, to agitate, to stir, to clarify. Legacy is not a to-do list. It's a tone you set, an invitation you extend.

So ask yourself, as you read: What do I want to echo once I've gone? Not just in spreadsheets and signatures, but in gestures, in courage, in culture. That is your true Legacy Frequency—not a static possession, but a living pattern. Not a monument, but a movement. And the more intention you pour into it now, the more powerfully it will ripple—through your lifetime and far beyond it.

Transcending Generational Cycles: How to Become the "First" in Your Lineage to Create Conscious Wealth—and How to Pass It On Intentionally

To transcend a generational cycle is to rewrite the script that life handed you at birth. When that cycle involves financial scarcity, shame around money, or inherited beliefs about unworthiness, the act of creating conscious wealth becomes nothing short of revolutionary. It is not merely about earning more, investing better, or leaving behind material assets. It is about interrupting the unconscious momentum of the past and redirecting it with intention, clarity, and care. Becoming the first in your family to embody this shift requires not only courage but deep inner literacy—a willingness to decode the emotional DNA that shaped your money story.

We often assume that wealth-building begins with strategy: the right budget, the right investment, the right opportunity. In truth, for many people—especially those breaking new ground within their lineage—the first threshold is *awareness*. Before one earns or builds, one must *unlearn*. We carry invisible scripts inherited from those who raised us, even if they never spoke a word about money. A parent's anxiety about bills, a grandparent's pride in self-sacrifice, or a sibling's discomfort with ambition—all of these become part of the internal environment from which our financial behaviour springs.

This is where the concept of financial epigenetics offers illuminating insight. Just as trauma and resilience can be passed through generations biologically, so too can attitudes and behaviours around money be culturally and emotionally transmitted. Researchers in the fields of psychology and intergenerational trauma have shown that children absorb not only what their caregivers explicitly teach, but also what they model, what they fear, and what they avoid. If wealth was absent or morally charged in your upbringing, you may unconsciously associate prosperity with betrayal, isolation, or danger.

To transcend these cycles, we must start by making them visible. Consider the story of Amira, a first-generation university graduate and successful marketing strategist who, by age thirty-three, was earning more in a year than her parents had earned in a decade. Despite this outward success, Amira found herself riddled with guilt and sabotaging her savings goals. Every financial milestone—whether it was buying a home or asking for a raise—was accompanied by discomfort, sometimes even panic. In therapy, she uncovered a deeply embedded belief: that surpassing her family's financial status would distance her from their love and invalidate their sacrifices. Her nervous system had encoded survival as sameness; excelling triggered a threat response.

Amira's real transformation began not with a financial planner, but with an inner commitment: to honour her roots without replicating their limits. She started having honest, vulnerable conversations with her parents, not to seek permission but to create emotional closure. She engaged in narrative therapy to separate her identity from inherited shame. Only after this internal work did the external flow begin to stabilise. She resumed investing, increased her giving, and began mentoring younger women from similar backgrounds. Her wealth-building became not just personal, but ancestral—a form of healing in motion.

Being the first in a lineage to create conscious wealth requires both boundary and bridge. Boundary, in the sense that you must refuse to repeat patterns that no longer serve. Bridge, in the sense that you remain connected to where you come from—not through loyalty to struggle, but through intentional contribution. This is where legacy thinking must begin *before* death. The way you model financial wholeness now becomes the template others in your family—siblings, children, cousins, mentees—may one day adopt.

Intentional transmission means moving beyond silence or secrecy. It means being transparent about your values, your choices, and your evolution. It does not mean flaunting. It means teaching. One of the most powerful ways to pass on a new frequency of wealth is to narrate not just what you've gained, but how you've grown. Children, especially, absorb nuance. When they hear you speak about both abundance and boundaries, giving and receiving, spending and saving—they learn that wealth is not static, but dynamic. They internalise the truth that money is not simply earned or lost, but *stewarded.*

And stewardship is the spiritual backbone of conscious wealth. It reframes money not as possession, but as energy—something to be directed, circulated, and sanctified. In many indigenous and ancestral cultures, wealth was not about individual accumulation but communal nourishment. Resources were pooled, redistributed, and celebrated not in isolation, but in context. To bring this ethos into modern wealth-building is to marry tradition with transformation. It is to ask: how can my success support not just my needs, but the unfolding of others' potential?

One of the key principles here is *reciprocity without depletion*. Many first-generation earners find themselves financially supporting extended family, often in unstructured or unsustainable ways. The emotional pressure can lead to burnout, resentment, or a sense of erasure. Conscious wealth requires learning how to give with discernment—not from guilt, but from sovereignty. It might mean setting up structured support: paying for education rather than recurring expenses, offering business capital instead of endless loans, or creating shared family funds with clear guidelines. These choices are not less generous; they are *more generative*—they plant seeds rather than enable dependency.

Passing wealth on intentionally also means preparing systems—not just stories. This includes wills, living trusts, ethical investment plans, and financial education. But it also includes legacy rituals: letters to heirs, values statements, gratitude ceremonies, storytelling gatherings. These are the containers that hold the emotional and spiritual aspects of wealth—ensuring that what is handed down is not just money, but meaning.

Consider the case of Raj and Priya, a couple in their forties who built a multimillion-dollar wellness brand. Coming from modest backgrounds, they were determined to raise their children with both financial stability and emotional intelligence. Rather than simply create a trust, they initiated annual "impact dialogues" with their children, aged ten and thirteen. These were dedicated weekends where they discussed causes they cared about, reviewed charitable donations, and allowed the children to pitch ideas for small family grants. Over time, their children began to understand not just the mechanics of money, but its purpose. Raj and Priya weren't just leaving behind assets—they were building financial *literacy, empathy, and intention.*

This kind of intergenerational leadership does not require vast sums. It requires *clarity*. Clarity about what matters, what heals, and what lasts. Whether you are the first in your family to earn six figures, buy a home, or start a business, your work is not merely economic—it is archetypal. You are re-writing the story of what is possible. And with that power comes responsibility: to embody the change, and to create pathways for others to walk with greater ease.

Ultimately, transcending generational cycles is not about escaping your origins. It is about *elevating* them—by choosing what to carry forward and what to lovingly release. It is a reclamation of agency, a declaration that you are not defined by the scarcity you inherited, but by the abundance you're willing to create and circulate.

And when done with integrity, this shift becomes a frequency—one that your descendants, and perhaps your entire community, will feel. Not as a loud proclamation, but as a quiet invitation: *You can live differently. You are allowed to thrive.* And in that simple yet radical truth lies the beginning of a new lineage.

Soul-Aligned Generosity: Giving from Overflow, Not Obligation

True generosity, when examined closely, is not measured by the size of the gift, but by the energy with which it is given. The act of giving—be it money, time, or presence—carries an invisible frequency that transmits more than the offering itself. It either expands both giver and receiver, or it subtly diminishes one to elevate the other. In the context of conscious wealth, generosity becomes more than an ethical impulse or a social responsibility. It becomes a spiritual practice—a sacred circulation of abundance that honours interconnection, agency, and wholeness. Soul-aligned generosity, in this light, is giving that arises from *overflow* rather than *obligation.* It is not performance, guilt, or appeasement; it is the natural outflow of a fulfilled source.

To give from overflow means that your offering is untainted by depletion. It is not extracted through sacrifice or driven by the fear of disapproval. It is the fruit of a full internal reservoir—emotional, spiritual, and financial. When generosity stems from this place, it uplifts the giver as much as the receiver. It reflects a worldview of sufficiency: the understanding that there is enough, and that sharing does not diminish but multiplies.

Yet in practice, much of our giving is entangled in subconscious programming. For many, especially those from collectivist cultures or marginalised communities, generosity has historically been a survival mechanism. Sharing resources was often necessary to ensure group endurance. Over time, this survival-based sharing was canonised as virtue, even when it depleted the individual. The result is a subtle but pervasive pattern: giving as a reflex, not a choice; as penance, not joy.

This is particularly true among first-generation wealth builders who carry a deep sense of loyalty to their roots. Their success, hard-earned and often lonely, becomes a silent contract: "I must now compensate for all that was lacked before me." They may find themselves financially supporting extended family, community causes, or even acquaintances, not because they feel called, but because they feel *compelled.* In this model, giving becomes a form of energetic leakage—a slow erosion of one's financial sovereignty masked as compassion.

The shift toward soul-aligned generosity begins with *discernment.* It requires asking not only "Can I give?" but "Is this giving clean?" Clean giving is devoid of resentment, hidden expectation, or self-negation. It is freely offered and internally congruent. It says, "This is mine to give, and I offer it with clarity and wholeness." This discernment is not selfishness—it is stewardship. When giving is aligned with soul rather than ego, it becomes sustainable, nourishing, and catalytic.

Take the example of Nina, a high-performing creative director who, after achieving significant financial success, felt pressure to contribute large sums to a family foundation established by her relatives. Though the cause was honourable—educational reform in underserved areas—Nina felt dissonance. She hadn't been consulted in the foundation's vision, and its operations lacked transparency. Still, she contributed for years, each time with a growing sense of misalignment. Eventually, she paused and redirected her resources toward a grassroots mentorship programme she personally co-founded with two former students. The act was no longer about optics or appeasement. It was about resonance. Her giving became not just charitable, but *alive.*

This example highlights a crucial element of soul-aligned generosity: *relationship.* Not all giving must be relational in the literal sense, but it must be relational in consciousness. It must reflect a connection—either to the people it supports, the values it furthers, or the impact it intends. Detached giving, while tax-efficient, rarely activates the deeper human circuitry of empathy, engagement, and expansion. Conversely, when giving is connected to your lived story, your growth arc, or your sense of purpose, it becomes regenerative.

Modern neuroscience reinforces this. Studies on altruism reveal that acts of voluntary, meaningful generosity activate the brain's reward centres, particularly the ventral striatum and prefrontal cortex. This neural activity isn't as strong when giving is coerced, performative, or ambivalent. In other words, our biology responds differently depending on the *spirit* of the giving. When aligned, generosity reinforces emotional resilience, reduces stress, and enhances wellbeing.

At a systemic level, soul-aligned generosity also invites us to reconsider *how* we give. Traditional philanthropy often positions the giver as superior—the benefactor, the saviour, the enlightened hand. This power dynamic perpetuates hierarchy, even when cloaked in benevolence. Conscious giving dismantles this paradigm. It acknowledges interdependence. It respects the agency of the receiver. It moves from charity to solidarity—from "I give because you need" to "I give because we are connected, and your flourishing is part of mine."

This philosophy is evident in the work of Anand Giridharadas, whose critique of elite philanthropy calls attention to how wealth can perpetuate the very inequalities it seeks to alleviate. His work reminds us that real generosity involves not only redistribution, but accountability. It asks hard questions: *Where did this wealth come from? Who was excluded in its accumulation? What structural changes must accompany my individual giving?* These inquiries do not negate the value of generosity. They deepen it. They ensure that our giving is not a balm for guilt but a beacon of consciousness.

Practically, this means integrating generosity into your financial architecture—not as an afterthought, but as a pillar. Whether it's a giving percentage built into your budget, a donor-advised fund aligned with your values, or informal community support structured with boundaries, the key is intentionality. Generosity should not destabilise your financial wellbeing. It should express it.

Moreover, giving from overflow requires that you *tend to your own cup first.* You cannot circulate what you have not cultivated. Emotional depletion, burnout, and resentment are signs not of failure, but of imbalance. They signal the need to pause, recalibrate, and restore your internal reserves. From this replenished place, generosity becomes joyful rather than burdensome. It becomes an act of affirmation, not amputation.

One elegant metaphor for this dynamic is the natural water cycle. A spring feeds a river, which nourishes the land, which replenishes the aquifer, which sustains the spring. Break the cycle at any point—excessive withdrawal, pollution, lack of rest—and the whole system collapses. Likewise, soul-aligned generosity requires circulation that honours the source. You are the source. Your wellness, your clarity, your alignment—these are not luxuries; they are prerequisites.

Finally, true abundance *demands* circulation. Hoarded wealth stagnates. It breeds fear, isolation, and distortion. Circulated wealth—shared with discernment, offered with heart—amplifies. It builds trust, connection, and continuity. It transforms the giver, the receiver, and the space between. This is not New Age optimism; it is economic reality. Studies in behavioural economics confirm that communities with higher levels of mutual aid and collective financial responsibility outperform those driven by competition and isolation, particularly in times of crisis.

Soul-aligned generosity is not about giving more. It is about giving *true*. It invites you to become a conduit of abundance—not just materially, but energetically. It challenges you to ask: Where does my giving come from? What does it sustain? What does it say about how I see the world?

And most importantly: What would it mean to give as if your wholeness depends on it—not because you must, but because you *can*? That is the essence of soul-aligned generosity. Not obligation, but overflow. Not depletion, but devotion. And in that space, giving becomes not a transaction—but a transmission.

Designing Your Impact Blueprint: Envisioning a Life of Purposeful Contribution

True wealth is not measured solely by what we accumulate, but by the ripple effect of how we live, give, and lead. In the context of conscious financial growth, designing an *impact blueprint* is the process of aligning your personal values, financial resources, and lived purpose into a cohesive strategy that leaves a meaningful imprint—on people, systems, and futures. It is a powerful shift away from passive legacy into active influence, from accumulation to activation. At its core, an impact blueprint is not about charity; it is about intentionality. It is the architecture of a life that shapes others not only through material wealth, but through time, skills, relationships, and spiritual resonance.

The concept borrows from strategic philanthropy and social entrepreneurship, but it expands beyond either. It asks: *What kind of presence do I want to be in the world?* What will people inherit from my decisions—not only financially, but emotionally and ethically? These questions are not reserved for billionaires or those nearing retirement. They are relevant at any stage of life, because impact does not begin when you're ready to 'give back'—it begins when you choose to *live forward.*

Designing your impact blueprint requires three essential pillars: self-awareness, structural clarity, and ongoing adaptation. First, the self-awareness component is foundational. You must understand your unique confluence of gifts, privileges, wounds, and aspirations. This is the psychic soil from which meaningful contribution grows. Too often, people attempt to create impact from abstraction—supporting causes that are trendy, disconnected, or performative. True resonance comes from integrating your lived experiences into your influence.

Take for instance the story of Malachi, a second-generation immigrant who built a successful software consultancy. His early years were shaped by systemic marginalisation, his mother's sacrifice, and the quiet resilience of his community. Initially, Malachi gave to large, international charities, but felt emotionally uninvested. After engaging in coaching and ancestral inquiry, he shifted course. He began funding grassroots tech education programmes for refugee youth in his home city—mirroring the support he never received. His blueprint wasn't built in spreadsheets—it was shaped by memory, empathy, and reclamation.

This brings us to the second pillar: structural clarity. Vision without strategy is sentiment. Designing your impact means putting framework to intention. This may involve creating a donor-advised fund, establishing a foundation, building a social enterprise, mentoring within a system, or investing in impact funds. But these vehicles should not be chosen reactively—they must serve the wider vision. Structure enables sustainability. It allows your impact to extend beyond mood, bandwidth, or performance. A blueprint anchors vision to reality.

Consider the case of Elise and Jordan, two artists who transitioned from gig-based incomes to consistent earnings through licensing and online teaching. As their financial stability increased, so did their desire to contribute. Rather than funnel money into abstract causes, they created a "creative commons grant" for emerging artists of colour to access studio space, mentorship, and mental health support. They pooled 10% of their net profit monthly into a community-run trust and created an application process co-designed with past grantees. Their giving model didn't mimic elite philanthropy—it emerged organically from their ecosystem. Their blueprint was simple, scalable, and embedded in their work.

The third pillar—ongoing adaptation—is often neglected in traditional legacy models. Too often, people design a blueprint and then ossify it: a foundation set in the past, static goals, or rigid bequests. But life evolves. Values deepen. Needs shift. A truly conscious impact blueprint is a living document. It is reviewed, revised, and reimagined. It is responsive to social change, economic upheaval, personal growth, and generational transition. It does not cling to form—it remains loyal to function: to make a difference in ways that are needed, not just nostalgic.

In practical terms, this might mean reviewing your impact vision annually alongside your financial review. It might involve asking your children, mentees, or collaborators how your contribution is landing. Is it empowering or dependent? Is it perpetuating control or cultivating autonomy? Is it driven by legacy or relevance? These questions create feedback loops that refine not only what you give, but *how* you give—and why.

Equally important is recognising that impact is not always visible. Some of the most transformative contributions are intimate, slow, and unseen by the public eye. Mentoring one young person through adulthood. Funding a cousin's therapy. Building a regenerative garden in a food desert. Creating art that heals intergenerational trauma. These acts don't always make headlines, but they create *field effects*—ripples of possibility that reshape how others think, feel, and act. Your impact blueprint must honour these micro-movements, not just macro-interventions.

This is where spirit meets structure. When your impact is driven by both strategic clarity and soulful resonance, it becomes magnetic. You attract aligned collaborators, catalyse unexpected outcomes, and model a form of leadership that transcends metrics. You stop performing generosity and start *embodying stewardship*. And this, perhaps, is the most radical part of an impact blueprint: it dissolves the binary between the giver and the beneficiary. You do not impact others as a saviour—you do so as a fellow participant in a shared unfolding.

Moreover, as you design this blueprint, you may find that your own healing accelerates. To give from an integrated place often brings resolution to internal wounds. It reclaims agency. It transforms shame into fuel, isolation into legacy. Impact, then, is not a destination—it is a *pathway of becoming*. It is a mirror that reflects who you are becoming while revealing what the world can receive through you.

Ultimately, your impact blueprint is a love letter to the future. It says: I did not only seek to succeed—I sought to serve. I did not only gather wealth—I circulated it with care. I did not only exist—I imprinted.

And that imprint—if crafted with consciousness—will last longer than your name, your brand, or your assets. It will live in the people you uplifted, the systems you reshaped, and the stories that outlived you. That is the true measure of wealth. And it begins not someday, but now. With one choice, one offering, one blueprint—written not just with money, but with meaning.

Death, Dignity, and the Wealth You Leave Behind: Preparing Financially and Spiritually for the End

Death is the only certainty we all share, yet it remains one of the most emotionally and financially neglected conversations of our time. Modern society, in its pursuit of longevity and material success, has cultivated an odd amnesia around mortality—as if ignoring it might delay its arrival. This denial, while culturally embedded, comes at a cost. It leaves families unprepared, wealth misdirected, and deeper legacies untold. For those seeking to live with consciousness and build wealth intentionally, confronting the end is not morbid. It is wise. It is dignified. And it is essential.

This chapter takes a bold and holistic look at death—not only through the lens of financial preparedness, but through the more nuanced terrain of energetic closure and legacy rituals. We explore what it means to die well, not just with a signed will, but with your essence transmitted, your affairs in order, and your relationships intact. True legacy begins not with what we leave behind, but with how we prepare to release what we've held.

The financial dimension of end-of-life planning is relatively straightforward in principle: wills, trusts, power of attorney, advanced healthcare directives, and estate taxes. Yet in practice, it is fraught with avoidance. According to recent global surveys, more than half of adults over the age of forty have not created a legal will. Even fewer have communicated their wishes clearly with their families. This vacuum often results in confusion, conflict, and costly litigation—turning grief into gridlock.

Creating a will is an act of clarity. But crafting an intentional estate plan is an act of care. It is an expression of love and responsibility that extends beyond one's lifetime. It answers questions you won't be present to resolve. Who will inherit what—and why? Who will manage your affairs if you're incapacitated? What values should guide the distribution of your assets? These decisions, when made early and updated regularly, spare your loved ones the burden of guessing your intentions.

Consider the example of Mateo and Ari, a same-sex couple in their fifties who had built a successful interior design firm together. Though they had shared everything for two decades, they had no formal estate documents. When Mateo suddenly passed from a stroke, his biological family—estranged for years—contested ownership of the couple's home and business assets. The grief was compounded by bureaucracy and betrayal. Only after an arduous legal battle did Ari retain what they had built together. Had there been a properly drafted will or trust, this outcome could have been avoided entirely.

Beyond legality lies a deeper layer: energetic closure. This concept refers to the emotional and spiritual preparation for death that transcends paperwork. It includes conversations that mend rifts, expressions of gratitude, blessings passed from elders to the next generation, and the transmission of stories, values, and teachings that no document can contain. Energetic closure is about leaving this world empty of regret, full of presence.

In many indigenous traditions, this dimension of preparation is central to death rituals. The dying are encouraged to recount their life experiences, confess unresolved tensions, and offer wisdom to their descendants. These conversations are not just cathartic—they are foundational. They root the next generation in a sense of belonging and identity. Yet in Western culture, where death is often medicalised and sequestered, these rituals are increasingly rare. As a result, families inherit assets, but not meaning.

Reintroducing such rituals into modern life requires intention. It might be as simple as recording a series of video messages to your children, narrating the choices you made, the values you held, and the love you felt but may not have always known how to express. It might be composing a "legacy letter," sharing your spiritual beliefs, financial lessons, and hopes for future generations. Or it might be conducting a ceremonial gathering—while you are still well—where you speak your blessings aloud and witness the impact of your life in real time.

Such acts are not just for the benefit of others. They are profoundly healing for the self. They offer a sense of completion, coherence, and peace. When done thoughtfully, they allow death to become not a rupture, but a rite of passage.

This is not to suggest that every death is neat or every family receptive. Some relationships remain fractured. Some histories are painful. But even in such cases, your preparation can prevent further harm. By clearly articulating your wishes, naming responsible executors, and creating structures that reflect your deepest values, you reduce the likelihood of ambiguity being weaponised. In doing so, you offer not only material inheritance, but emotional clarity.

The concept of "death cleaning," popularised by the Swedish practice of *döstädning*, adds another layer of mindfulness. This process involves gradually decluttering one's life of physical possessions that no longer serve, with the awareness that someone else will one day have to manage them. It is not a grim task—it is an act of grace. It acknowledges the impermanence of things and creates space for what matters most to remain.

Furthermore, your death planning can—and should—extend into the structures of your wealth. Are your investments aligned with your ethics? Does your giving reflect your convictions? Have you established endowments or impact funds that will continue your work? Conscious wealth does not stop at accumulation—it evolves into *circulation*. You have the opportunity to create vehicles that continue flowing your values long after you're gone.

One powerful example is that of Ravi, a physician and teacher who, in the last decade of his life, created a scholarship fund for rural students pursuing integrative medicine. But he didn't stop at money. He compiled a set of teachings, recorded meditations, and stories from his career, all housed in a digital repository accessible to his future recipients. His legacy was not just funded—it was *felt*. His passing was mourned, but his presence remained.

This kind of legacy planning doesn't require vast wealth—only deliberate design. Whether through modest savings, creative gifts, or deeply personal reflections, the point is to ensure that what you have built—internally and externally—does not vanish unshared. Death becomes not a void, but a vessel.

In the final accounting, the wealth you leave behind is not just what's on your balance sheet. It's who you became while you were alive. It's the integrity with which you navigated power, the generosity with which you shared, and the wisdom you were willing to articulate. Preparing for death with financial and spiritual intelligence is not morose—it is liberating. It frees your loved ones. It clarifies your impact. It gives dignity to your departure.

You are not only the author of your life—you are the curator of your legacy. The way you meet your ending is part of your story. Make it conscious. Make it complete. And in doing so, you make your wealth—material and energetic—a lasting gift, not just to your heirs, but to the evolution of humanity.

Interactive Vision Board: The Legacy Map – Designing a Multi-Generational Money Mission

Legacy is often perceived as a static concept—something etched in stone after one's departure. But in the context of conscious wealth and generational stewardship, legacy is not a monument to the past. It is a living design for the future. It evolves, breathes, and adapts with each generation it touches. The *Legacy Map* is a guided visioning tool that reframes legacy not as a final bequest, but as an ongoing mission—a dynamic blueprint for how your wealth, values, and wisdom will continue to serve across lifetimes. This approach challenges the outdated notion of inheritance as mere property transfer and replaces it with a purposeful, participatory model of multi-generational intention.

The concept of a Legacy Map draws from diverse disciplines—strategic philanthropy, family governance, financial planning, visual learning, and even spiritual ritual. At its core, it functions as both a reflective exercise and a tactical framework. The purpose is not simply to visualise what you will leave behind, but to *align your long-term wealth trajectory with your deepest convictions.* It invites you to imagine not just what you are building for your children or successors, but with them. This distinction is profound: legacy becomes less about what is *given* and more about what is *co-created.*

A Legacy Map differs from a typical vision board in that it is not solely focused on personal milestones or material symbols of success. Rather, it integrates dimensions of financial literacy, emotional legacy, community impact, spiritual continuity, and systemic awareness. It invites the question: What values do I want my wealth to perpetuate? What types of decisions should this money enable, not just today but fifty years from now? How do I ensure that my resources fuel empowerment, not entitlement?

The process begins with introspection. Before laying down any visual markers or strategic goals, the map requires a personal inventory. This includes revisiting the pivotal moments in your life where money shaped meaning—times of scarcity, abundance, giving, receiving, and reframing. These stories contain clues. They reveal the themes that have governed your relationship with wealth and expose the beliefs you have either internalised or transcended. Mapping these origin points is not sentimental; it is strategic. Because without understanding your own money narrative, it becomes nearly impossible to construct one that can transcend generations with clarity.

Once this reflective groundwork is laid, the visioning begins. The map invites you to plot five primary vectors: values, vision, vehicles, voice, and velocity. *Values* represent the foundational principles you wish your wealth to embody—integrity, justice, creativity, resilience, or community. *Vision* outlines the specific impacts you wish to have—educational access, environmental regeneration, cultural preservation, or entrepreneurial empowerment. *Vehicles* are the financial and structural tools that will carry your vision—such as trusts, donor-advised funds, investment portfolios, or business ventures. *Voice* captures the narrative you want to be remembered by—not just in legal documents but in letters, stories, rituals, and teachings. And *velocity* maps the desired pace and rhythm of your legacy's unfolding—whether your impact is meant to stretch slowly across time or ignite a rapid transformation in the present.

These categories do not operate in silos; they are inherently interconnected. For instance, if one of your values is equity, and your vision is to fund future generations of social entrepreneurs from underserved communities, your vehicle may include an impact fund managed in part by your descendants, with your voice represented through an annual storytelling gathering that contextualises the fund's origin. The velocity might be planned across thirty years, with periodic recalibrations every five. Such specificity transforms vague intention into a grounded roadmap.

Real-world examples bring the Legacy Map concept to life. Consider the case of Laila, a civil rights attorney who amassed modest but stable wealth through careful investing and property ownership. Rather than wait until her death to distribute her estate, she engaged her adult children in a collective design process. Together, they created a multi-decade giving strategy that blended their passions—Laila's commitment to justice, her daughter's expertise in education, and her son's interest in environmental policy. They built a shared giving calendar, rotating who chooses the cause each quarter, with mandatory reflection sessions built in. They also drafted legacy letters and recorded short videos explaining the historical injustices and aspirations that shaped their decisions. The map was not a poster on the wall. It was a living contract of co-stewardship.

The psychological benefits of this process are profound. Engaging in legacy mapping reduces the fear of irrelevance that often accompanies ageing. It transforms end-of-life planning into a creative act. For the younger generation, it removes the ambiguity and entitlement that so often breeds conflict after inheritance. When legacy becomes a dialogue rather than a monologue, families grow stronger, more cohesive, and more future-oriented. They begin to see wealth not as a finite resource, but as an evolving ecosystem of energy, insight, and impact.

Critically, the Legacy Map also includes *ritual*. This is not a token gesture. Ritual, in this context, is the intentional embedding of meaning into action. Whether it is lighting a candle during your legacy visioning session, incorporating ancestral stories into your financial meetings, or designing a rite of passage for children who reach a milestone age and inherit a portion of the family's giving fund—these small ceremonies ground the map in embodied experience. They create memory. They signal importance. They root abstract values in tangible practices.

This approach also integrates well with other modalities. For those who use somatic therapies, narrative coaching, or family constellation work, the Legacy Map becomes a complementary tool. It offers a canvas to reframe intergenerational money trauma and transmute it into conscious direction. It helps illuminate invisible loyalties that may be sabotaging financial growth—such as a subconscious belief that surpassing one's parents is disloyal—and replaces them with purposeful recalibration.

A truly powerful Legacy Map transcends personal goals and dares to shape culture. It sees money not just as personal security but as social influence. It asks: *How can I use my capital to challenge inequity, nourish creativity, or shift paradigms?* Legacy, then, becomes not the shadow of your life, but its most luminous continuation. It allows you to move from ownership to orchestration.

And importantly, it need not be perfect. A Legacy Map is iterative. It is reviewed, reshaped, and re-envisioned as your life evolves. The goal is not permanence but alignment. Not rigidity but resonance. It is your compass, not your cage.

In a world increasingly driven by short-term metrics, transactional success, and generational divides, creating a multi-generational money mission through a Legacy Map is a radical act of foresight. It affirms that your wealth—material, emotional, intellectual, and spiritual—matters not just now, but in the unfolding of futures you may never witness. It dignifies your life's work by ensuring that its essence does not vanish, but vibrates forward.

Ultimately, the Legacy Map is not about what you leave behind. It's about what you set in motion. And when created with clarity, care, and courage, it becomes not just a tool for inheritance—but a testament to intentional living.

Conclusion
The Currency of Consciousness

For generations, wealth has been weighed by static measures—net worth, property deeds, dividend statements, the cold comfort of account balances. Yet, as we draw the curtain on this book, a richer truth surfaces: wealth is not what you clutch, but what you move. It's a shift not only in thinking, but in being—a recalibration of prosperity from hoarding to flowing, from ownership to orchestration. In this emerging paradigm, currency is not forged solely in mint or market, but in motive. It pulses through your decisions, your exchanges, even the way you sit with a stranger at dinner and split the bill. This flow doesn't just shape your financial story—it spills outward, imprinting the emotional and ethical contours of your community.

This chapter isn't a neat wrap-up. It's more like a breath before the leap—a call to integrate, to absorb what's come before and step into the lived experience of it. You're invited now to embody this convergence of financial savvy and spiritual sensibility. Not as theory, but as ritual. This isn't about becoming a master of markets or a magician of manifestation; it's about becoming a steward—one who understands money as movement, not measure. Because when consciousness enters the equation, money stops being a source of strain or status. It starts becoming a conduit—for coherence, for choice, for trust.

Across these pages, you've peeled back inherited assumptions, sifted through subconscious habits, and explored the neurobiological, quantum, and somatic dimensions of your financial reality. You've met exercises that weren't merely informative, but catalytic—designed to get under your skin in the best possible way. You've questioned scarcity's gospel, dismantled superiority's pedestal, reimagined the humble budget as a kind of spiritual scaffolding, and come to see abundance not as excess, but as alignment. But let's not mistake introspection for completion. The work doesn't finish until your wealth becomes kinetic—until it moves through you with direction, not drift.

This movement—this flow—is not charity cloaked in virtue. It's not about giving away what you don't need. It's about reciprocity, about recognising that money does not move in a vacuum. Every pound, every rupee, every dollar carries a trace—of your mood, your clarity, your fear, your integrity. So here's the deeper invitation: pause before you spend. Ask, "What am I fuelling?" "Whose reality am I underwriting with this choice?" and perhaps most poignantly, "Is this how I want my life force to circulate?"

Take, for instance, Nina—a veteran financial adviser to the ultra-wealthy. For years, she was the architect behind high-performing portfolios. But a brush with mortality jolted her into reassessment. Her spreadsheets remained, but the soul of her work shifted. She began encouraging her clients to feel their investments—not just analyse them. To direct funds toward climate resilience, worker dignity, regenerative projects—ventures that paid dividends not only in currency, but in conscience. Her clients didn't just see different returns; they became different people. Their sense of sufficiency rose. Their anxiety around wealth diminished. Their strategies didn't just change—their states did.

This, then, is the pulse of conscious currency: money as medium, not as end. A means by which your ethics become visible, your values audible, your presence unmistakable. We're no longer talking about control, or conquest. We're talking about collaboration—with self, with system, with soul.

Now, this doesn't mean tossing aside the practicalities. Keep the spreadsheets. Keep the forecasts. But let them breathe. Let them reflect not just numbers, but nuance. When you budget, bring awareness. When you invest, check for integrity. When you spend, listen for resonance. Ask the odd, inconvenient questions: "Does this purchase reflect who I'm becoming?" "Does this contract me or open something wider?" Not every answer will be easy. That's the point.

More broadly, this reimagined relationship with wealth beckons you into quiet leadership—not the podium kind, but the lived kind. The kind that shifts family cultures, reshapes dinner table conversations, redraws the contours of a workplace. It asks you to be the person who speaks openly about money without shame. Who models boundaries with grace. Who brings empathy into earnings and transparency into transactions. Who teaches their children to pair emotional intelligence with financial fluency. Not loudly. Not perfectly. But consistently.

This leadership is subtle. It shows up in the way you respond to financial pressure. In the care you take while splitting resources. In the silence you maintain when a boastful brag circles the room—and you simply smile, choosing depth over display. These gestures—small as they seem—are where consciousness shows itself. Not in the spotlight, but in the seam.

And let's be honest: this isn't about flawless execution. Expect stumbles. There will be moments of contraction, ego flares, scarcity's old voice whispering its familiar script. That's not failure. That's the feedback loop of growth. This isn't about maintaining some performative alignment. It's about remaining responsive—willing to shift when you've drifted. Money consciousness isn't linear. It's evolutionary. It spirals. It ripples. It hums.

To anchor this, many readers find value in personal rituals—simple, recurring acts that keep money tethered to meaning. You might host monthly reflections—not just to track expenses, but to gauge your emotional temperature around them. Or journal weekly on how your financial choices are shaping your sense of self. Or sit each season with your accounts and ask, "What changed me, and what did I change?" These rituals aren't tasks. They're tendings. They ground awareness in rhythm, allowing consciousness to root.

And in the end—here's the quiet truth—your wealth will not be measured by digits. It will be felt in your freedom. In the calm that enters your breath when your choices mirror your values. In the joy of watching your resources touch lives—uplift, restore, inspire.

This book was never about money alone. It's been about agency. Presence. Possibility. About remembering that you are not a bystander in the marketplace—you are a composer of systems that heal or harm, constrict or expand, silence or empower.

So as you step out from these pages and back into the fabric of your life, carry this: you were not made to hoard. You were made to harmonise. To become a channel, not just of prosperity, but of purpose. To let your transactions carry transformation. Your choices, consciousness.

And in doing so, you change more than your accounts. You change the field. You change the future.

One intentional flow at a time.

Tying It All Together—Your New Relationship with Wealth

The final act of any meaningful transformation is integration. It is where insight becomes embodiment, where learning becomes lifestyle. Over the course of this book, you have travelled through a multidimensional exploration of money—not as a static resource to acquire, but as a living current that mirrors your consciousness. You have examined inherited beliefs, rewired self-sabotaging narratives, embraced the vibrational science of value, and explored the subtle yet potent intersection of spirituality, neurobiology, and finance. Now, in tying it all together, we move from theory to rhythm. This is not about wrapping things up—it is about *opening up* to a new way of being in relationship with wealth.

At the heart of this new paradigm is a radical but grounded truth: wealth is not merely what you *hold*, but how you *flow* it. This redefinition is deceptively simple. But it shifts everything. In traditional paradigms, wealth is framed as accumulation—amassing assets, fortifying security, and measuring success through visible indicators. In this evolved framework, wealth is reframed as *circulation with intention*—a dynamic interplay between giving and receiving, saving and sharing, building and surrendering. It asks not just how much you have, but how well it aligns, moves, uplifts, and regenerates.

Consider the difference between a reservoir and a river. A reservoir may hold vast water, but if it stagnates, it grows toxic. A river, on the other hand, nourishes every environment it passes through—

even while flowing toward uncertainty. Conscious wealth behaves more like a river. It flows in alignment with purpose, adjusts course with awareness, and allows abundance to be both a personal experience and a collective gift.

This orientation has profound implications. For one, it dissolves the artificial divide between financial intelligence and spiritual integrity. You no longer have to choose between spreadsheets and soul, pragmatism and purpose. You are now equipped to build budgets as rituals of respect, invest with both strategy and intuition, and give not from guilt or duty, but from genuine overflow. You understand that manifestation without action is fantasy, and that financial planning without embodied resonance is hollow. This integration—the sacred and the systemic—is what gives your wealth true momentum.

To live this new relationship with wealth, however, requires *consistency*. Not perfection. Not performance. But daily, conscious participation in your own unfolding. It requires asking yourself with regularity: "Am I in alignment with what I most value?" "Does this financial decision reflect who I am becoming?" "Is my money flowing toward expansion or contraction, toward fear or towards freedom?"

Take, for example, the story of Ravi and Anya, two educators who began this journey feeling trapped between their modest salaries and expansive dreams. They had tried every budgeting app, every manifestation workshop, and still felt stuck in scarcity cycles. Through conscious financial reflection, they realised that their emotional resistance to receiving was tied to childhood narratives about self-sacrifice and guilt around abundance. As they engaged with embodiment practices, nervous system regulation, and value-aligned spending strategies, something shifted—not just in their income, but in their *identity*. They began offering paid mentorship in their areas of passion, created a joint fund for community micro-loans, and restructured their spending to prioritise creative joy. Within a year, they had doubled their household income—not through hustle, but through harmony. Their money began to reflect who they were *at their core*.

This is the essence of the new relationship with wealth: it emerges not from scarcity-fuelled ambition, but from soul-aligned resonance. When your nervous system feels safe, your body becomes receptive. When your story is integrated, your energy becomes magnetic. And when your money is an extension of your mission, it finds its way into places that matter.

But integration is not only inward. It is communal. The final frontier of financial consciousness is *service.* When you begin to understand that your wealth is part of a larger field of collective energy, your choices take on a new depth. You move from accumulation for ego to distribution for impact. From legacy as inheritance to legacy as *living influence.* This does not mean self-erasure. It means self-expansion. It means recognising that as you rise, you carry others with you—not through obligation, but through design.

You may choose to mentor young entrepreneurs, seed ethical businesses, support regenerative agriculture, or fund scholarships in under-resourced communities. You may build family rituals that teach the next generation not just how to earn, but how to *discern.* You may create investment structures that channel money into innovation, healing, and justice. These choices do not require you to be a millionaire. They require you to be *intentional.* To move from passive spending to participatory stewardship.

Indeed, one of the most radical acts in this economy is to direct your money with meaning. To pause before a purchase and ask: "Is this aligned?" To review your investment portfolio and ask: "Does this reflect the future I believe in?" To teach your children not that money is evil or scarce, but that money is *energy*—and with energy comes responsibility.

This mindset also protects against the regression into fear-based patterns. When financial setbacks occur—and they will—you are no longer destabilised. You understand that your worth is not your income. That your flow is not your fault. That every contraction invites recalibration. You have tools: breathwork, reframing, nervous system practices, gratitude rituals. You are not at the mercy of external circumstances. You are an active participant in your own return to flow.

Moreover, this new relationship invites *joy*. It restores delight to the act of earning, giving, saving, and spending. It makes room for celebration without shame, generosity without depletion, investment without dread. It gives you permission to thrive—*and* to redefine what thriving means.

And so, as this chapter invites you to tie it all together, it does not offer closure. It offers *continuity*. Because financial evolution is not a checklist. It is a rhythm. A pulse. A practice. Your relationship with wealth will keep changing—as you grow, as the world changes, as your desires refine. What matters is that you remain attuned. That you keep returning to centre. That you let money be a mirror—not of who you were, but of who you are *becoming*.

The world needs financially conscious humans now more than ever. People who can channel abundance without arrogance, steward resources with reverence, and model a form of prosperity that uplifts rather than extracts. You are now part of that movement. A quiet revolution of conscious capital, where money is no longer just a means, but a *message*.

Let it say: I am awake. I am aligned. I am in flow. And through this flow, I uplift all that I touch.

About the Author

Arman Lefevre is a financial energy strategist and transformational coach who helps people bridge the gap between wealth and well-being. With a unique approach that blends financial education, mindset coaching, and intuitive alignment, Arman has guided thousands toward achieving both prosperity and peace. Drawing from both modern economics and ancient wisdom traditions, his work empowers readers to shift their relationship with money from one of stress to one of sustainable flow. His writing blends grounded tools with soulful insight—ideal for those seeking more than just spreadsheets.

www.ingramcontent.com/pod-product-compliance
Lightning Source LLC
Chambersburg PA
CBHW031342230926
51848CB00002B/350
* 9 7 8 9 3 7 1 3 4 6 0 2 3 *